Neural Networks with R

Smart models using CNN, RNN, deep learning, and artificial intelligence principles

Giuseppe Ciaburro
Balaji Venkateswaran

BIRMINGHAM - MUMBAI

Neural Networks with R

First published: September 2017

Production reference: 1220917

Published by Packt Publishing Ltd.
Livery Place
35 Livery Street
Birmingham
B3 2PB, UK.
ISBN 978-1-78839-787-2

www.packtpub.com

Credits

Authors
Giuseppe Ciaburro
Balaji Venkateswaran

Reviewer
Juan Tomás Oliva Ramos

Commissioning Editor
Sunith Shetty

Acquisition Editor
Varsha Shetty

Content Development Editor
Cheryl Dsa

Technical Editor
Suwarna Patil

Copy Editors
Safis Editing
Alpha Singh
Vikrant Phadkay

Project Coordinator
Nidhi Joshi

Proofreader
Safis Editing

Indexer
Mariammal Chettiyar

Graphics
Tania Dutta

Production Coordinator
Arvindkumar Gupta

About the Authors

Giuseppe Ciaburro; holds a master's degree in chemical engineering from Università degli Studi di Napoli Federico II, and a master's degree in acoustic and noise control from Seconda Università degli Studi di Napoli. He works at the Built Environment Control Laboratory of Università degli Studi della Campania "Luigi Vanvitelli".

He has over 15 years of work experience in programming, first in the field of combustion and then in acoustics and noise control. His core programming knowledge is in Python and R, and he has extensive experience of working with MATLAB. An expert in acoustics and noise control, Giuseppe has wide experience in teaching professional computer courses (about 15 years), dealing with e-learning as an author. He has several publications to his credit: monographs, scientific journals, and thematic conferences. He is currently researching machine learning applications in acoustics and noise control.

Balaji Venkateswaran is an AI expert, data scientist, machine learning practitioner, and database architect. He has 17+ years of experience in investment banking payment processing, telecom billing, and project management. He has worked for major companies such as ADP, Goldman Sachs, MasterCard, and Wipro. Balaji is a trainer in data science, Hadoop, and Tableau. He holds a postgraduate degree PG in business analytics from Great Lakes Institute of Management, Chennai.

Balaji has expertise relating to statistics, classification, regression, pattern recognition, time series forecasting, and unstructured data analysis using text mining procedures. His main interests are neural networks and deep learning.

Balaji holds various certifications in IBM SPSS, IBM Watson, IBM big data architect, cloud architect, CEH, Splunk, Salesforce, Agile CSM, and AWS.

If you have any questions, don't hesitate to message him on LinkedIn (linkedin.com/in/balvenkateswaran); he will be more than glad to help fellow data scientists.

"I would like to thank my parents and the three As in my life - wife Aruna, son Aadarsh and baby Abhitha who have been very supportive in this endeavor. I would also like to thank the staff of Packt publishers who were very helpful throughout the journey."

About the Reviewer

Juan Tomás Oliva Ramos is an environmental engineer from the university of Guanajuato, Mexico, with a master's degree in administrative engineering and quality. He has more than 5 years of experience in management and development of patents, technological innovation projects, and development of technological solutions through the statistical control of processes. He has been a teacher of statistics, entrepreneurship, and technological development of projects since 2011. He became an entrepreneur mentor, and started a new department of technology management and entrepreneurship at instituto Tecnologico Superior de Purisima del Rincon.

Juan is a *Alfaomega* reviewer and has worked on the book *Wearable designs for Smart watches, Smart TVs and Android mobile devices*.

He has developed prototypes through programming and automation technologies for the improvement of operations, which have been registered for patents.

I want to thank God for giving me the wisdom and humility to review this book. I thank Packt for giving me the opportunity to review this amazing book and to collaborate with a group of committed people. I want to thank my beautiful wife, Brenda; our two magic princesses, Regina and Renata; and our next member, Angel Tadeo; all of you give me the strength, happiness, and joy to start a new day. Thanks for being my family.

www.PacktPub.com

For support files and downloads related to your book, please visit www.PacktPub.com.

Did you know that Packt offers eBook versions of every book published, with PDF and ePub files available? You can upgrade to the eBook version at www.PacktPub.com and as a print book customer, you are entitled to a discount on the eBook copy. Get in touch with us at service@packtpub.com for more details.

At www.PacktPub.com, you can also read a collection of free technical articles, sign up for a range of free newsletters and receive exclusive discounts and offers on Packt books and eBooks.

https://www.packtpub.com/mapt

Get the most in-demand software skills with Mapt. Mapt gives you full access to all Packt books and video courses, as well as industry-leading tools to help you plan your personal development and advance your career.

Why subscribe?

- Fully searchable across every book published by Packt
- Copy and paste, print, and bookmark content
- On demand and accessible via a web browser

Customer Feedback

Thanks for purchasing this Packt book. At Packt, quality is at the heart of our editorial process. To help us improve, please leave us an honest review on this book's Amazon page at https://www.amazon.com/dp/1788397878.

If you'd like to join our team of regular reviewers, you can e-mail us at customerreviews@packtpub.com. We award our regular reviewers with free eBooks and videos in exchange for their valuable feedback. Help us be relentless in improving our products!

Table of Contents

Preface

Neural networks are one of the most fascinating machine learning models for solving complex computational problems efficiently. Neural networks are used to solve a wide range of problems in different areas of AI and machine learning.

This book explains the niche aspects of neural networking and provides you with the foundation to get started with advanced topics. The book begins with neural network design using the `neuralnet` package; then you'll build solid knowledge of how a neural network learns from data and the principles behind it. This book covers various types of neural networks, including recurrent neural networks and convoluted neural networks. You will not only learn how to train neural networks but also explore generalization of these networks. Later, we will delve into combining different neural network models and work with the real-world use cases.

By the end of this book, you will learn to implement neural network models in your applications with the help of the practical examples in the book.

What this book covers

Chapter 1, *Neural Network and Artificial Intelligence Concepts*, introduces the basic theoretical concepts of **Artificial Neural Networks** (**ANN**) and **Artificial Intelligence** (**AI**). It presents the simple applications of ANN and AI with usage of math concepts. Some introduction to R ANN functions is also covered.

Chapter 2, *Learning Processes in Neural Networks*, shows how to do exact inferences in graphical models and show applications as expert systems. Inference algorithms are the base components for learning and using these types of models. The reader must at least understand their use and a bit about how they work.

Chapter 3, *Deep Learning Using Multilayer Neural Networks*, is about understanding deep learning and neural network usage in deep learning. It goes through the details of the implementation using R packages. It covers the many hidden layers set up for deep learning and uses practical datasets to help understand the implementation.

Chapter 4, *Perceptron Neural Network – Basic Models*, helps understand what a perceptron is and the applications that can be built using it. This chapter covers an implementation of perceptrons using R.

Chapter 5, *Training and Visualizing a Neural Network in R,* covers another example of training a neural network with a dataset. It also gives a better understanding of neural networks with a graphical representation of input, hidden, and output layers using the plot() function in R.

Chapter 6, *Recurrent and Convolutional Neural Networks,* introduces **Recurrent Neural Networks** (**RNN**) and **Convolutional Neural Networks** (**CNN**) with their implementation in R. Several examples are proposed to understand the basic concepts.

Chapter 7, *Use Cases of Neural Networks – Advanced Topics,* presents neural network applications from different fields and how neural networks can be used in the AI world. This will help the reader understand the practical usage of neural network algorithms. The reader can enhance his or her skills further by taking different datasets and running the R code.

What you need for this book

This book is focused on neural networks in an R environment. We have used R version 3.4.1 to build various applications and the open source and enterprise-ready professional software for R, RStudio version 1.0.153. We focus on how to utilize various R libraries in the best possible way to build real-world applications. In that spirit, we have tried to keep all the code as friendly and readable as possible. We feel that this will enable our readers to easily understand the code and readily use it in different scenarios.

Who this book is for

This book is intended for anyone who has a statistics background with knowledge in R and wants to work with neural networks to get better results from complex data. If you are interested in artificial intelligence and deep learning and want to level up, then this book is what you need!

Conventions

In this book, you will find a number of text styles that distinguish between different kinds of information. Here are some examples of these styles and an explanation of their meaning.

Code words in text, database table names, folder names, filenames, file extensions, pathnames, dummy URLs, user input, and Twitter handles are shown as follows: "The line in R includes the `neuralnet()` library in our program."

Any command-line input or output is written as follows:

```
mydata=read.csv('Squares.csv',sep=",",header=TRUE)
mydata
attach(mydata)
names(mydata)
```

New terms and **important words** are shown in bold. Words that you see on the screen, for example, in menus or dialog boxes, appear in the text like this: "A reference page in the **Help** browser."

Warnings or important notes appear in a box like this.

Tips and tricks appear like this.

Reader feedback

Feedback from our readers is always welcome. Let us know what you think about this book-what you liked or disliked. Reader feedback is important for us as it helps us develop titles that you will really get the most out of.

To send us general feedback, simply e-mail feedback@packtpub.com, and mention the book's title in the subject of your message.

If there is a topic that you have expertise in and you are interested in either writing or contributing to a book, see our author guide at www.packtpub.com/authors.

Customer support

Now that you are the proud owner of a Packt book, we have a number of things to help you to get the most from your purchase.

Downloading the example code

You can download the example code files for this book from your account at http://www.packtpub.com. If you purchased this book elsewhere, you can visit http://www.packtpub.com/support and register to have the files emailed directly to you. You can download the code files by following these steps:

1. Log in or register to our website using your email address and password.
2. Hover the mouse pointer on the **SUPPORT** tab at the top.
3. Click on **Code Downloads & Errata**.
4. Enter the name of the book in the **Search** box.
5. Select the book for which you're looking to download the code files.
6. Choose from the drop-down menu where you purchased this book from.
7. Click on **Code Download**.

Once the file is downloaded, please make sure that you unzip or extract the folder using the latest version of:

- WinRAR / 7-Zip for Windows
- Zipeg / iZip / UnRarX for Mac
- 7-Zip / PeaZip for Linux

The code bundle for the book is also hosted on GitHub at https://github.com/PacktPublishing/Neural-Networks-with-R. We also have other code bundles from our rich catalog of books and videos available at https://github.com/PacktPublishing/. Check them out!

Errata

Although we have taken every care to ensure the accuracy of our content, mistakes do happen. If you find a mistake in one of our books-maybe a mistake in the text or the code-we would be grateful if you could report this to us. By doing so, you can save other readers from frustration and help us improve subsequent versions of this book. If you find any errata, please report them by visiting http://www.packtpub.com/submit-errata, selecting your book, clicking on the **Errata Submission Form** link, and entering the details of your errata. Once your errata are verified, your submission will be accepted and the errata will be uploaded to our website or added to any list of existing errata under the Errata section of that title. To view the previously submitted errata, go to https://www.packtpub.com/books/content/support and enter the name of the book in the search field. The required information will appear under the Errata section.

Piracy

Piracy of copyrighted material on the internet is an ongoing problem across all media. At Packt, we take the protection of our copyright and licenses very seriously. If you come across any illegal copies of our works in any form on the internet, please provide us with the location address or website name immediately so that we can pursue a remedy. Please contact us at copyright@packtpub.com with a link to the suspected pirated material. We appreciate your help in protecting our authors and our ability to bring you valuable content.

Questions

If you have a problem with any aspect of this book, you can contact us at questions@packtpub.com, and we will do our best to address the problem.

1
Neural Network and Artificial Intelligence Concepts

From the scientific and philosophical studies conducted over the centuries, special mechanisms have been identified that are the basis of human intelligence. Taking inspiration from their operations, it was possible to create machines that imitate part of these mechanisms. The problem is that they have not yet succeeded in imitating and integrating all of them, so the **Artificial Intelligence (AI)** systems we have are largely incomplete.

A decisive step in the improvement of such machines came from the use of so-called **Artificial Neural Networks (ANNs)** that, starting from the mechanisms regulating natural neural networks, plan to simulate human thinking. Software can now imitate the mechanisms needed to win a chess match or to translate text into a different language in accordance with its grammatical rules.

This chapter introduces the basic theoretical concepts of ANN and AI. Fundamental understanding of the following is expected:

- Basic high school mathematics; differential calculus and functions such as *sigmoid*
- R programming and usage of R libraries

We will go through the basics of neural networks and try out one model using R. This chapter is a foundation for neural networks and all the subsequent chapters.

We will cover the following topics in this chapter:

- ANN concepts
- Neurons, perceptron, and multilayered neural networks
- Bias, weights, activation functions, and hidden layers
- Forward and backpropagation methods
- Brief overview of **Graphics Processing Unit (GPU)**

At the end of the chapter, you will be able to recognize the different neural network algorithms and tools which R provides to handle them.

Introduction

The brain is the most important organ of the human body. It is the central processing unit for all the functions performed by us. Weighing only 1.5 kilos, it has around 86 billion neurons. A neuron is defined as a cell transmitting nerve impulses or electrochemical signals. The brain is a complex network of neurons which process information through a system of several interconnected neurons. It has always been challenging to understand the brain functions; however, due to advancements in computing technologies, we can now program neural networks artificially.

The discipline of ANN arose from the thought of mimicking the functioning of the same human brain that was trying to solve the problem. The drawbacks of conventional approaches and their successive applications have been overcome within well-defined technical environments.

AI or machine intelligence is a field of study that aims to give cognitive powers to computers to program them to learn and solve problems. Its objective is to simulate computers with human intelligence. AI cannot imitate human intelligence completely; computers can only be programmed to do some aspects of the human brain.

Machine learning is a branch of AI which helps computers to program themselves based on the input data. Machine learning gives AI the ability to do data-based problem solving. ANNs are an example of machine learning algorithms.

Deep learning (DL) is complex set of neural networks with more layers of processing, which develop high levels of abstraction. They are typically used for complex tasks, such as image recognition, image classification, and hand writing identification.

Most of the audience think that neural networks are difficult to learn and use it as a black box. This book intends to open the black box and help one learn the internals with implementation in R. With the working knowledge, we can see many use cases where neural networks can be made tremendously useful seen in the following image:

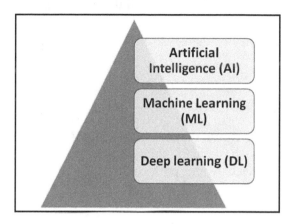

Inspiration for neural networks

Neural networks are inspired by the way the human brain works. A human brain can process huge amounts of information using data sent by human senses (especially vision). The processing is done by neurons, which work on electrical signals passing through them and applying flip-flop logic, like opening and closing of the gates for signal to transmit through. The following images shows the structure of a neuron:

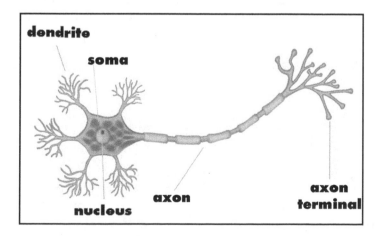

The major components of each neuron are:

- **Dendrites**: Entry points in each neuron which take input from other neurons in the network in form of electrical impulses
- **Cell Body**: It generates inferences from the dendrite inputs and decides what action to take
- **Axon terminals**: They transmit outputs in form of electrical impulses to next neuron

Each neuron processes signals only if it exceeds a certain threshold. Neurons either fire or do not fire; it is either *0* or *1*.

AI has been a domain for sci-fi movies and fiction books. ANNs within AI have been around since the 1950s, but we have made them more dominant in the past 10 years due to advances in computing architecture and performance. There have been major advancements in computer processing, leading to:

- Massive parallelism
- Distributed representation and computation
- Learning and generalization ability
- Fault tolerance
- Low energy consumption

In the domain of numerical computations and symbol manipulation, solving problems on-top of centralized architecture, modern day computers have surpassed humans to a greater extent. Where they actually lag behind with such an organizing structure is in the domains of pattern recognition, noise reduction, and optimizing. A toddler can recognize his/her mom in a huge crowd, but a computer with a centralized architecture wouldn't be able to do the same.

This is where the biological neural network of the brain has been outperforming machines, and hence the inspiration to develop an alternative loosely held, decentralized architecture mimicking the brain.

ANNs are massively parallel computing systems consisting of an extremely large number of simple processors with many interconnections.

One of the leading global news agencies, Guardian, used big data in digitizing the archives by uploading the snapshots of all the archives they had had. However, for a user to copy the content and use it elsewhere is the limitation here. To overcome that, one can use an ANN for text pattern recognition to convert the images to text file and then to any format according to the needs of the end-users.

How do neural networks work?

Similar to the biological neuron structure, ANNs define the neuron as a central processing unit, which performs a mathematical operation to generate one output from a set of inputs. The output of a neuron is a function of the weighted sum of the inputs plus the bias. Each neuron performs a very simple operation that involves activating if the total amount of signal received exceeds an activation threshold, as shown in the following figure:

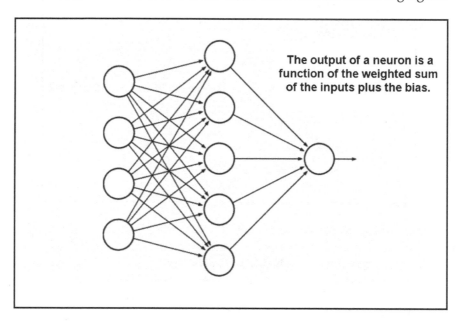

The output of a neuron is a function of the weighted sum of the inputs plus the bias.

The function of the entire neural network is simply the computation of the outputs of all the neurons, which is an entirely deterministic calculation. Essentially, ANN is a set of mathematical function approximations. We would now be introducing new terminology associated with ANNs:

- Input layer
- Hidden layer
- Output layer
- Weights
- Bias
- Activation functions

Layered approach

Any neural network processing a framework has the following architecture:

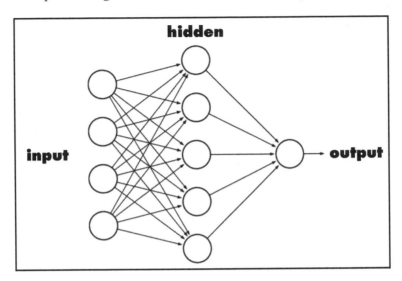

There is a set of inputs, a processor, and a set of outputs. This layered approach is also followed in neural networks. The inputs form the **input layer**, the **middle layer(s)** which performs the processing is called the **hidden layer(s)**, and the **output(s)** forms the output layer.

Our neural network architectures are also based on the same principle. The hidden layer has the magic to convert the input to the desired output. The understanding of the hidden layer requires knowledge of weights, bias, and activation functions, which is our next topic of discussion.

Weights and biases

Weights in an ANN are the most important factor in converting an input to impact the output. This is similar to slope in linear regression, where a weight is multiplied to the input to add up to form the output. Weights are numerical parameters which determine how strongly each of the neurons affects the other.

For a typical neuron, if the inputs are x_1, x_2, and x_3, then the synaptic weights to be applied to them are denoted as w_1, w_2, and w_3.

Output is

$$y = f(x) = \sum x_i w_i$$

where *i* is *1* to the number of inputs.

Simply, this is a matrix multiplication to arrive at the weighted sum.

Bias is like the intercept added in a linear equation. It is an additional parameter which is used to adjust the output along with the weighted sum of the inputs to the neuron.

The processing done by a neuron is thus denoted as :

$$output = sum\left(weights * inputs\right) + bias$$

A function is applied on this output and is called an **activation function**. The input of the next layer is the output of the neurons in the previous layer, as shown in the following image:

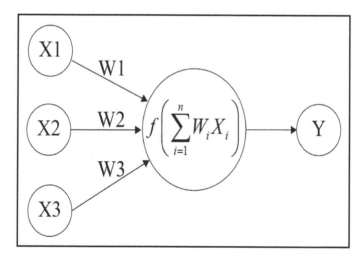

Training neural networks

Training is the act of presenting the network with some sample data and modifying the weights to better approximate the desired function.

There are two main types of training: supervised learning and unsupervised learning.

Supervised learning

We supply the neural network with inputs and the desired outputs. Response of the network to the inputs is measured. The weights are modified to reduce the difference between the actual and desired outputs.

Unsupervised learning

We only supply inputs. The neural network adjusts its own weights, so that similar inputs cause similar outputs. The network identifies the patterns and differences in the inputs without any external assistance.

Epoch

One iteration or pass through the process of providing the network with an input and updating the network's weights is called an **epoch**. It is a full run of feed-forward and backpropagation for update of weights. It is also one full read through of the entire dataset.

Typically, many epochs, in the order of tens of thousands at times, are required to train the neural network efficiently. We will see more about epochs in the forthcoming chapters.

Activation functions

The abstraction of the processing of neural networks is mainly achieved through the activation functions. An activation function is a mathematical function which converts the input to an output, and adds the magic of neural network processing. Without activation functions, the working of neural networks will be like linear functions. A linear function is one where the output is directly proportional to input, for example:

$$y = 2x + 1$$
$$y = f(x)$$

A linear function is a polynomial of one degree. Simply, it is a straight line without any curves.

However, most of the problems the neural networks try to solve are nonlinear and complex in nature. To achieve the nonlinearity, the activation functions are used. Nonlinear functions are high degree polynomial functions, for example:

$$y = x^2$$
$$y = \sin(x)$$

The graph of a nonlinear function is curved and adds the complexity factor.

Activation functions give the nonlinearity property to neural networks and make them true universal function approximators.

Different activation functions

There are many activation functions available for a neural network to use. We shall see a few of them here.

Linear function

The simplest activation function, one that is commonly used for the output layer activation function in neural network problems, is the linear activation function represented by the following formula:

$$y = f(x) = x$$

The output is same as the input and the function is defined in the range (*-infinity, +infinity*). In the following figure, a linear activation function is shown:

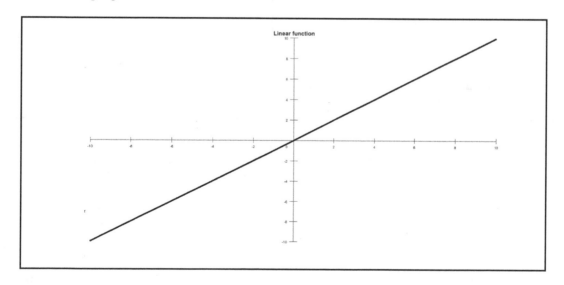

Unit step activation function

A unit step activation function is a much-used feature in neural networks. The output assumes value *0* for negative argument and *1* for positive argument. The function is as follows:

$$f(x) = o \; when \; x < o,$$
$$1 \; when \; x >= o$$

The range is between *(0,1)* and the output is binary in nature. These types of activation functions are useful for binary schemes. When we want to classify an input model in one of two groups, we can use a binary compiler with a unit step activation function. A unit step activation function is shown in the following figure:

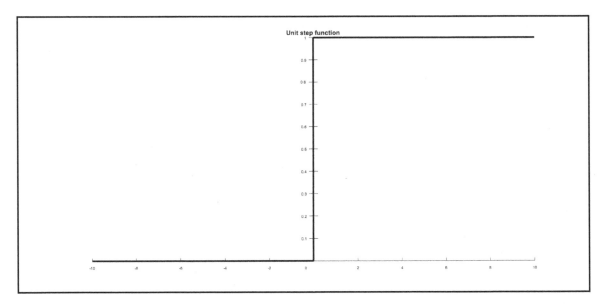

Sigmoid

The *sigmoid* function is a mathematical function that produces a sigmoidal curve; a characteristic curve for its *S* shape. This is the earliest and often used activation function. This squashes the input to any value between *0* and *1*, and makes the model logistic in nature. This function refers to a special case of logistic function defined by the following formula:

$$f(x) = 1/(1 + e^{-x})$$

In the following figure is shown a sigmoid curve with an *S* shape:

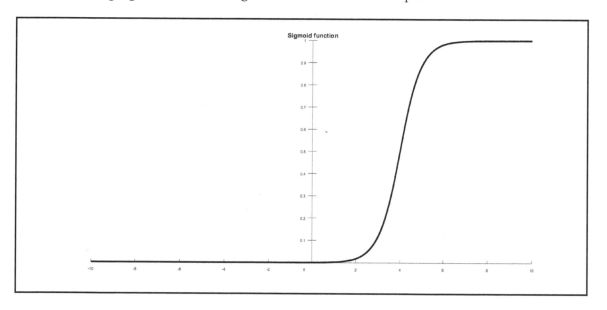

Hyperbolic tangent

Another very popular and widely used activation feature is the *tanh* function. If you look at the figure that follows, you can notice that it looks very similar to *sigmoid*; in fact, it is a scaled *sigmoid* function. This is a nonlinear function, defined in the range of values *(-1, 1)*, so you need not worry about activations blowing up. One thing to clarify is that the gradient is stronger for *tanh* than *sigmoid* (the derivatives are more steep). Deciding between *sigmoid* and *tanh* will depend on your gradient strength requirement. Like the *sigmoid*, *tanh* also has the missing slope problem. The function is defined by the following formula:

$$f(x) = \tanh(x)$$

In the following figure is shown a hyberbolic tangent activation function:

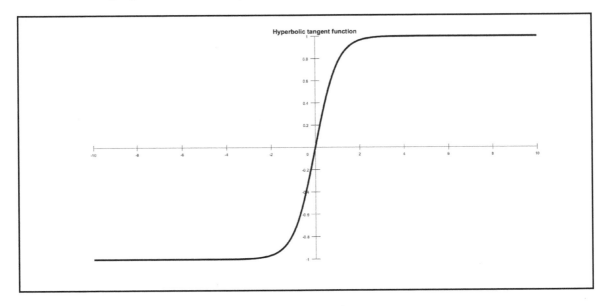

This looks very similar to *sigmoid*; in fact, it is a scaled *sigmoid* function.

Rectified Linear Unit

Rectified Linear Unit (ReLU) is the most used activation function since 2015. It is a simple condition and has advantages over the other functions. The function is defined by the following formula:

$$f(x) = o \ when \ x < o,$$
$$x \ when \ x >= o$$

In the following figure is shown a ReLU activation function:

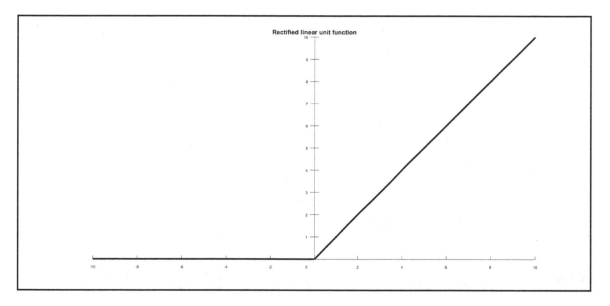

The range of output is between *0* and infinity. ReLU finds applications in computer vision and speech recognition using deep neural nets. There are various other activation functions as well, but we have covered the most important ones here.

Which activation functions to use?

Given that neural networks are to support nonlinearity and more complexity, the activation function to be used has to be robust enough to have the following:

- It should be differential; we will see why we need differentiation in backpropagation. It should not cause gradients to vanish.
- It should be simple and fast in processing.
- It should not be zero centered.

The *sigmoid* is the most used activation function, but it suffers from the following setbacks:

- Since it uses logistic model, the computations are time consuming and complex
- It cause gradients to vanish and no signals pass through the neurons at some point of time
- It is slow in convergence
- It is not zero centered

These drawbacks are solved by ReLU. ReLU is simple and is faster to process. It does not have the vanishing gradient problem and has shown vast improvements compared to the *sigmoid* and *tanh* functions. ReLU is the most preferred activation function for neural networks and DL problems.

ReLU is used for hidden layers, while the output layer can use a `softmax` function for logistic problems and a linear function of regression problems.

Perceptron and multilayer architectures

A perceptron is a single neuron that classifies a set of inputs into one of two categories (usually *1* or *-1*). If the inputs are in the form of a grid, a perceptron can be used to recognize visual images of shapes. The perceptron usually uses a step function, which returns *1* if the weighted sum of the inputs exceeds a threshold, and *0* otherwise.

When layers of perceptron are combined together, they form a multilayer architecture, and this gives the required complexity of the neural network processing. **Multi-Layer Perceptrons** (**MLPs**) are the most widely used architecture for neural networks.

Forward and backpropagation

The processing from input layer to hidden layer(s) and then to the output layer is called **forward propagation**. The *sum(input*weights)+bias* is applied at each layer and then the activation function value is propagated to the next layer. The next layer can be another hidden layer or the output layer. The construction of neural networks uses large number of hidden layers to give rise to **Deep Neural Network (DNN)**.

Once the output is arrived at, at the last layer (the output layer), we compute the error (the predicted output minus the original output). This error is required to correct the weights and biases used in forward propagation. Here is where the derivative function is used. The amount of weight that has to be changed is determined by **gradient descent**.

The backpropagation process uses the partial derivative of each neuron's activation function to identify the slope (or gradient) in the direction of each of the incoming weights. The gradient suggests how steeply the error will be reduced or increased for a change in the weight. The backpropagation keeps changing the weights until there is greatest reduction in errors by an amount known as the **learning rate**.

Learning rate is a scalar parameter, analogous to step size in numerical integration, used to set the rate of adjustments to reduce the errors faster. Learning rate is used in backpropagation during adjustment of weights and bias.

More the learning rate, the faster the algorithm will reduce the errors and faster will be the training process:

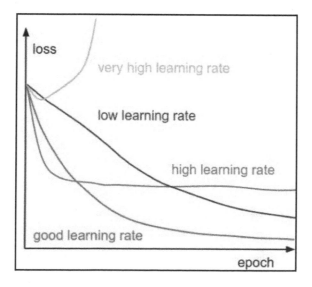

Step-by-step illustration of a neuralnet and an activation function

We shall take a step-by-step approach to understand the forward and reverse pass with a single hidden layer. The input layer has one neuron and the output will solve a binary classification problem (predict 0 or 1). In the following figure is shown a forward and reverse pass with a single hidden layer:

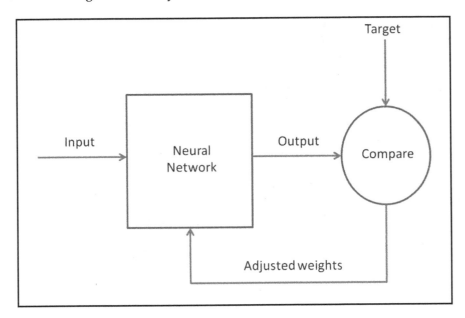

Next, let us analyze in detail, step by step, all the operations to be done for network training:

1. Take the input as a matrix.
2. Initialize the weights and biases with random values. This is one time and we will keep updating these with the error propagation process.
3. Repeat the steps 4 to 9 for each training pattern (presented in random order), until the error is minimized.
4. Apply the inputs to the network.
5. Calculate the output for every neuron from the input layer, through the hidden layer(s), to the output layer.
6. Calculate the error at the outputs: actual minus predicted.

7. Use the output error to compute error signals for previous layers. The partial derivative of the activation function is used to compute the error signals.
8. Use the error signals to compute weight adjustments.
9. Apply the weight adjustments.

Steps 4 and 5 are forward propagation and steps 6 through 9 arc backpropagation.

The learning rate is the amount that weights are updated is controlled by a configuration parameter.

The complete pass back and forth is called a **training cycle** or **epoch**. The updated weights and biases are used in the next cycle. We keep recursively training until the error is very minimal.

We shall cover more about the forward and backpropagation in detail throughout this book.

Feed-forward and feedback networks

The flow of the signals in neural networks can be either in only one direction or in recurrence. In the first case, we call the neural network architecture feed-forward, since the input signals are fed into the input layer, then, after being processed, they are forwarded to the next layer, just as shown in the following figure. MLPs and radial basis functions are also good examples of feed-forward networks. In the following figure is shown an MLPs architecture:

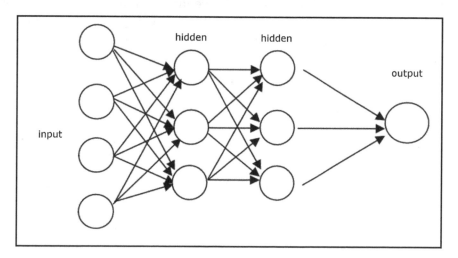

When the neural network has some kind of internal recurrence, meaning that the signals are fed back to a neuron or layer that has already received and processed that signal, the network is of the type feedback, as shown in the following image:

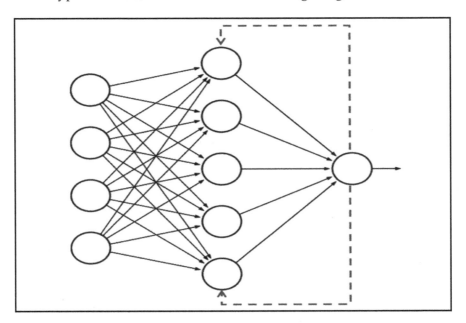

The special reason to add recurrence in a network is the production of a dynamic behavior, particularly when the network addresses problems involving time series or pattern recognition, that require an internal memory to reinforce the learning process. However, such networks are particularly difficult to train, eventually failing to learn. Most of the feedback networks are single layer, such as the **Elman** and **Hopfield** networks, but it is possible to build a recurrent multilayer network, such as echo and recurrent MLP networks.

Gradient descent

Gradient descent is an iterative approach for error correction in any learning model. For neural networks during backpropagation, the process of iterating the update of weights and biases with the error times derivative of the activation function is the gradient descent approach. The steepest descent step size is replaced by a similar size from the previous step. Gradient is basically defined as the slope of the curve and is the derivative of the activation function:

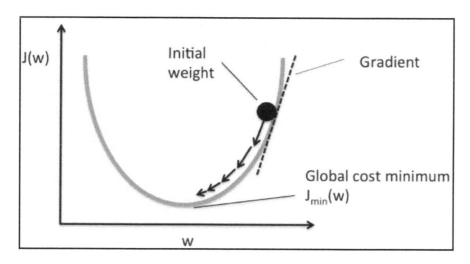

The objective of deriving gradient descent at each step is to find the global cost minimum, where the error is the lowest. And this is where the model has a good fit for the data and predictions are more accurate.

Gradient descent can be performed either for the full batch or stochastic. In full batch gradient descent, the gradient is computed for the full training dataset, whereas **Stochastic Gradient Descent (SGD)** takes a single sample and performs gradient calculation. It can also take mini-batches and perform the calculations. One advantage of SGD is faster computation of gradients.

Taxonomy of neural networks

The basic foundation for ANNs is the same, but various neural network models have been designed during its evolution. The following are a few of the ANN models:

- **Adaptive Linear Element** (**ADALINE**), is a simple perceptron which can solve only linear problems. Each neuron takes the weighted linear sum of the inputs and passes it to a bi-polar function, which either produces a *+1* or *-1* depending on the sum. The function checks the sum of the inputs passed and if the net is >= *0*, it is *+1*, else it is *-1*.
- **Multiple ADALINEs** (**MADALINE**), is a multilayer network of ADALINE units.
- Perceptrons are single layer neural networks (single neuron or unit), where the input is multidimensional (vector) and the output is a function on the weight sum of the inputs.
- Radial basis function network is an ANN where a radial basis function is used as an activation function. The network output is a linear combination of radial basis functions of the inputs and some neuron parameters.
- Feed-forward is the simplest form of neural networks. The data is processed across layers without any loops are cycles. We will study the following feed-forward networks in this book:
  - Autoencoder
  - Probabilistic
  - Time delay
  - Covolutional
- **Recurrent Neural Networks** (**RNNs**), unlike feed-forward networks, propagate data forward and also backwards from later processing stages to earlier stages. The following are the types of RNNs; we shall study them in our later chapters:
  - Hopfield networks
  - Boltzmann machine
  - **Self Organizing Maps** (**SOMs**)
  - **Bidirectional Associative Memory** (**BAM**)
  - **Long Short Term Memory** (**LSTM**)

The following images depict **(a) Recurrent neural network** and **(b) Forward neural network**:

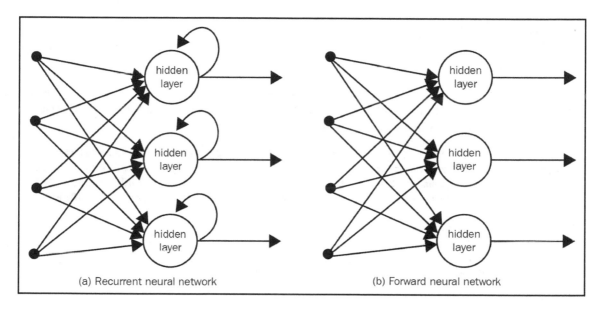

(a) Recurrent neural network   (b) Forward neural network

Simple example using R neural net library - neuralnet()

Consider a simple dataset of a square of numbers, which will be used to train a `neuralnet` function in R and then test the accuracy of the built neural network:

INPUT	OUTPUT
0	0
1	1
2	4
3	9
4	16
5	25
6	36

7	49
8	64
9	81
10	100

Our objective is to set up the weights and bias so that the model can do what is being done here. The output needs to be modeled on a function of input and the function can be used in future to determine the output based on an input:

```
########################################################################
###Chapter 1 - Introduction to Neural Networks - using R ##############
###Simple R program to build, train and test neural Networks###########
########################################################################

#Choose the libraries to use
library("neuralnet")

#Set working directory for the training data
setwd("C:/R")
getwd()

#Read the input file
mydata=read.csv('Squares.csv',sep=",",header=TRUE)
mydata
attach(mydata)
names(mydata)

#Train the model based on output from input
model=neuralnet(formula = Output~Input,
                data = mydata,
                hidden=10,
                threshold=0.01 )
print(model)

#Lets plot and see the layers
plot(model)

#Check the data - actual and predicted
final_output=cbind (Input, Output,
                    as.data.frame(model$net.result) )
colnames(final_output) = c("Input", "Expected Output",
                           "Neural Net Output" )
print(final_output)
########################################################################
```

Let us go through the code line-by-line

To understand all the steps in the code just proposed, we will look at them in detail. Do not worry if a few steps seem unclear at this time, you will be able to look into it in the following examples. First, the code snippet will be shown, and the explanation will follow:

```
library("neuralnet")
```

The line in R includes the library `neuralnet()` in our program. `neuralnet()` is part of **Comprehensive R Archive Network (CRAN)**, which contains numerous R libraries for various applications.

```
mydata=read.csv('Squares.csv',sep=",",header=TRUE)
mydata
attach(mydata)
names(mydata)
```

This reads the CSV file with separator , (comma), and header is the first line in the file. `names()` would display the header of the file.

```
model=neuralnet(formula = Output~Input,
                data = mydata,
                hidden=10,
                threshold=0.01 )
```

The training of the output with respect to the input happens here. The `neuralnet()` library is passed the output and input column names (`ouput~input`), the dataset to be used, the number of neurons in the hidden layer, and the stopping criteria (`threshold`).

A brief description of the `neuralnet` package, extracted from the official documentation, is shown in the following table:

neuralnet-package:
Description:
Training of neural networks using the backpropagation, resilient backpropagation with (Riedmiller, 1994) or without weight backtracking (Riedmiller, 1993), or the modified globally convergent version by Anastasiadis et al. (2005). The package allows flexible settings through custom-choice of error and activation function. Furthermore, the calculation of generalized weights (Intrator O & Intrator N, 1993) is implemented.
Details:
Package: `neuralnet` Type: Package Version: 1.33 Date: 2016-08-05 License: GPL (>=2)

Authors:
Stefan Fritsch, Frauke Guenther (email: `guenther@leibniz-bips.de`) Maintainer: Frauke Guenther (email: `guenther@leibniz-bips.de`)

Usage:

`neuralnet(formula, data, hidden = 1, threshold = 0.01, stepmax = 1e+05, rep = 1,`
`startweights = NULL, learningrate.limit = NULL, learningrate.factor = list(minus = 0.5,`
`plus = 1.2), learningrate=NULL, lifesign = "none", lifesign.step = 1000, algorithm =`
`"rprop+", err.fct = "sse", act.fct = "logistic", linear.output = TRUE, exclude = NULL,`
`constant.weights = NULL, likelihood = FALSE)`

Meaning of the arguments:
`formula`: A symbolic description of the model to be fitted. `data`: A dataframe containing the variables specified in formula. `hidden`: A vector of integers specifying the number of hidden neurons (vertices) in each layer. `threshold`: A numeric value specifying the threshold for the partial derivatives of the error function as stopping criteria. `stepmax`: The maximum steps for the training of the neural network. Reaching this maximum leads to a stop of the neural network's training process. `rep`: The number of repetitions for the neural network's training. `startweights`: A vector containing starting values for the weights. The weights will not be randomly initialized. `learningrate.limit`: A vector or a list containing the lowest and highest limit for the learning rate. Used only for RPROP and GRPROP. `learningrate.factor`: A vector or a list containing the multiplication factors for the upper and lower learning rate, used only for RPROP and GRPROP. `learningrate`: A numeric value specifying the learning rate used by traditional backpropagation. Used only for traditional backpropagation. `lifesign`: A string specifying how much the function will print during the calculation of the neural network- `'none'`, `'minimal'`, or `'full'`. `lifesign.step`: An integer specifying the step size to print the minimal threshold in full lifesign mode. `algorithm`: A string containing the algorithm type to calculate the neural network. `err.fct`: A differentiable function that is used for the calculation of the error. `act.fct`: A differentiable function that is used for smoothing the result of the cross product of the covariate or neurons and the weights. `linear.output`: Logical. If `act.fct` should not be applied to the output neurons set linear output to TRUE, otherwise to FALSE. `exclude`: A vector or a matrix specifying the weights that are excluded from the calculation. `constant.weights`: A vector specifying the values of the weights that are excluded from the training process and treated as fix. `likelihood`: Logical. If the error function is equal to the negative log-likelihood function, the information criteria AIC and BIC will be calculated. Furthermore the usage of confidence. interval is meaningful.

After giving a brief glimpse into the package documentation, let's review the remaining lines of the proposed code sample:

```
print(model)
```

This command prints the model that has just been generated, as follows:

```
$result.matrix
                                          1
error                        0.001094100442
reached.threshold            0.009942937680
steps                    34563.000000000000
Intercept.to.1layhid1       12.859227998180
Input.to.1layhid1           -1.267870997079
Intercept.to.1layhid2       11.352189417430
Input.to.1layhid2           -2.185293148851
Intercept.to.1layhid3        9.108325110066
Input.to.1layhid3           -2.242001064132
Intercept.to.1layhid4      -12.895335140784
Input.to.1layhid4            1.334791491801
Intercept.to.1layhid5       -2.764125889399
Input.to.1layhid5            1.037696638808
Intercept.to.1layhid6       -7.891447011323
Input.to.1layhid6            1.168603081208
Intercept.to.1layhid7       -9.305272978434
Input.to.1layhid7            1.183154841948
Intercept.to.1layhid8       -5.056059256828
Input.to.1layhid8            0.939818815422
Intercept.to.1layhid9       -0.716095585596
Input.to.1layhid9           -0.199246231047
Intercept.to.1layhid10      10.041789457410
Input.to.1layhid10          -0.971900813630
Intercept.to.Output         15.279512257145
1layhid.1.to.Output        -10.701406269616
1layhid.2.to.Output         -3.225793088326
1layhid.3.to.Output         -2.935972228783
1layhid.4.to.Output         35.957437333162
1layhid.5.to.Output         16.897986621510
1layhid.6.to.Output         19.159646982676
1layhid.7.to.Output         20.437748965610
1layhid.8.to.Output         16.049490298968
1layhid.9.to.Output         16.328504039013
1layhid.10.to.Output        -4.900353775268
```

Let's go back to the code analysis:

```
plot(model)
```

This preceding command plots the neural network for us, as follows:

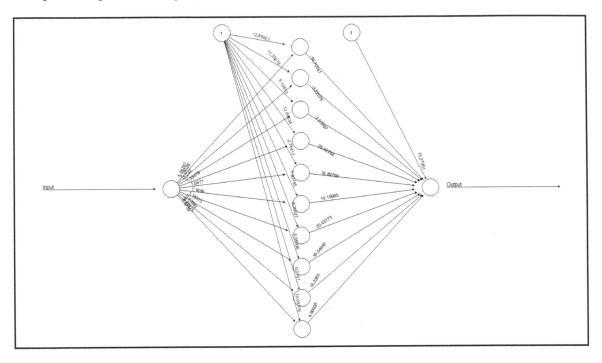

```
final_output=cbind (Input, Output,
                    as.data.frame(model$net.result) )
colnames(final_output) = c("Input", "Expected Output",
                    "Neural Net Output" )
print(final_output)
```

This preceding code prints the final output, comparing the output predicted and actual as:

```
> print(final_output)
   Input Expected Output Neural Net Output
1     0               0      -0.0108685813
2     1               1       1.0277796553
3     2               4       3.9699671691
4     3               9       9.0173879001
5     4              16      15.9950295615
6     5              25      25.0033272826
7     6              36      35.9947137155
8     7              49      49.0046689369
9     8              64      63.9972090104
10    9              81      81.0008391011
11   10             100      99.9997950184
```

Implementation using nnet() library

To improve our practice with the `nnet` library, we look at another example. This time we will use the data collected at a restaurant through customer interviews. The customers were asked to give a score to the following aspects: service, ambience, and food. They were also asked whether they would leave the tip on the basis of these scores. In this case, the number of inputs is 2 and the output is a categorical value (`Tip=1` and `No-tip=0`).

The input file to be used is shown in the following table:

No	CustomerWillTip	Service	Ambience	Food	TipOrNo
1	1	4	4	5	Tip
2	1	6	4	4	Tip
3	1	5	2	4	Tip
4	1	6	5	5	Tip
5	1	6	3	4	Tip
6	1	3	4	5	Tip
7	1	5	5	5	Tip
8	1	5	4	4	Tip
9	1	7	6	4	Tip
10	1	7	6	4	Tip
11	1	6	7	2	Tip
12	1	5	6	4	Tip
13	1	7	3	3	Tip
14	1	5	1	4	Tip
15	1	7	5	5	Tip
16	0	3	1	3	No-tip
17	0	4	6	2	No-tip
18	0	2	5	2	No-tip
19	0	5	2	4	No-tip
20	0	4	1	3	No-tip

21	0	3	3	4	No-tip
22	0	3	4	5	No-tip
23	0	3	6	3	No-tip
24	0	4	4	2	No-tip
25	0	6	3	6	No-tip
26	0	3	6	3	No-tip
27	0	4	3	2	No-tip
28	0	3	5	2	No-tip
29	0	5	5	3	No-tip
30	0	1	3	2	No-tip

This is a classification problem with three inputs and one categorical output. We will address the problem with the following code:

```
####################################################################
##Chapter 1 - Introduction to Neural Networks - using R ############
###Simple R program to build, train and test neural networks #######
### Classification based on 3 inputs and 1 categorical output ######
####################################################################

###Choose the libraries to use
library(NeuralNetTools)
library(nnet)

###Set working directory for the training data
setwd("C:/R")
getwd()

###Read the input file
mydata=read.csv('RestaurantTips.csv',sep=",",header=TRUE)
mydata
attach(mydata)
names(mydata)

##Train the model based on output from input
model=nnet(CustomerWillTip~Service+Ambience+Food,
          data=mydata,
          size =5,
          rang=0.1,
          decay=5e-2,
          maxit=5000)
```

```
print (model)
plotnet (model)
garson (model)


################################################################
```

Let us go through the code line-by-line

To understand all the steps in the code just proposed, we will look at them in detail. First, the code snippet will be shown, and the explanation will follow.

```
library(NeuralNetTools)
library(nnet)
```

This includes the libraries `NeuralNetTools` and `nnet()` for our program.

```
###Set working directory for the training data
setwd("C:/R")
getwd()
###Read the input file
mydata=read.csv('RestaurantTips.csv',sep=",",header=TRUE)
mydata
attach(mydata)
names(mydata)
```

This sets the working directory and reads the input CSV file.

```
##Train the model based on output from input
model=nnet(CustomerWillTip~Service+Ambience+Food,
  data=mydata,
  size =5,
  rang=0.1,
  decay=5e-2,
  maxit=5000)
print(model)
```

This calls the `nnet()` function with the arguments passed. The output is as follows. `nnet()` processes the forward and backpropagation until convergence:

```
> model=nnet(CustomerWillTip~Service+Ambience+Food,data=mydata, size =5,
rang=0.1, decay=5e-2, maxit=5000)
# weights:   26
initial   value 7.571002
iter  10 value 5.927044
iter  20 value 5.267425
iter  30 value 5.238099
iter  40 value 5.217199
```

```
iter   50 value 5.216688
final    value 5.216665
converged
```

A brief description of the `nnet` package, extracted from the official documentation, is shown in the following table:

nnet-package: Feed-forward neural networks and multinomial log-linear models
Description:
Software for feed-forward neural networks with a single hidden layer, and for multinomial log-linear models.
Details:
Package: `nnet` Type: Package Version: 7.3-12 Date: 2016-02-02 License: GPL-2 | GPL-3
Author(s):
Brian Ripley *William Venables*
Usage:
`nnet(formula, data, weights,subset, na.action, contrasts = NULL)`
Meaning of the arguments:
`Formula`: A formula of the form class ~ *x1* + *x2* + ... `data`: Dataframe from which variables specified in formula are preferentially to be taken `weights`: (Case) weights for each example; if missing, defaults to *1* `subset`: An index vector specifying the cases to be used in the training sample `na.action`: A function to specify the action to be taken if NAs are found `contrasts`: A list of contrasts to be used for some or all of the factors appearing as variables in the model formula

After giving a brief glimpse into the package documentation, let's review the remaining lines of the proposed in the following code sample:

```
print(model)
```

This command prints the details of the `net ()` as follows:

```
> print(model)
a 3-5-1 network with 26 weights
inputs: Service Ambience Food
output(s): CustomerWillTip
options were - decay=0.05
```

To plot the `model`, use the following command:

```
plotnet(model)
```

The plot of the `model` is as follows; there are five nodes in the single hidden layer:

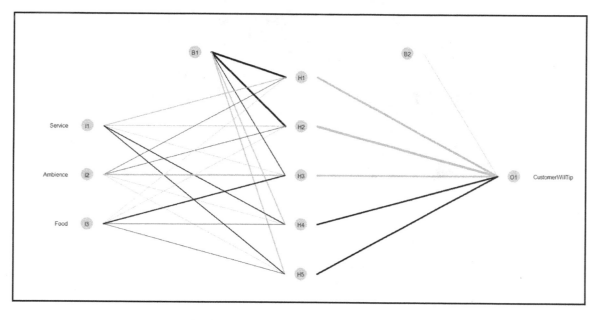

Using `NeuralNetTools`, it's possible to obtain the relative importance of input variables in neural networks using `garson` algorithm:

```
garson(model)
```

This command prints the various input parameters and their importance to the output prediction, as shown in the following figure:

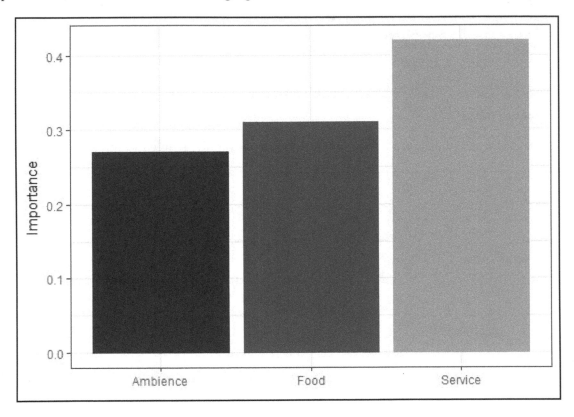

From the chart obtained from the application of the Garson algorithm, it is possible to note that, in the decision to give the tip, the service received by the customers has the greater influence.

We have seen two neural network libraries in R and used them in simple examples. We would deep dive with several practical use cases throughout this book.

Deep learning

DL forms an advanced neural network with numerous hidden layers. DL is a vast subject and is an important concept for building AI. It is used in various applications, such as:

- Image recognition
- Computer vision
- Handwriting detection
- Text classification
- Multiclass classification
- Regression problems, and more

We would see more about DL with R in the future chapters.

Pros and cons of neural networks

Neural networks form the basis of DL, and applications are enormous for DL, ranging from voice recognition to cancer detection. The pros and cons of neural networks are described in this section. The pros outweigh the cons and give neural networks as the preferred modeling technique for data science, machine learning, and predictions.

Pros

The following are some of the advantages of neural networks:

- Neural networks are flexible and can be used for both regression and classification problems. Any data which can be made numeric can be used in the model, as neural network is a mathematical model with approximation functions.
- Neural networks are good to model with nonlinear data with large number of inputs; for example, images. It is reliable in an approach of tasks involving many features. It works by splitting the problem of classification into a layered network of simpler elements.
- Once trained, the predictions are pretty fast.
- Neural networks can be trained with any number of inputs and layers.
- Neural networks work best with more data points.

Cons

Let us take a look at some of the cons of neural networks:

- Neural networks are black boxes, meaning we cannot know how much each independent variable is influencing the dependent variables.
- It is computationally very expensive and time consuming to train with traditional CPUs.
- Neural networks depend a lot on training data. This leads to the problem of over-fitting and generalization. The mode relies more on the training data and may be tuned to the data.

Best practices in neural network implementations

The following are some best practices that will help in the implementation of neural network:

- Neural networks are best implemented when there is good training data
- More the hidden layers in an MLP, the better the accuracy of the model for predictions
- It is best to have five nodes in the hidden layer
- ReLU and **Sum of Square of Errors** (**SSE**) are respectively best techniques for activation function and error deduction

Quick note on GPU processing

The increase in processing capabilities has been a tremendous booster for usage of neural networks in day-to-day problems. GPU is a specialized processor designed to perform graphical operations (for example, gaming, 3D animation, and so on). They perform mathematically intensive tasks and are additional to the CPU. The CPU performs the operational tasks of the computer, while the GPU is used to perform heavy workload processing.

The neural network architecture needs heavy mathematical computational capabilities and GPU is the preferred candidate here. The vectorized dot matrix product between the weights and inputs at every neuron can be run in parallel through GPUs. The advancements in GPUs is popularizing neural networks. The applications of DL in image processing, computer vision, bioinformatics, and weather modeling are benefiting through GPUs.

Summary

In this chapter, we saw an overview of ANNs. Neural networks implementation is simple, but the internals are pretty complex. We can summarize neural network as a universal mathematical function approximation. Any set of inputs which produce outputs can be made a black box mathematical function through a neural network, and the applications are enormous in the recent years.

We saw the following in this chapter:

- Neural network is a machine learning technique and is data-driven
- AI, machine learning, and neural networks are different paradigms of making machines work like humans
- Neural networks can be used for both supervised and unsupervised machine learning
- Weights, biases, and activation functions are important concepts in neural networks
- Neural networks are nonlinear and non-parametric
- Neural networks are very fast in prediction and are most accurate in comparison with other machine learning models
- There are input, hidden, and output layers in any neural network architecture
- Neural networks are based on building MLP, and we understood the basis for neural networks: weights, bias, activation functions, feed-forward, and backpropagation processing
- Forward and backpropagation are techniques to derive a neural network model

Neural networks can be implemented through many programming languages, namely Python, R, MATLAB, C, and Java, among others. The focus of this book will be building applications using R. DNN and AI systems are evolving on the basis of neural networks. In the forthcoming chapter, we will drill through different types of neural networks and their various applications.

2
Learning Process in Neural Networks

Just as there are many different types of learning and approaches to human learning, so we can say about the machines as well. To ensure that a machine will be able to learn from experience, it is important to define the best available methodologies depending on the specific job requirements. This often means choosing techniques that work for the present case and evaluating them from time to time, to determine if we need to try something new.

We have seen the basics of neural networks in Chapter 1, *Neural Network and Artificial Intelligence Concepts*, and also two simple implementations using R. In this chapter, we will deal with the learning process, that is how to train, test, and deploy a neural network machine learning model. The training phase is used for learning, to fit the parameters of the neural networks. The testing phase is used to assess the performance of fully-trained neural networks. Finally, inthe deployment phase, actual data is passed through the model to get the prediction.

The following is the list of concepts covered in this chapter:

- Learning process
- Supervised learning
- Unsupervised learning
- Training, testing, and deploying a model
- Evaluation metrics-error measurement and fine tuning; measuring accuracy of a model
- Supervised learning model using neural networks
- Unsupervised learning model using neural networks
- Backpropagation

By the end of the chapter, we will understand the basic concepts of the learning process and how to implementit in the R environment. We will discover different types of algorithms to implement a neural network. We will learn how to train, test, and deploy a model. We will know how to perform a correct valuation procedure.

What is machine learning?

What do we mean by the term machine learning? The definition is quite difficult, to do so, we are asking large field of scientists to help. We can mention an artificial intelligence pioneer's quote:

> *"Field of study that gives computers the ability to learn without being explicitly programmed."*

> –Arthur Samuel

Machine learning is about training a model or an algorithm with data and then using the model to predict any new data. For example, a toddler is taught how to walk from his crawling phase. Initially, the toddler's parents hold the toddler's hand to help him up, and he is taught through the data that is given. On the basis of these procedures, if an obstacle presents itself in the toddler's path or if there is a turn somewhere, the toddler is able to navigate on his own after the training. The data used for training is the training data and the recipient continues to learn even after the formal training.

Machines too can be taught like toddlers to do a task based on training. First, we feed enough data to tell the machine what needs to be done on what circumstances. After the training, the machine can perform automatically and can also learn to fine-tune itself. This type of training the machine is called **machine learning**.

The main difference between machine learning and programming is that there is no coding/programming involved in machine learning, while programming is about giving the machine a set of instructions to perform. In machine learning, the data is the only input provided and the model is based on the algorithm we have decided to use.

The algorithm to be used is based on various factors of the data: the features (or independent variables), the type of dependent variable(s), the accuracy of the model, and the speed of training and prediction of the model.

Based on the independent variable(s) of the machine learning data, there are three different ways to train a model:

- Supervised learning
- Unsupervised learning
- Reinforcement learning

The following figure shows thedifferentalgorithms to train a machine learning model:

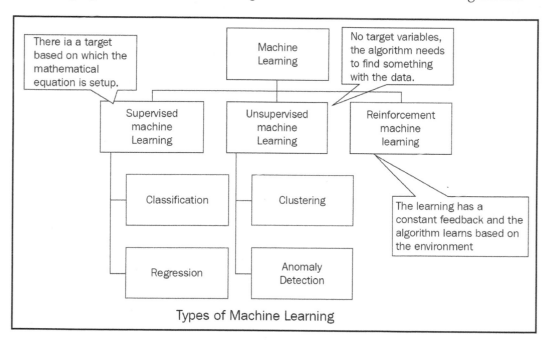

In the following sections, we will go through them on by one.

Supervised learning

Supervised learning is a learning method where there is a part of the training data which acts as a teacher to the algorithm to determine the model. The machine is taught what to learn from the target data. The target data, or dependent or response variables, are the outcome of the collective action of the independent variables. The network training is done with the target data and its behavior with patterns of input data. The target labels are known in advance and the data is fed to the algorithm to derive the model.

Most of neural network usage is done using supervised learning. The weights and biases are adjusted based on the output values. The output can be categorical (like true/false or 0/1/2) or continuous (like 1,2,3, and so on). The model is dependent on the type of output variables, and in the case of neural networks, the output layer is built on the type of target variable.

 For neural networks, all the independent and dependent variables need to be numeric, as a neural network is based on mathematical models. It is up to the data scientist to convert the data to numbers to be fed into the model.

Supervised learning is depicted by the following diagram:

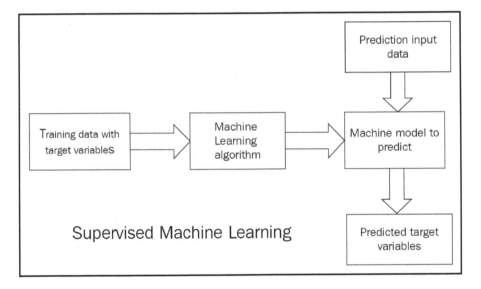

Unsupervised learning

In unsupervised learning (or self organization), the output layer is trained to organize the input data into another set of data without the need of a target variable. The input data is analyzed and patterns are found in it to derive the output, as shown in the following figure. Since there is no teacher (or target variable), this type of learning is called**unsupervised learning**.

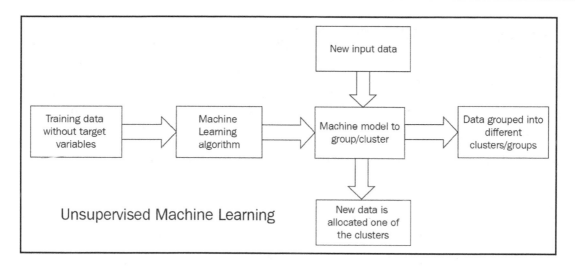

The different techniques available for unsupervised learning are as follows:

- Clustering (K-means, hierarchical)
- Association techniques
- Dimensionality reduction
- **Self Organizing Map(SOM)**/ Kohonen networks

To summarize, the two main types of machine learning are depicted in the following figure:

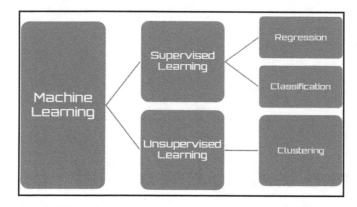

For neural networks, we have both the types available, using different ways available in R.

Reinforcement learning

Reinforcement learning is a type of machine learning where there is constant feedback given to the model to adapt to the environment. There is a performance evaluation at each step to improve the model. For neural networks, there is a special type called **Q-learning**, combined with neuron to implement reinforcement learning in the backpropagation feedback mechanism. The details are out of scope of this book.

The following are the three types of learnings we have covered so far:

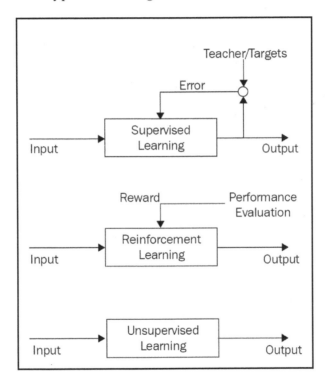

Training and testing the model

Training and testing the model forms the basis for further usage of the model for prediction in predictive analytics. Given a dataset of *100* rows of data, which includes the predictor and response variables, we split the dataset into a convenient ratio (say *70:30*) and allocate *70* rows for training and *30* rows for testing. The rows are selected in random to reduce bias.

Once the training data is available, the data is fed to the neural network to get the massive universal function in place. The training data determines the weights, biases, and activation functions to be used to get to output from input. Until recently, we could not say that a weight has a positive or a negative influence on the target variable. But now we've been able to shed some light inside the black box. For example, by plotting a trained neural network, we can discover trained synaptic weights and basic information about the training process.

Once the sufficient convergence is achieved, the model is stored in memory and the next step is testing the model. We pass the *30* rows of data to check if the actual output matches with the predicted output from the model. The evaluation is used to get various metrics which can validate the model. If the accuracy is too wary, the model has to be re-built with change in the training data and other parameters passed to the neural net function. We will cover more about the evaluation metrics later in this chapter.

After training and testing, the model is said to be deployed, where actual data is passed through the model to get the prediction. For example, the use case may be determining a fraud transaction or a home loan eligibility check based on various input parameters.

The training, testing, and deployment is represented in the following figure:

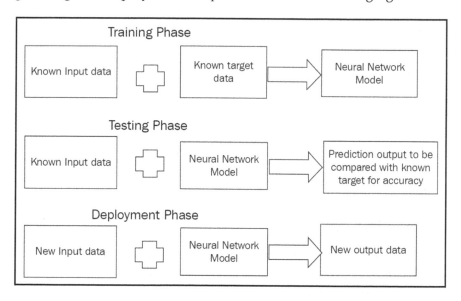

So far, we have focused on the various algorithms available; it is now time to dedicate ourselves to the data that represents the essential element of each analysis.

The data cycle

The data forms a key component for model building and the learning process. The data needs to be collected, cleaned, converted, and then fed to the model for learning. The overall data life cycle is shown as follows:

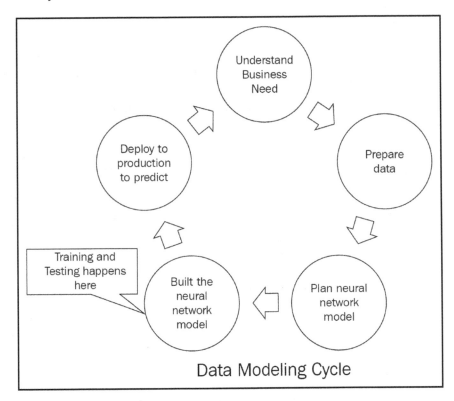

Data Modeling Cycle

One of the critical requirements for modeling is having good and balanced data. This helps in higher accuracy models and better usage of the available algorithms. A data scientist's time is mostly spent on cleansing the data before building the model.

We have seen the training and testing before deployment of the model. For testing, the results are captured as evaluation metrics, which helps us decide if we should use a particular model or change it instead.

We will see the evaluation metrics next.

Evaluation metrics

Evaluating a model involves checking if the predicted value is equal to the actual value during the testing phase. There are various metrics available to check the model, and they depend on the state of the target variable.

For a binary classification problem, the predicted target variable and the actual target variable can be in any of the following four states:

Predicted	Actual
Predicted = TRUE	*Actual = TRUE*
Predicted = TRUE	*Actual = FALSE*
Predicted = FALSE	*Actual = TRUE*
Predicted = FALSE	*Actual = FALSE*

When we have the predicted and actual values as same values, we are said to be accurate. If all predicted and actual values are same (either all *TRUE* or all *FALSE*), the model is *100* percent accurate. But, this is never the case.

Since neural networks are approximation models, there is always a bit of error possible. All the four states mentioned in the previous table are possible.

We define the following terminology and metrics for a model:

- **True Positives (TP):**All cases wherethe predicted and actual are both *TRUE* (good accuracy).
- **True Negative (TN):**All cases when predicted is *FALSE* and the actual is also *FALSE* (good accuracy).
- **False Positive(FP):**This is a case when we predict something as positive (*TRUE*), but it is actually negative. It is like a false alarm or an FP error. An example is when a male is predicted to be pregnant by a pregnancy test kit. All cases when predicted is *TRUE*, while the actual is *FALSE*. This is also called**type 1 error**.
- **False Negative (FN):**When we predict something as *FALSE*, but in actuality it is *TRUE*, then the case is called FN. For example, when a pregnant female is predicted as not being pregnant by a pregnancy test kit, it is an FN case. All cases when predicted is *FALSE* and actual *TRUE*. This is also called**type 2 error**.

Confusion matrix

When the values of the classification are plotted in a *nxn* matrix (*2x2* in case of binary classification), the matrix is called the **confusion matrix**. All the evaluation metrics can be derived from the confusion matrix itself:

	Predicted value	Predicted value
Actual values	*TRUE*	*FALSE*
TRUE	*TP*	*FN*
FALSE	*FP*	*TN*

Now, let's look at some evaluation metrics in detail.

True Positive Rate

True Positive Rate (**TPR**) or sensitivity or recall or hit rate is a measure of how many true positives were identified out of all the positives identified:

$$TPR = \frac{TP}{P} = \frac{TP}{TP + FN}$$

Ideally, the model is better if we have this closer to one.

True Negative Rate

True Negative Rate (**TNR**) or specificity is the ratio of true negatives and total number of negatives we have predicted:

$$TNR = \frac{TN}{N} = \frac{TN}{TN + FP}$$

If this ratio is closer to zero, the model is more accurate.

Accuracy

Accuracy is the measure of how good our model is. It is expected to be closer to 1, if our model is performing well.

Accuracy is the ratio of correct predictions and all the total predictions:

$$ACC = \frac{TP + TN}{P + N} = \frac{TP + TN}{TP + TN + FP + FN}$$

Precision and recall

Precision and recall are again ratios between the *TP* with (*TP+FP*) and *TP* with (*TP+FN*) respectively. These ratios determine how relevant our predictions are compared to the actual.

Precision is defined as how many selected items are relevant. That is, how many of the predicted ones are actually correctly predicted.

The equation is:

$$Precision = \frac{TP}{TP + FP}$$

If precision is closer to one, we are more accurate in our predictions.

Recall, on the other hand, tells how many relevant items we selected. Mathematically, it is:

$$Recall = \frac{TP}{TP + FN}$$

The following diagram depicts clearly the discussion we have done so far:

F-score

F-score, or F1-score, is another measure of accuracy. Technically, it is the harmonic mean of precision and recall:

$$F = 2 \cdot \frac{\text{precision} \cdot \text{recall}}{\text{precision} + \text{recall}}$$

Receiver Operating Characteristic curve

A **Receiver Operating Characteristic(ROC)** curve is a graphical visual that illustrates the predictive ability of a binary classifier system. The ROC curve is created by plotting a graph of the TPR against the **False Positive Rate** (**FPR**) at various threshold settings. This gives us **Sensitivity** versus (**1 - Specificity**). A ROC curve typically looks like this:

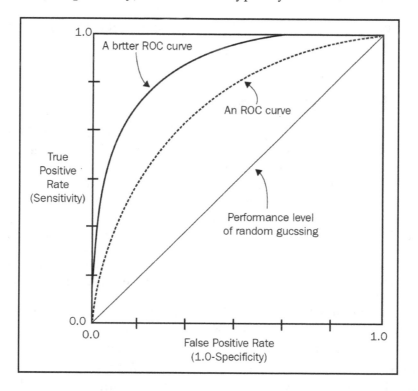

After acquiring the necessary skills, we are ready to analyze in detail the algorithms used for building the neural networks.

Learning in neural networks

As we saw in Chapter 1, *Neural Network and Artificial Intelligence Concepts*, neural networks is a machine learning algorithm that has the ability to learn from data and give us predictions using the model built. It is a universal function approximation, that is, any input, output data can be approximated to a mathematical function.

The forward propagation gives us an initial mathematical function to arrive at output(s) based on inputs by choosing random weights. The difference between the actual and predicted is called the error term. The learning process in a feed-forward neural network actually happens during the backpropagation stage. The model is fine tuned with the weights by reducing the error term in each iteration. Gradient descent is used in the backpropagation process.

Let us cover the backpropagation in detail in this chapter, as it is an important machine learning aspect for neural networks.

Back to backpropagation

We have covered the forward propagation in detail in `Chapter 1`, *Neural Network and Artificial Intelligence Concepts*, and a little about backpropagation using gradient descent. Backpropagation is one of the important concepts for understanding neural networks and it relies on calculus to update the weights and biases in each layer. Backpropagation of errors is similar to *learning from mistakes*. We correct ourselves in our mistakes (errors) in every iteration, until we reach a point called **convergence**. The goal of backpropagation is to correct the weights in each layer and minimize the overall error at the output layer.

Neural network learning heavily relies on backpropagation in feed-forward networks. The usual steps of forward propagation and error correction are explained as follows:

1. Start the neural network forward propagation by assigning random weights and biases to each of the neurons in the hidden layer.
2. Get the sum of *sum(weight*input) + bias* at each neuron.
3. Apply the activation function (*sigmoid*) at each neuron.
4. Take this output and pass it onto the next layer neuron.
5. If the layer is the output layer, apply the weights and get thesum of *sum(weight*input) + bias* at each output layer neuron.
6. Again, apply the activation function at the output layer neuron.
7. This forms the output of the neural network at the output layer for one forward pass.
8. Now, with the training data, we can identify the error term at each output neuron, by subtracting the actual output and the activation function output value.

9. The total of the errors is arrived at by using the followingformula:

$$E = \frac{1}{2}(t-y)^2,$$

where

E is the squared error,

t is the target output for a training sample, and

y is the actual output of the output neuron.

A factor of *1/2* is used to cancel the exponent when the error function E is subsequently differentiated.

10. The gradient descent technique requires calculation of the partial derivative of the error term (E) with respect to the weights of the network. Calculating the partial derivative of the full error with respect to the weight $w_{ij}$is done using the **chain rule**of differentiation:

$$\frac{\partial E}{\partial w_{ij}} = \frac{\partial E}{\partial o_j} \frac{\partial o_j}{\partial net_j} \frac{\partial net_j}{\partial w_{ij}}$$

The derivative is defined as the rate of change of a value, the gradient descent uses the derivative (or slope) to minimize the error term and arrive at a correct set of weights.

11. The first factor is partial derivative of the error term with respect to the output at that particular neuron *j*and o_j is equal to *y*:

$$\frac{\partial E}{\partial o_j} = \frac{\partial E}{\partial y} \frac{\partial}{\partial y} \frac{1}{2}(t-y)^2 = y - t$$

12. The second factor in the chain rule is the partial derivative of the output of neuron o_j with respect to its input, and is the partial derivative of the activation function (the *sigmoid* function):

$$\frac{\partial o_j}{\partial \text{net}_j} = \frac{\partial}{\partial \text{net}_j} \varphi\left(\text{net}_j\right) = \varphi\left(\text{net}_j\right)\left(1 - \varphi\left(\text{net}_j\right)\right)$$

Here net_j is the input to the neuron.

13. The third term in the chain rule is simply o_i.

$$\frac{\partial \text{net}_j}{\partial w_{ij}} \frac{\partial}{\partial w_{ij}} \left(\sum_{k=1}^{n} w_{kj} o_k\right) = \frac{\partial}{\partial w_{ij}} w_{kj} o_k = o_i$$

14. Combining steps 11, 12, and 13, we get:

$$\frac{\partial E}{\partial w_{ij}} = o_i \delta_j$$

with

$$\delta_j = \frac{\partial E}{\partial o_j} \frac{\partial o_j}{\partial \text{net}_j} = \begin{cases} \left(o_j - t_j\right) o_j \left(1 - o_j\right) & \text{if } j \text{ is an output neuron,} \\ \left(\sum_{\ell \in L} \delta_\ell w_{j\ell}\right) o_j \left(1 - o_j\right) & \text{if } j \text{ is an inner neuron.} \end{cases}$$

15. The weight w_{ij} at each neuron (any layer) is updated with this partial derivative, combined with the learning rate.

These steps are repeated until we have convergence of very low error term or a specified number of times.

All the steps are taken care of internally in the R packages available. We can supply the learning rate along with various other parameters.

The backpropagation is illustrated as follows:

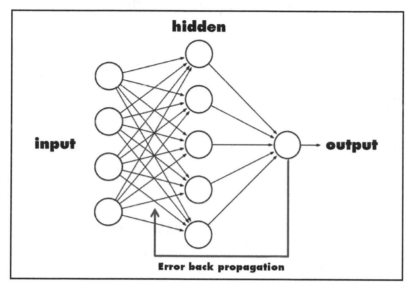

As with all things in life, even an algorithm has further improvement margins. In the next section, we'll see how to do it.

Neural network learning algorithm optimization

The procedure used to carry out the learning process in a neural network is called the training algorithm.The learning algorithm is what the machine learning algorithm chooses as model with the best optimization. The aim is to minimize the loss function and provide more accuracy. Here we illustrate some of the optimization techniques, other than gradient descent.

The **Particle Swarm Optimization** (**PSO**) methodis inspired by observations of social and collective behavior on the movements of bird flocks in search of food or survival. It is similar to a fish school trying to move together. We know the position and velocity of the particles, and PSO aims at searching a solution set in a large space controlled by mathematical equations on position and velocity.It is bio-inspired from biological organism behavior for collective intelligence.

Simulated annealing is a method that works on a probabilistic approach to approximate the global optimum for the cost function. The method searches for a solution in large space with simulation.

Evolutionary methods are derived from the evolutionary process in biology, and evolution can be in terms of reproduction, mutation, selection, and recombination. A fitness function is used to determine the performance of a model, and based on this function, we select our final model.

The **Expectation Maximization(EM)** methodis a statistical learning method that uses an iterative method to find maximum likelihood or maximum posterior estimate, thus minimizing the error.

Supervised learning in neural networks

As previously mentioned, supervised learning is a learning method where there is a part of training data which acts as a teacher to the algorithm to determine the model. In the following section, an example of a regression predictive modeling problem is proposed to understand how to solve it with neural networks.

Boston dataset

The dataset describes 13 numerical properties of houses in Boston suburbs, and is concerned with modeling the price of houses in those suburbs in thousands of dollars. As such, this is a regression predictive modeling problem. Input attributes include things like crime rate, proportion of non-retail business acres, chemical concentrations, and more. In the following list are shown all the variables followed by a brief description:

- Number of instances: *506*
- Number of attributes: *13* continuous attributes (including `class` attribute `MEDV`), and one binary-valued attribute

Each of the attributes is detailed as follows:

1. `crim`per capita crime rate by town.
2. `zn` proportion of residential land zoned for lots over *25,000* square feet.
3. `indus` proportion of non-retail business acres per town.
4. `chas` Charles River dummy variable (= *1* if tract bounds river; *0* otherwise).

5. `nox` nitric oxides concentration (parts per *10* million).

6. `rm` average number of rooms per dwelling.

7. `age` proportion of owner-occupied units built prior to *1940*.

8. `dis` weighted distances to five Boston employment centres

9. `rad` index of accessibility to radial highways.

10. `tax` full-value property-tax rate per *$10,000*.

11. `ptratio` pupil-teacher ratio by town.

12. `black` *1000(Bk - 0.63)^2* where *Bk* is the proportion of blacks by town.

13. `lstat` percent lower status of the population.

14. `medv` median value of owner-occupied homes in *$1000's*.

Of these, `medv` is the response variable, while the other thirteen variables are possible predictors. The goal of this analysis is to fit a regression model that best explains the variation in `medv`.

There is a relation between the first thirteen columns and the `medv` response variable. We can predict the `medv` value based on the input thirteen columns.

 This dataset is already provided with R libraries (`MASS`), as we will see later, so we do not have to worry about retrieving the data.

Neural network regression with the Boston dataset

In this section, we will run a regression neural network for the `Boston` dataset. The `medv` value is predicted for the test data. The train to test split is *70:30*. The `neuralnet` function is used to model the data with a neural network:

```
###########################################################################
###Chapter 2 - Introduction to Neural Networks - using R ###########
###Simple R program to build, train, test regression neural networks#
#########################flename: Boston.r#########################
###########################################################################

library("neuralnet")
library(MASS)
```

```
set.seed(1)

data = Boston

max_data <- apply(data, 2, max)
min_data <- apply(data, 2, min)
data_scaled <- scale(data,center = min_data, scale = max_data - min_data)

index = sample(1:nrow(data),round(0.70*nrow(data)))
train_data <- as.data.frame(data_scaled[index,])
test_data <- as.data.frame(data_scaled[-index,])

n = names(data)
f = as.formula(paste("medv ~", paste(n[!n %in% "medv"], collapse = " + ")))
net_data = neuralnet(f,data=train_data,hidden=10,linear.output=T)
plot(net_data)

predict_net_test <- compute(net_data,test_data[,1:13])

predict_net_test_start <- predict_net_test$net.result*(max(data$medv)-
min(data$medv))+min(data$medv)
test_start <- as.data.frame((test_data$medv)*(max(data$medv)-
min(data$medv))+min(data$medv))
MSE.net_data <- sum((test_start -
predict_net_test_start)^2)/nrow(test_start)

Regression_Model <- lm(medv~., data=data)
summary(Regression_Model)
test <- data[-index,]
predict_lm <- predict(Regression_Model,test)
MSE.lm <- sum((predict_lm - test$medv)^2)/nrow(test)

MSE.net_data
MSE.lm
#################################################################################
```

Don't worry, now we will explain in detail the whole code,line by line.

```
library("neuralnet")
library(MASS)
```

The first two lines of the code are simple, as they load the libraries we will use for later calculations. Specifically, the `neuralnet` library will help us to build and train the network, while the `MASS` library will serve us to load the `Boston` dataset that we have previously introduced in detail.

Remember, to install a library that is not present in the initial distribution of R, you must use the `install.package` function. This is the main function to install packages. It takes a vector of names and a destination library, downloads the packages from the repositories and installs them.

In our case, for example, to install the neuralnet package, we should write:

install.neuralnet

Finally, it should be emphasized that this function should be used only once and not every time you run the code. Instead, load the library through the following command and must be repeated every time you run the code:

library (neuralnet)

The function set.seed sets the seed of R's random number generator, which is useful for creating simulations or random objects that can be reproduced:

set.seed(1)

You have to use this function every time you want to get a reproducible random result. In this case, the random numbers are the same, and they would continue to be the same no matter how far out in the sequence we go.

The following command loads the Boston dataset, which, as we anticipated, is contained in the MASS library and saves it in a given frame:

data = Boston

Use the `str` function to view a compactly display the structure of an arbitrary R object. In our case, using `str(data)`, we will obtain the following results:

```
> str(data)
'data.frame': 506 obs. of 14 variables:
 $ crim : num 0.00632 0.02731 0.02729 0.03237 0.06905 ...
 $ zn : num 18 0 0 0 0 0 12.5 12.5 12.5 12.5 ...
 $ indus : num 2.31 7.07 7.07 2.18 2.18 2.18 7.87 7.87 7.87 7.87 ...
 $ chas : int 0 0 0 0 0 0 0 0 0 0 ...
 $ nox : num 0.538 0.469 0.469 0.458 0.458 0.458 0.524 0.524 0.524 0.524
...
 $ rm : num 6.58 6.42 7.18 7 7.15 ...
 $ age : num 65.2 78.9 61.1 45.8 54.2 58.7 66.6 96.1 100 85.9 ...
 $ dis : num 4.09 4.97 4.97 6.06 6.06 ...
 $ rad : int 1 2 2 3 3 3 5 5 5 5 ...
 $ tax : num 296 242 242 222 222 222 311 311 311 311 ...
```

```
$ ptratio: num 15.3 17.8 17.8 18.7 18.7 18.7 15.2 15.2 15.2 15.2 ...
$ black : num 397 397 393 395 397 ...
$ lstat : num 4.98 9.14 4.03 2.94 5.33 ...
$ medv : num 24 21.6 34.7 33.4 36.2 28.7 22.9 27.1 16.5 18.9 ...
```

The result obtained for the given object is shown in the following figure:

	crim	zn	indus	chas	nox	rm	age	dis	rad	tax	ptratio	black	lstat	medv
1	0.00632	18.0	2.31	0	0.5380	6.575	65.2	4.0900	1	296	15.3	396.90	4.98	24.0
2	0.02731	0.0	7.07	0	0.4690	6.421	78.9	4.9671	2	242	17.8	396.90	9.14	21.6
3	0.02729	0.0	7.07	0	0.4690	7.185	61.1	4.9671	2	242	17.8	392.83	4.03	34.7
4	0.03237	0.0	2.18	0	0.4580	6.998	45.8	6.0622	3	222	18.7	394.63	2.94	33.4
5	0.06905	0.0	2.18	0	0.4580	7.147	54.2	6.0622	3	222	18.7	396.90	5.33	36.2
6	0.02985	0.0	2.18	0	0.4580	6.430	58.7	6.0622	3	222	18.7	394.12	5.21	28.7
7	0.08829	12.5	7.87	0	0.5240	6.012	66.6	5.5605	5	311	15.2	395.60	12.43	22.9
8	0.14455	12.5	7.87	0	0.5240	6.172	96.1	5.9505	5	311	15.2	396.90	19.15	27.1
9	0.21124	12.5	7.87	0	0.5240	5.631	100.0	6.0821	5	311	15.2	386.63	29.93	16.5
10	0.17004	12.5	7.87	0	0.5240	6.004	85.9	6.5921	5	311	15.2	386.71	17.10	18.9
11	0.22489	12.5	7.87	0	0.5240	6.377	94.3	6.3467	5	311	15.2	392.52	20.45	15.0
12	0.11747	12.5	7.87	0	0.5240	6.009	82.9	6.2267	5	311	15.2	396.90	13.27	18.9
13	0.09378	12.5	7.87	0	0.5240	5.889	39.0	5.4509	5	311	15.2	390.50	15.71	21.7
14	0.62976	0.0	8.14	0	0.5380	5.949	61.8	4.7075	4	307	21.0	396.90	8.26	20.4
15	0.63796	0.0	8.14	0	0.5380	6.096	84.5	4.4619	4	307	21.0	380.02	10.26	18.2
16	0.62739	0.0	8.14	0	0.5380	5.834	56.5	4.4986	4	307	21.0	395.62	8.47	19.9
17	1.05393	0.0	8.14	0	0.5380	5.935	29.3	4.4986	4	307	21.0	386.85	6.58	23.1
18	0.78420	0.0	8.14	0	0.5380	5.990	81.7	4.2579	4	307	21.0	386.75	14.67	17.5
19	0.80271	0.0	8.14	0	0.5380	5.456	36.6	3.7965	4	307	21.0	288.99	11.69	20.2

Showing 1 to 19 of 506 entries

Let's go back to parse the code:

```
max_data <- apply(data, 2, max)
min_data <- apply(data, 2, min)
data_scaled <- scale(data,center = min_data, scale = max_data - min_data)
```

We needthis snippet of code to normalize the data.

Remember, it is good practice to normalize the data before training a neural network.With normalization, data units are eliminated, allowing you to easily compare data from different locations.

This is an extremely important procedure in building a neural network, as it avoids unnecessary results or very difficult training processes resulting in algorithm convergence problems. You can choose different methods for scaling the data (**z-normalization, min-max scale,** and so on). For this example, we will use the min-max method (usually called feature scaling) to get all the scaled data in the range *[0,1]*. The formula to achieve this is the following:

$$x_{scaled} = \frac{x - x_{min}}{x_{max} - x_{min}}$$

Before applying the method chosen for normalization, you must calculate the minimum and maximum values of each database column. To do this, we use the `apply` function. This function returns a vector or an array or a list of values obtained by applying a function to margins of an array or matrix. Let's understand the meaning of the arguments used.

```
max_data <- apply(data, 2, max)
```

The first argument of the `apply` function specifies the dataset to apply the function, in our case, the dataset named `data`. The second argument must contain a vector giving the subscripts which the function will be applied over. In our case, one indicates rows and 2 indicates columns. The third argument must contain the function to be applied; in our case, the `max` function.

To normalize the data, we use the `scale` function, which is a generic function whose default method centers and/or scales the columns of a numeric matrix.

```
index = sample(1:nrow(data),round(0.70*nrow(data)))
train_data <- as.data.frame(data_scaled[index,])
test_data <- as.data.frame(data_scaled[-index,])
```

In the first line of the code just suggested, the dataset is split into *70:30*, with the intention of using *70* percent of the data at our disposal to train the network and the remaining *30* percent to test the network. In the second and third lines, the data of the dataframe named `data` is subdivided into two new dataframes, called `train_data` and `test_data`.

```
n = names(data)
f = as.formula(paste("medv ~", paste(n[!n %in% "medv"], collapse = " + ")))
net_data = neuralnet(f,data=train_data,hidden=10,linear.output=T)
plot(net_data)
```

Everything so far has only been used to prepare the data. It is now time to build the network. To do this, we first recover all the variable names using the `names` function. This function will get or set the name of an object.

Next, we build`formula` that we will use to build the network, so we use the `neuralnet` function to build and train the network. In this case, we will create a network with only one hidden layer with `10` nodes. Finally, we`plot` the neural network,as shown in the following figure:

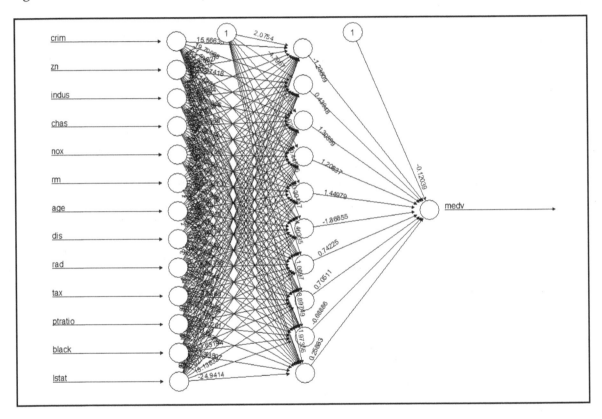

Now that we have the network, what do we do? Of course, we use it to make predictions. We had set aside *30* percent of the available data to do this:

```
predict_net_test <- compute(net_data,test_data[,1:13])
```

In our case, we applied the function to the `test_data` dataset, using only the first `13` columns representing the input variables of the network:

```
predict_net_test_start <- predict_net_test$net.result*(max(data$medv)-
min(data$medv))+min(data$medv)
test_start <- as.data.frame((test_data$medv)*(max(data$medv)-
min(data$medv))+min(data$medv))
MSE.net_data <- sum((predict_net_test_start -
test_start)^2)/nrow(test_start)
```

But how do we figure out whether the forecasts the network is able to perform are accurate? We can use the **Mean Squared Error** (**MSE**) as a measure of how far away our predictions are from the real data.

In this regard, it is worth remembering that before we built the network we had normalized the data. Now, in order to be able to compare, we need to step back and return to the starting position. Once the values of the dataset are restored, we can calculate the *MSE* through the following equation:

$$MSE = \frac{\sum_{i=1}^{n}\left(y_{predict} - y_{actual}\right)^2}{n}$$

Well, we have calculated *MSE* now with what do we compare it to? To get an idea of the accuracy of the network prediction, we can build a linear regression model:

```
Regression_Model <- lm(medv~., data=data)
summary(Regression_Model)
test <- data[-index,]
predict_lm <- predict(Regression_Model,test)
MSE.lm <- sum((predict_lm - test$medv)^2)/nrow(test)
```

We build a linear regression model using the `lm` function. This function is used to fit linear models. It can be used to perform regression, single stratum analysis of variance, and analysis of covariance.To produce result summaries of the results of model fitting obtained, we have used the `summary` function, which returns the following results:

```
> summary(Regression_Model)

Call:
lm(formula = medv ~ ., data = data)

Residuals:
 Min 1Q Median 3Q Max
-15.5944739 -2.7297159 -0.5180489 1.7770506 26.1992710

Coefficients:
 Estimate Std. Error t value Pr(>|t|)
(Intercept) 36.4594883851 5.1034588106 7.14407 0.00000000000328344 ***
crim -0.1080113578 0.0328649942 -3.28652 0.00108681 **
zn 0.0464204584 0.0137274615 3.38158 0.00077811 ***
indus 0.0205586264 0.0614956890 0.33431 0.73828807
chas 2.6867338193 0.8615797562 3.11838 0.00192503 **
nox -17.7666112283 3.8197437074 -4.65126 0.00000424564380765 ***
rm 3.8098652068 0.4179252538 9.11614 < 0.000000000000000222 ***
age 0.0006922246 0.0132097820 0.05240 0.95822931
dis -1.4755668456 0.1994547347 -7.39800 0.00000000000060135 ***
rad 0.3060494790 0.0663464403 4.61290 0.00000507052902269 ***
tax -0.0123345939 0.0037605364 -3.28001 0.00111164 **
ptratio -0.9527472317 0.1308267559 -7.28251 0.00000000000130884 ***
black 0.0093116833 0.0026859649 3.46679 0.00057286 ***
lstat -0.5247583779 0.0507152782 -10.34715 < 0.000000000000000222 ***
---
Signif. codes: 0 '***' 0.001 '**' 0.01 '*' 0.05 '.' 0.1 ' ' 1

Residual standard error: 4.745298 on 492 degrees of freedom
Multiple R-squared: 0.7406427, Adjusted R-squared: 0.7337897
F-statistic: 108.0767 on 13 and 492 DF, p-value: < 0.00000000000000022204
```

Also, for the regression model, we calculate themean MSE. Finally, in order to assess the performance of the network, it is compared with a multiple linear regression model calculated with the same database as follows:

```
MSE.net_data
MSE.lm
```

The results are:

```
> MSE.net_data
[1] 12.0692812
> MSE.lm
[1] 26.99265692
```

From the analysis of the results, it is possible to note that the neural network has a lower MSE than the linear regression model.

Unsupervised learning in neural networks

In this section, we present unsupervised learning models in neural network,named competitive learning andKohonen SOM. Kohonen SOM was invented by a professor named Teuvo Kohonen and is a way to represent multidimensional data in much lower dimensions:*1D* or *2D*. It can classify data without supervision. Unsupervised learning aims at finding hidden patterns within the dataset and clustering them into different classes of data.

There are many unsupervised learning techniques, namely K-means clustering, dimensionality reduction, EM, and so on. The common feature is that there is no input-output mapping and we work only on the input values to create a group or set of outputs.

For the case of neural networks, they can be used for unsupervised learning. They can group data into different buckets (clustering) or abstract original data into a different set of output data points (feature abstraction or dimensionality reduction). Unsupervised techniques require less processing power and memory than supervised technique.

In unsupervised neural networks, there is no target variable and we cannot do backpropagation. Instead, we keep adjusting the weights without the error measure and try to group similar data together. There are two methods we will see for unsupervised neural networks:

- Competitive learning
- Kohonen SOMs

Competitive learning

Here, the neural network nodes compete with each other for the right to respond to a subset of the input data. The hidden layer is called the **competitive layer**. Every competitive neuron has its own weight and we calculate the similarity measure between the individual input vector and the neuron weight. For each input vector, the hidden neurons compete with each other to see which one is the *most* similar to the particular input vector:

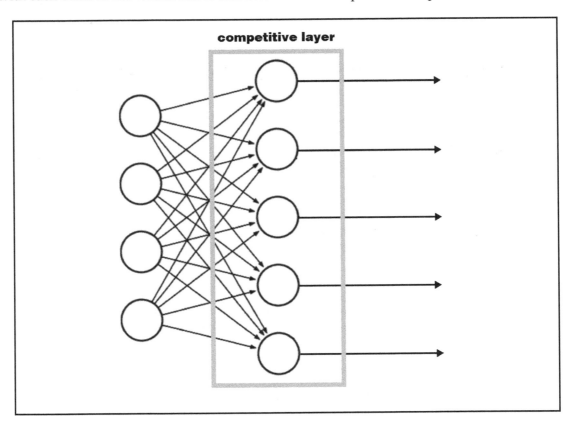

The output neurons are said to be in competition for input patterns.

- During training, the output neuron that provides the highest activation to a given input pattern is declared the weights of the winner and is moved closer to the input pattern, whereas the rest of the neurons are left unchanged
- This strategy is also called **winner-takes-all**, since only the winning neuron is updated:

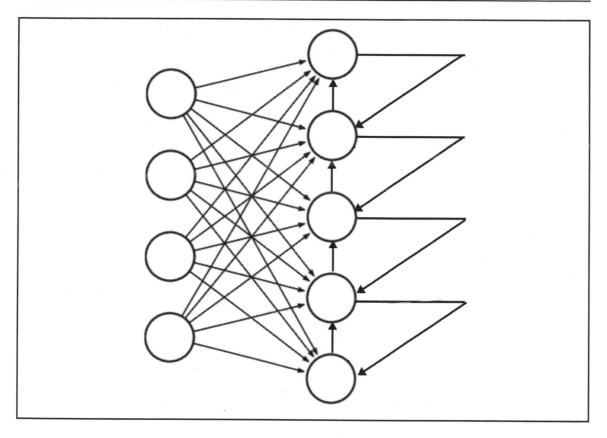

Let us see a simple competitive learning algorithm example to find three neurons within the given input data:

1. We will have threeinput neurons in the input layer. Each input to the neuron is a continuous variable and let the weight at each input neuron be a random number between *0.0* and *1.0*. The output of each node is the product of the three weights and its input.

2. Each competitive layer neuron receives the sum of the product of weights and inputs.

3. The competitive layer node with the highest output is regarded as the winner. The input is then categorized as being within the cluster corresponding to that node.

4. The winner updates each of its weights, moving the weight from the connections that gave it weaker signals to the ones that gave it stronger signals.

Thus, as we receive more data, each node converges on the center of the cluster that it has come to represent. It activates more strongly for inputs belonging to this cluster and more weakly for inputs that belong to other clusters.

There are basically two stopping conditions of competitive learning:

- **Predefined number of epochs**: Only Nepochs are run and this prevents the algorithm from running for a relatively long time without convergence
- **Minimum value of weight update**: The algorithm is run until we have a minimum value of weight update

Kohonen SOM

The concept of competitive learning combined with neighborhood neurons gives us Kohonen SOMs. Every neuron in the output layer has two neighbors. The neuron that fires the greatest value updates its weights in competitive learning, but in SOM, the neighboring neurons also update their weights at a relatively slow rate. The number of neighborhood neurons that the network updates the weights is based on the dimension of the problem.

For a *2D* problem, the SOM is represented as follows:

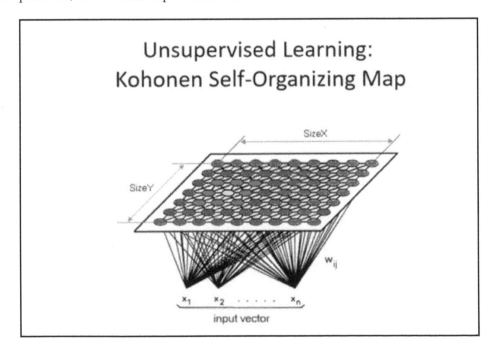

Diagrammatically, this is how the SOM maps different colors into different clusters:

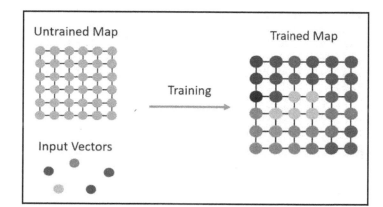

Let us understand the working of Kohonen SOM step-by-step:

1. The number of inputs and the clusters that define the SOM structure and each node's weights are initialized.
2. A vector is chosen at random from the set of training data and is presented to the network.
3. Every node in the network is examined to calculate which one's weights are most similar to the input vector. The winning node is commonly known as the **Best Matching Unit** (**BMU**).
4. The radius of the neighborhood of the BMU is calculated. This value starts large and is typically set to be the radius of the network, diminishing each time-step.
5. Any neurons found within the radius of the BMU, calculated in step 4, are adjusted to make them more like the input vector. The closer a neuron is to the BMU, the more its weights are altered.
6. Repeat from step 2 for N iterations.

The steps are repeated for a set of N epochs or until a minimum weight update is obtained.

SOMs are used in the fields of clustering (grouping of data into different buckets), data abstraction (deriving output data from inputs), and dimensionality reduction (reducing the number of input features).SOMs handle the problem in a way similar to **Multi Dimensional Scaling** (**MDS**), but instead of minimizing the distances, they try regroup topology, or in other words, they try to keep the same neighbors.

Let us see an example of SOM implementation in R. The kohonen package is a package to be installed to use the functions offered in R for SOM.

The following R program explains some functions from the kohonen package :

```
#########################################################################
###Chapter 2 - Introduction to Neural Networks - using R     ##########
###Usuervised ML technique using Kohonen package  #################
####################### filename: kohonen.r########################
#########################################################################
library("kohonen")

data("wines")
str(wines)
head(wines)
View (wines)

set.seed(1)
som.wines = som(scale(wines), grid = somgrid(5, 5, "hexagonal"))
som.wines
dim(getCodes(som.wines))

plot(som.wines, main = "Wine data Kohonen SOM")
par(mfrow = c(1, 1))
plot(som.wines, type = "changes", main = "Wine data: SOM")

training = sample(nrow(wines), 150)
Xtraining = scale(wines[training, ])
Xtest = scale(wines[-training, ],
              center = attr(Xtraining, "scaled:center"),
              scale = attr(Xtraining, "scaled:scale"))
trainingdata = list(measurements = Xtraining,
              vintages = vintages[training])
testdata = list(measurements = Xtest, vintages = vintages[-training])
mygrid = somgrid(5, 5, "hexagonal")
som.wines = supersom(trainingdata, grid = mygrid)

som.prediction = predict(som.wines, newdata = testdata)
table(vintages[-training], som.prediction$predictions[["vintages"]])
#########################################################################
```

The code uses a wine dataset, which contains adata frame with 177 rows and 13 columns; the object vintages contains the class labels. This data is obtained from the chemical analyses of wines grown in the same region in Italy (Piemonte) but derived from three different cultivars, namely, the Nebbiolo, Barberas, and Grignolino grapes. The wine from the Nebbiolo grape is called **Barolo**. The data consists of the amounts of several constituents found in each of the three types of wines, as well as some spectroscopic variables.

Now, let's see the outputs at each section of the code.

```
library("kohonen")
```

The first line of the code is simple, as it loads the library we will use for later calculations. Specifically, the `kohonen` library will help us to train SOMs. Also, interrogation of the maps and prediction using trained maps are supported.

 Remember, to install a library that is not present in the initial distribution of R, you must use the `install.package` function. This is the main function to install packages. It takes a vector of names and a destination library, downloads the packages from the repositories and installs them.

```
data("wines")
str(wines)
head(wines)
view (wines)
```

These lines load the `wines` dataset, which, as we anticipated, is contained in the R distribution, and saves it in a dataframe named `data`. Then, we use the `str` function to view a compactly display the structure of the dataset. The function `head` is used to return the first or last parts of the dataframe. Finally, the `view` function is used to invoke a spreadsheet-style data viewer on the dataframe object, as shown in the following figure:

	alcohol	malic acid	ash	ash alkalinity	magnesium	tot. phenols	flavonoids	non-flav. phenols	proanth	col. int.	col. hue	OD ratio	proline
1	13.20	1.78	2.14	11.2	100	2.65	2.76	0.26	1.28	4.38	1.050	3.40	1050
2	13.16	2.36	2.67	18.6	101	2.80	3.24	0.30	2.81	5.68	1.030	3.17	1185
3	14.37	1.95	2.50	16.8	113	3.85	3.49	0.24	2.18	7.80	0.860	3.45	1480
4	13.24	2.59	2.87	21.0	118	2.80	2.69	0.39	1.82	4.32	1.040	2.93	735
5	14.20	1.76	2.45	15.2	112	3.27	3.39	0.34	1.97	6.75	1.050	2.85	1450
6	14.39	1.87	2.45	14.6	96	2.50	2.52	0.30	1.98	5.25	1.020	3.58	1290
7	14.06	2.15	2.61	17.6	121	2.60	2.51	0.31	1.25	5.05	1.060	3.58	1295
8	14.83	1.64	2.17	14.0	97	2.80	2.98	0.29	1.98	5.20	1.080	2.85	1045
9	13.86	1.35	2.27	16.0	98	2.98	3.15	0.22	1.85	7.22	1.010	3.55	1045
10	14.10	2.16	2.30	18.0	105	2.95	3.32	0.22	2.38	5.75	1.250	3.17	1510
11	14.12	1.48	2.32	16.8	95	2.20	2.43	0.26	1.57	5.00	1.170	2.82	1280
12	13.75	1.73	2.41	16.0	89	2.60	2.76	0.29	1.81	5.60	1.150	2.90	1320
13	14.75	1.73	2.39	11.4	91	3.10	3.69	0.43	2.81	5.40	1.250	2.73	1150
14	14.38	1.87	2.38	12.0	102	3.30	3.64	0.29	2.96	7.50	1.200	3.00	1547
15	13.63	1.81	2.70	17.2	112	2.85	2.91	0.30	1.46	7.30	1.280	2.88	1310
16	14.30	1.92	2.72	20.0	120	2.80	3.14	0.33	1.97	6.20	1.070	2.65	1280
17	13.83	1.57	2.62	20.0	115	2.95	3.40	0.40	1.72	6.60	1.130	2.57	1130
18	14.19	1.59	2.48	16.5	108	3.30	3.93	0.32	1.86	8.70	1.230	2.82	1680

Showing 1 to 18 of 177 entries

We will continue to analyze the code:

```
set.seed(1)
som.wines = som(scale(wines), grid = somgrid(5, 5, "hexagonal"))
dim(getCodes(som.wines))
plot(som.wines, main = "Wine data Kohonen SOM")
```

After loading the wine data and setting seed for reproducibility, we call som to create a *5x5* matrix, inwhich the features have to be clustered. The function internally does the kohonen processing and the result can be seen by the clusters formed with the features. There are *25* clusters created, each of which has a combined set of features having common pattern, as shown in the following image:

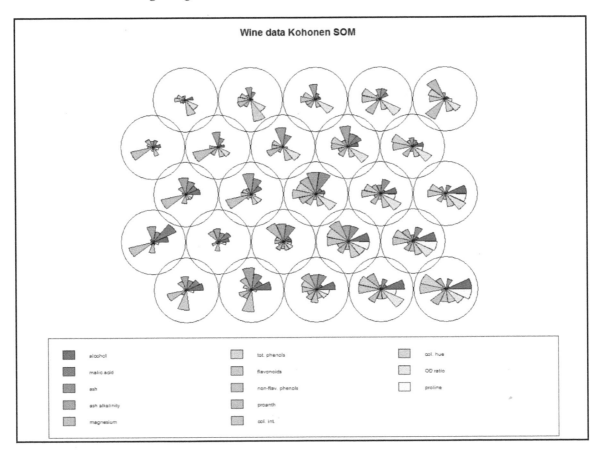

The next part of the code plots the mean distance to the closest unit versus the number of iterations done by `som`:

```
graphics.off()
par(mfrow = c(1, 1))
plot(som.wines, type = "changes", main = "Wine data: SOM")
```

In the following figure is shownmean distance to closest unit versus the number of iterations:

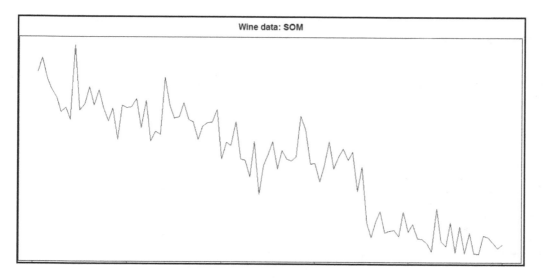

Next, we create a `training` dataset with 150 rows and `test` dataset with27 rows. We run the SOM and predict with the test data. The`supersom`function is used here. Here, the model is supervised SOM:

```
training = sample(nrow(wines), 150)
Xtraining = scale(wines[training, ])
Xtest = scale(wines[-training, ],
              center = attr(Xtraining, "scaled:center"),
              scale = attr(Xtraining, "scaled:scale"))
trainingdata = list(measurements = Xtraining,
                    vintages = vintages[training])
testdata = list(measurements = Xtest, vintages = vintages[-training])
mygrid = somgrid(5, 5, "hexagonal")
som.wines = supersom(trainingdata, grid = mygrid)

som.prediction = predict(som.wines, newdata = testdata)
table(vintages[-training], som.prediction$predictions[["vintages"]])
```

Finally, we invoke the `table` function that uses the cross-classifying factors to build a contingency table of the counts at each combination of factor levels, as shown next:

```
> table(vintages[-training], som.prediction$predictions[["vintages"]])

           Barbera Barolo Grignolino
Barbera          5      0          0
Barolo           0     11          0
Grignolino       0      0         11
```

The `kohonen` package features standard SOMs and two extensions: for classification and regression purposes, and for data mining. Also, it has extensive graphics capability for visualization.

The following table lists the functions available in the `kohonen` package:

Function name	Description
som	Standard SOM
xyf, bdk	Supervised SOM; two parallel maps
supersom	SOM with multiple parallel maps
plot.kohonen	Generic plotting function
summary.kohonen	Generic summary function
map.kohonen	Map data to the most similar neuron
predict.kohonen	Generic function to predict properties

Summary

In this chapter, we explored the machine learning field and we saw the learning process in a neural network. We learned to distinguish between supervised learning, unsupervised learning, and reinforcement learning. To understand in detail the necessary procedures, we also learned how to train and test the model.

Afterwards, we discovered the meaning of the data cycle and how the data must be collected, cleaned, converted, and then fed to the model for learning.So we went deeper into the evaluation model to see if the expected value is equal to the actual value during the test phase. We analyzed the different metrics available to control the model that depends on the status of the target variable.

Then we discovered one of the concepts important for understanding the neural networks, the backpropagation algorithm, that is based on computing to update weights and bias ions at each level.

Finally, we covered two practical programs in R for the learning process, by applyingthe `neuralnet` and the `kohonen` libraries. We can systematically use these basics for further building of complex networks.

In the next chapter, we will discover the **Deep Neural Network (DNN)**. We will see some basics of theH2O package. Overall, `H2O` is a highly user-friendly package that can be used to train feed-forward networks or deep auto-encoders. It supports distributed computations and provides a web interface. By including the `H2O` package, like any other package in R, we can do all kind of modeling and processing of DNN.

Deep Learning Using Multilayer Neural Networks

3

Deep learning is the recent hot trend in machine learning/AI. It is all about building advanced neural networks. By making multiple hidden layers work in a neural network model, we can work with complex nonlinear representations of data. We create deep learning using base neural networks. Deep learning has numerous use cases in real life, such as, driverless cars, medical diagnostics, computer vision, speech recognition, **Natural Language Processing** (**NLP**), handwriting recognition, language translation, and many other fields.

In this chapter, we will deal with the deep learning process: how to train, test, and deploy a **Deep Neural Network** (**DNN**). We will look at the different packages available in R to handle DNNs. We will understand how to build and train a DNN with the neuralnet package. Finally, we will analyze an example of training and modeling a DNN using h2o, the scalable open-memory learning platform, to create models with large datasets and implement prediction with high-precision methods.

The following are the topics covered in this chapter:

- Types of DNNs
- R packages for deep learning
- Training and modeling a DNN with neuralnet
- The h2o library

By the end of the chapter, we will understand the basic concepts of deep learning and how to implement it in the R environment. We will discover different types of DNNs. We will learn how to train, test, and deploy a model. We will know how to train and model a DNN using h2o.

Introduction of DNNs

With the advent of big data processing infrastructure, GPU, and GP-GPU, we are now able to overcome the challenges with shallow neural networks, namely overfitting and vanishing gradient, using various activation functions and L1/L2 regularization techniques. Deep learning can work on large amounts of labeled and unlabeled data easily and efficiently.

As mentioned, deep learning is a class of machine learning wherein learning happens on multiple levels of neuron networks. The standard diagram depicting a DNN is shown in the following figure:

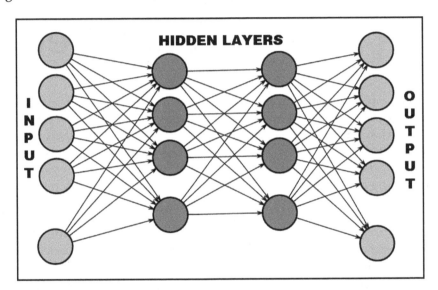

From the analysis of the previous figure, we can notice a remarkable analogy with the neural networks we have studied so far. We can then be quiet, unlike what it might look like, deep learning is simply an extension of the neural network. In this regard, most of what we have seen in the previous chapters is valid. In short, a DNN is a multilayer neural network that contains two or more hidden layers. Nothing very complicated here. By adding more layers and more neurons per layer, we increase the specialization of the model to train data but decrease the performance on the test data.

As we anticipated, DNN are derivatives of ANN. By making the number of hidden layers more than one, we build DNNs. There are many variations of DNNs, as illustrated by the different terms shown next:

- **Deep Belief Network** (**DBN**): It is typically a feed-forward network in which data flows from one layer to another without looping back. There is at least one hidden layer and there can be multiple hidden layers, increasing the complexity.
- **Restricted Boltzmann Machine** (**RBM**): It has a single hidden layer and there is no connection between nodes in a group. It is a simple MLP model of neural networks.
- **Recurrent Neural Networks** (**RNN**) and **Long Short Term Memory** (**LSTM**): These networks have data flowing in any direction within groups and across groups.

As with any machine learning algorithm, even DNNs require building, training, and evaluating processes. A basic workflow for deep learning in shown in the following figure:

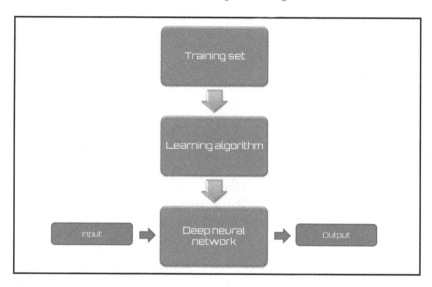

The workflow we have seen in the previous figure remembers very closely that typical of a supervised learning algorithm. But what makes it different from other machine learning algorithms?

Almost all machine learning algorithms demonstrate their limits in identifying the characteristics of raw input data, especially when they are complex and lacking an apparent order, such as in images. Usually, this limit is exceeded through the help of humans, who are concerned with identifying what the machine can not do. Deep learning removes this step, relying on the training process to find the most useful models through input examples. Also in that case human intervention is necessary in order to make choices before starting training, but automatic discovery of features makes life much easier. What makes the neural networks particularly advantageous, compared to the other solutions offered by machine learning, is the great generalization ability of the model.

These features have made deep learning very effective for almost all tasks that require automatic learning; although it is particularly effective in a case of complex hierarchical data. Its underlying ANN forms highly nonlinear representations; these are usually composed of multiple layers together with nonlinear transformations and custom architectures.

Essentially, deep learning works really well with messy data from the real world, making it a key instrument in several technological fields of the next few years. Until recently, it was a dark and daunting area to know, but its success has brought many great resources and projects that make it easier than ever to start.

Now that we know what the DNNs are, let's see what tools the R development environment offers us to deal with this particular topic.

R for DNNs

In the previous section, we clarified some key concepts that are at the deep learning base. We also understood the features that make the use of deep learning particularly convenient. Moreover, its rapid diffusion is also due to the great availability of a wide range of frameworks and libraries for various programming languages.

The R programming language is widely used by scientists and programmers, thanks to its extreme ease of use. Additionally, there is an extensive collection of libraries that allow professional data visualization and analysis with the most popular algorithms. The rapid diffusion of deep learning algorithms has led to the creation of an ever-increasing number of packages available for deep learning, even in R.

The following table shows the various packages/interfaces available for deep learning using R:

CRAN package	Supported taxonomy of neural network	Underlying language/ vendor
MXNet	Feed-forward, CNN	C/C++/CUDA
darch	RBM, DBN	C/C++
deepnet	Feed-forward, RBM, DBN, autoencoders	R
h2o	Feed-forward network, autoencoders	Java
nnet and neuralnet	Feed-forward	R
Keras	Variety of DNNs	Python/keras.io
TensorFlow	Variety of DNNs	C++, Python/Google

MXNet is a modern, portable, deep learning library that can support multiple machines. The world's largest companies and universities have adopted MXNet as a machine learning framework. These include Amazon, Intel, Data, Baidu, Microsoft, Wolfram Research, Carnegie Mellon, MIT, University of Washington, and Hong Kong University of Science and Technology.

MXNet is an open source framework that allows for fast modeling, and supports a flexible programming model in multiple programming languages (C ++, Python, Julia, MATLAB, JavaScript, Go, R, Scala, Perl, and Wolfram Language).

The MXNet framework supports R programming language. The MXNet R package provides flexible and efficient GPU computing and a state-of-the-art deepening at R. It allows us to write a seamless tensorial/ matrix calculation with multiple GPUs in R. It also allows us to build and customize the state-of-the-art deep learning models in R and apply them to activities such as image classification and data science challenges.

The darch framework is based on the code written by G. E. Hinton and R. R. Salakhutdinov, and is available in the MATLAB environment for DBN. This package can generate neural networks with many levels (deep architectures) and form them with an innovative method developed by the authors. This method provides a pre-formation with the contrasting divergence method published by G. Hinton (2002) and fine-tuning with common training algorithms known as backpropagation or conjugated gradients. In addition, fine-tuning supervision can be improved with maxout and dropout, two recently developed techniques to improve fine-tuning for deep learning.

The `deepnet` library is a relatively small, yet quite powerful package with variety of architectures to pick from. This library implements some deep learning architectures and neural network algorithms, including backpropagation, RBM, DBN, deep autoencoder, and so on. Unlike the other libraries we have analyzed, it was specifically written for R. It has several functions, including:

- `nn.train`: For training single or multiple hidden layers neural network by BP
- `nn.predict`: For predicting new samples by trained neural network
- `dbn.dnn.train`: For training a DNN with weights initialized by DBN
- `rbm.train`: For training an RBM

The `h2o` R package has functions for building general linear regression, K-means, Naive Bayes, **Principal Component Analysis (PCA)**, forests, and deep learning (multilayer `neuralnet` models). `h2o` is an external package to CRAN and is built using Java, and is available for a variety of platforms. It is an open source math engine for big data that computes parallel distributed machine learning algorithms.

The packages `nnet` and `neuralnet` have been widely discussed in the previous chapters. These are two packages for the management of neural networks in R. They are also able to build and train multicore neural networks, so they rely on deep learning.

`Keras` is an open source neural network library written in Python. Designed to enable fast experimentation with DNNs, it focuses on being minimal, modular, and extensible. The library contains numerous implementations of commonly used neural network building blocks, such as layers, objectives, activation functions, optimizers, and a host of tools to make working with image and text data easier. The code is hosted on GitHub, and community support forums include the GitHub issues page, a Gitter channel, and a Slack channel.

`TensorFlow` is an open source software library for machine learning. It contains a system for building and training neural networks to detect and decipher patterns and correlations, with methods similar to those adopted by human learning. It is used both for search and for Google production.

Multilayer neural networks with neuralnet

After understanding the basics of deep learning, it's time to apply the skills acquired to a practical case. We've seen in the previous section that two libraries we know are listed in packages available in *R for DNNs* section. I refer to the `nnet` and `neuralnet` packages that we learned to use in the previous chapters through practical examples. Since we have some practice with the `neuralnet` library, I think we should start our practical exploration of the amazing world of deep learning from here.

To start, we introduce the dataset we will use to build and train the network. It is named the `College` dataset, and it contains statistics for a large number of US colleges, collected from the 1995 issue of *US News and World Report*. This dataset was taken from the `StatLib` library, which is maintained at Carnegie Mellon University, and was used in the *ASA Section on Statistical Graphics*.

Things for us are further simplified because we do not have to retrieve the data and then import it into R, as these data are contained in a R package. I refer to the `ISLR` package. We just have to install the package and load the relative library. But we will see this later, when we explain the codices in detail. Now let's just look at the content of the dataset `College`. It is a dataframe with `777` observations on the following `18` variables:

- `Private`: A factor with levels `No` and `Yes` indicating private or public university
- `Apps`: Number of applications received
- `Accept`: Number of applications accepted
- `Enroll`: Number of new students enrolled
- `Top10perc`: Percentage of new students from top 10 percent of H.S. class
- `Top25perc`: Percentage of new students from top 25 percent of H.S. class
- `F.Undergrad`: Number of full time undergraduates
- `P.Undergrad`: Number of part time undergraduates
- `Outstate`: Out-of-state tuition
- `Room.Board`: Room and board costs
- `Books`: Estimated book costs
- `Personal`: Estimated personal spending
- `PhD`: Percentage of faculty with Ph.D.s
- `Terminal`: Percentage of faculty with terminal degree
- `S.F.Ratio`: Student-faculty ratio

- `perc.alumni`: Percentage of alumni who donate
- `Expend`: Instructional expenditure per student
- `Grad.Rate`: Graduation rate

Our aim will be to build a multilayer neural network capable of predicting whether the school is public or private, based on the values assumed by the other 17 variables:

```
#####################################################################
############Chapter 3 - Deep Learning with neuralnet#################
#####################################################################
library("neuralnet")
library(ISLR)

data = College
View(data)

max_data <- apply(data[,2:18], 2, max)
min_data <- apply(data[,2:18], 2, min)
data_scaled <- scale(data[,2:18],center = min_data, scale = max_data -
min_data)

Private = as.numeric(College$Private)-1
data_scaled = cbind(Private,data_scaled)

index = sample(1:nrow(data),round(0.70*nrow(data)))
train_data <- as.data.frame(data_scaled[index,])
test_data <- as.data.frame(data_scaled[-index,])

n = names(train_data)
f <- as.formula(paste("Private ~", paste(n[!n %in% "Private"], collapse = "
+ ")))
deep_net = neuralnet(f,data=train_data,hidden=c(5,3),linear.output=F)
plot(deep_net)

predicted_data <- compute(deep_net,test_data[,2:18])
print(head(predicted_data$net.result))
predicted_data$net.result <-
sapply(predicted_data$net.result,round,digits=0)

table(test_data$Private,predicted_data$net.result)
```

As usual, we will analyze the code line-by-line, by explaining in detail all the features applied to capture the results.

```
library("neuralnet")
library(ISLR)
```

As usual, the first two lines of the initial code are used to load the libraries needed to run the analysis.

TIP

Remember, to install a library that is not present in the initial distribution of R, you must use the `install.package` function. This is the main function to install packages. It takes a vector of names and a destination library, downloads the packages from the repositories and installs them. This function should be used only once and not every time you run the code.

```
data = College
View(data)
```

This command loads the `College` dataset, which as we anticipated is contained in the `ISLR` library, and saves it in a given dataframe. Use the `View` function to view a compact display of the structure of an arbitrary R object. The following figure shows some of the data contained in the `College` dataset:

	Private	Apps	Accept	Enroll	Top10perc	Top25perc	F.Undergrad	P.Undergrad	Outstate	Room.Board	Books	Personal	PhD	Terminal	S.F.Ratio	perc.alumni	Expend	Grad.Rate
Abilene Christian University	Yes	1660	1232	721	23	52	2885	537	7440	3300	450	2200	70	78	18.1	12	7041	60
Adelphi University	Yes	2186	1924	512	16	29	2683	1227	12280	6450	750	1500	29	30	12.2	16	10527	56
Adrian College	Yes	1428	1097	336	22	50	1036	99	11250	3750	400	1165	53	66	12.9	30	8735	54
Agnes Scott College	Yes	417	349	137	60	89	510	63	12960	5450	450	675	92	97	7.7	37	19016	59
Alaska Pacific University	Yes	193	146	55	16	44	249	869	7560	4120	800	1500	76	72	11.9	2	10922	15
Albertson College	Yes	587	479	158	38	62	678	41	13500	3335	500	675	67	73	9.4	11	9727	55
Albertus Magnus College	Yes	353	340	103	17	45	416	230	13290	5720	500	1500	90	93	11.5	26	8861	63
Albion College	Yes	1899	1720	489	37	68	1594	32	13868	4826	450	850	89	100	13.7	37	11487	73
Albright College	Yes	1038	839	227	30	63	973	306	15595	4400	300	500	79	84	11.3	23	11644	80
Alderson-Broaddus College	Yes	582	498	172	21	44	799	78	10468	3380	660	1800	40	41	11.5	15	8991	52
Alfred University	Yes	1732	1425	472	37	75	1830	110	16548	5406	500	600	82	88	11.3	31	10932	73
Allegheny College	Yes	2652	1900	484	44	77	1707	44	17080	4440	400	600	73	91	9.9	41	11711	76
Allentown Coll. of St. Francis de Sales	Yes	1179	780	290	38	64	1130	638	9690	4785	600	1000	60	84	13.3	21	7940	74
Alma College	Yes	1267	1080	385	44	73	1306	28	12572	4552	400	400	79	87	15.3	32	9305	68
Alverno College	Yes	494	313	157	23	46	1317	1235	8352	3640	650	2449	36	69	11.1	26	8127	55
American International College	Yes	1420	1093	220	9	22	1018	287	8700	4780	450	1400	78	84	14.7	19	7355	69
Amherst College	Yes	4302	992	418	83	96	1593	5	19760	5300	660	1598	93	98	8.4	63	21424	100
Anderson University	Yes	1216	908	423	19	40	1819	281	10100	3520	550	1100	48	61	12.1	14	7994	59
Andrews University	Yes	1130	704	322	14	23	1586	326	9996	3090	900	1320	62	66	11.5	18	10908	46
Angelo State University	No	3540	2001	1016	24	54	4190	1512	5130	3592	500	2000	60	62	23.1	5	4010	34
Antioch University	Yes	713	661	252	25	44	712	23	15476	3336	400	1100	69	82	11.3	35	42926	48
Appalachian State University	No	7313	4664	1910	20	63	9940	1035	6806	2540	96	2000	83	96	18.3	14	5854	70
Aquinas College	Yes	619	516	219	20	51	1251	767	11208	4124	350	1615	55	65	12.7	25	6584	65
Arizona State University Main campus	No	12809	10308	3761	24	49	22593	7585	7434	4850	700	2100	86	93	18.9	5	4602	48
Arkansas College (Lyon College)	Yes	708	334	166	46	74	530	182	8644	3922	500	800	79	88	12.8	24	14579	54
Arkansas Tech University	No	1734	1729	951	12	52	3602	939	3460	2650	450	1000	57	60	19.6	5	4739	48
Assumption College	Yes	2135	1700	491	23	59	1706	689	12000	5920	500	500	93	93	13.8	30	7100	88
Auburn University-Main Campus	No	7548	6791	3070	25	57	16262	1716	6300	3933	600	1908	85	91	16.7	18	6642	69
Augsburg College	Yes	662	513	257	12	30	2074	726	11902	4372	540	950	65	65	12.8	31	7836	58
Augustana College IL	Yes	1879	1658	497	36	69	1950	38	13353	4173	540	821	78	83	12.7	40	9220	71
Augustana College	Yes	761	725	306	21	58	1337	300	10990	3244	600	1021	66	70	10.4	30	6671	69
Austin College	Yes	948	798	295	42	74	1120	15	11280	4342	400	1150	81	95	13.0	33	11361	71

Showing 1 to 33 of 777 entries

How it is possible to note for each college are listed a series of statistics; the rows represent the observations on the columns instead are present the detected features:

```
max_data <- apply(data[,2:18], 2, max)
min_data <- apply(data[,2:18], 2, min)
data_scaled <- scale(data[,2:18],center = min_data, scale = max_data -
min_data)
```

In this snippet of code we need to normalize the data.

 TIP Remember, it is good practice to normalize the data before training a neural network. With normalization, data units are eliminated, allowing you to easily compare data from different locations.

For this example, we will use the **min-max method** (usually called feature **scaling**) to get all the scaled data in the range *[0,1]*. Before applying the method chosen for normalization, you must calculate the minimum and maximum values of each database column. This procedure has already been adopted in the example we analyzed in Chapter 2, *Learning Process in Neural Networks*.

The last line scales the data by adopting the expected normalization rule. Note that we performed normalization only on the last *17* rows (from *2* to *18*), excluding the first column, Private, that contains a factor with levels No and Yes, indicating private or public university. This variable will be our target in the network we are about to build. To get a confirmation of what we say, check the typologies of the variables contained in the dataset. To do this, we will use the function str to view a compactly display the structure of an arbitrary R object:

```
> str(data)
'data.frame': 777 obs. of 18 variables:
 $ Private : Factor w/ 2 levels "No","Yes": 2 2 2 2 2 2 2 2 2 2 ...
 $ Apps : num 1660 2186 1428 417 193 ...
 $ Accept : num 1232 1924 1097 349 146 ...
 $ Enroll : num 721 512 336 137 55 158 103 489 227 172 ...
 $ Top10perc : num 23 16 22 60 16 38 17 37 30 21 ...
 $ Top25perc : num 52 29 50 89 44 62 45 68 63 44 ...
 $ F.Undergrad: num 2885 2683 1036 510 249 ...
 $ P.Undergrad: num 537 1227 99 63 869 ...
 $ Outstate : num 7440 12280 11250 12960 7560 ...
 $ Room.Board : num 3300 6450 3750 5450 4120 ...
 $ Books : num 450 750 400 450 800 500 500 450 300 660 ...
 $ Personal : num 2200 1500 1165 875 1500 ...
 $ PhD : num 70 29 53 92 76 67 90 89 79 40 ...
 $ Terminal : num 78 30 66 97 72 73 93 100 84 41 ...
 $ S.F.Ratio : num 18.1 12.2 12.9 7.7 11.9 9.4 11.5 13.7 11.3 11.5 ...
```

```
$ perc.alumni: num 12 16 30 37 2 11 26 37 23 15 ...
$ Expend : num 7041 10527 8735 19016 10922 ...
$ Grad.Rate : num 60 56 54 59 15 55 63 73 80 52 ...
```

As anticipated, the first variable is of the `Factor` type, with two `levels`: `No` and `Yes`. For the remaining `17` variables, these are of the numeric type. As anticipated in `Chapter 1`, *Neural Network and Artificial Intelligence Concepts*, only numeric data can be used in the model, as neural network is a mathematical model with approximation functions. So we have a problem with the first variable, `Private`. Do not worry, the problem can be easily resolved; just turn it into a numeric variable:

```
Private = as.numeric(College$Private)-1
data_scaled = cbind(Private,data_scaled)
```

In this regard, the first line transforms the `Private` variable into numeric, while the second line of code is used to reconstruct the dataset with that variable and the remaining *17* appropriately normalized variables. To do this, we use the `cbind` function, that takes a sequence of vector, matrix, or dataframe arguments and combines by columns or rows, respectively:

```
index = sample(1:nrow(data),round(0.70*nrow(data)))
train_data <- as.data.frame(data_scaled[index,])
test_data <- as.data.frame(data_scaled[-index,])
```

The time has come to split the data for training and testing of the network. In the first line of the code just suggested, the dataset is split into *70:30*, with the intention of using *70* percent of the data at our disposal to train the network and the remaining *30* percent to test the network. In the third line, the data of the dataframe named data is subdivided into two new dataframes, called `train_data` and `test_data`:

```
n = names(train_data)
f <- as.formula(paste("Private ~", paste(n[!n %in% "Private"], collapse = "
+ ")))
```

In this piece of code, we first recover all the variable names using the `names` function. This function gets or sets the name of an object. Next, we build the formula that we will use to build the network, so we use the `neuralnet` function to build and train the network. Everything so far has only been used to prepare the data. Now it is time to build the network:

```
deep_net = neuralnet(f,data=train_data,hidden=c(5,3),linear.output=F)
```

This is the key line of the code. Here the network is built and trained; let's analyze it in detail. We had anticipated that we would use the `neuralnet` library to build our DNN. But what has changed with respect to the cases which we have built a single hidden layer network? Everything is played in the `hidden` argument setting.

> Remember that the `hidden` argument must contain a vector of integers specifying the number of hidden neurons (vertices) in each layer.

In our case, we set the hidden layer to contain the vector *(5,3)*, which corresponds to two hidden levels with respective five neurons in the first hidden layer and three neurons in the second.

```
plot(deep_net)
```

The previous line simply plots the network diagram, as shown in the following figure:

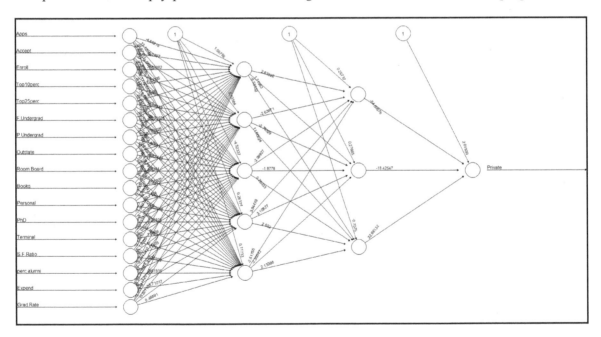

As we can see, the network is built and trained, and we only have to verify its ability to predict:

```
predicted_data <- compute(deep_net,test_data[,2:18])
print(head(predicted_data$net.result))
```

To predict the data reserved for testing, we can use the `compute` method. This is a method for objects of class `nn`, typically produced by the `neuralnet` function. Computes the outputs of all the neurons for specific arbitrary covariate vectors given a trained neural network. It's crucial to make sure that the order of the covariates is the same in the new matrix or dataframe as in the original neural network. Subsequently, to visualize, the first lines of the prediction result is used the `print` function, shown as follows:

```
> print(head(predicted_data$net.result))
  [,1]
Abilene Christian University 0.1917109322
Adelphi University           1.0000000000
Adrian College               1.0000000000
Agnes Scott College          1.0000000000
Albertus Magnus College      1.0000000000
Albion College               1.0000000000
```

As can be seen, the forecast results are provided in the form of decimal numbers, which approach the values of the two expected classes (one and zero), but do not exactly assume these values. We need to assume these values precisely, so we can make a comparison with the current values. To do this, we will use the `sapply()` function to round these off to either zero or one class, so we can evaluate them against the test labels:

```
predicted_data$net.result <-
sapply(predicted_data$net.result,round,digits=0)
```

As anticipated, the `sapply()` function has rounded the prediction results in the two available classes. Now we have everything we need to make a comparison in order to assess the DNN as a prediction tool:

```
table(test_data$Private,predicted_data$net.result)
```

To make a comparison, we rely on the confusion matrix. To build it, just use the `table` function. Indeed, the `table` function uses the cross-classifying factors to construct a contingency table of counts at each combination of factor levels.

The confusion matrix is a specific table layout that allows visualization of the performance of an algorithm. Each row represents the instances in an actual class, while each column represents the instances in a predicted class. The term confusion matrix results from the fact that it makes it easy to see if the system is confusing two classes.

Let's see then the results obtained:

```
> table(test_data$Private,predicted_data$net.result)

     0   1
0   49   8
1    9 167
```

Let us understand the results. Let us first remember that in a confusion matrix, the terms on the main diagonal represent the number of correct predictions, that is, the number of instances of the predicted class that coincide with the instances of the actual class. It seems that in our simulation, things have gone well. In fact, we got 49 occurrences of class 0 (No) and 167 of class 1 (Yes). But let's now analyze the other two terms, these represent the mistakes made by the model.

As defined in Chapter 2, *Learning Process in Neural Networks*, 8 are FN and 9 are FP. In this regard, we recall that FN means the number of negative predictions that are positive in actual data, while FPs are the number of positive predictions that are negative in actual data. We can check this by again using the table function:

```
> table(test_data$Private)
   0   1
  57 176
```

These represent the actual results, in particular, 57 results belonging to class 0 and 176 to class 1. By summing the data contained in the rows of the confusion matrix, we get exactly those values in fact results:

```
> 49 + 8
[1] 57
> 9 + 167
[1] 176
```

Now we again use the table function to obtain the occurrences in the predicted data:

```
> table(predicted_data$net.result)
   0   1
  58 175
```

These represent the results of the prediction, in particular, 58 results belonging to class 0 and 175 to class 1. By summing the data contained in the columns of the confusion matrix, we get exactly those values in fact results:

```
> 49 + 9
[1] 58
> 8 + 167
[1] 175
```

At this point, we calculate the accuracy of the simulation by using the data contained in the confusion matrix. Let's remember that accuracy is defined by the following equation:

$$Accuracy = \frac{TP+TN}{P+N} = \frac{TP+TN}{TP+TN+FP+FN}$$

Here:

$$TP = TRUE\ POSITIVE$$

$$TN = TRUE\ NEGATIVE$$

$$FP = FALSE\ POSITIVE$$

$$FN = TRUE\ NEGATIVE$$

Let us take a look at this in the following code sample:

```
> Acc = (49 + 167) / (49 + 167 + 9 + 8)
> Acc
[1] 0.9270386266
```

We've got an accuracy of around 93 percent, confirming that our model is able to predict data with a good result.

Training and modeling a DNN using H2O

In this section, we will cover an example of training and modeling a DNN using h2o. h2o is an open source, in-memory, scalable machine learning and AI platform used to build models with large datasets and implement predictions with high-accuracy methods. The h2o library is adapted at a large scale in numerous organizations to operationalize data science and provide a platform to build data products. h2o can run on individual laptops or large clusters of high-performance scalable servers. It works very fast, exploiting the machine architecture advancements and GPU processing. It has high-accuracy implementations of deep learning, neural networks, and other machine learning algorithms.

As said earlier, the h2o R package has functions for building general linear regression, K-means, Naive Bayes, PCA, forests, and deep learning (multilayer neuralnet models). The h2o package is an external package to CRAN and is built using Java. It is available for a variety of platforms.

We will install h2o in R using the following code:

```
install.packages("h2o")
```

We obtain the following results:

```
> install.packages("h2o")
Installing package into 'C:/Users/Giuseppe/Documents/R/win-library/3.4'
(as 'lib' is unspecified)
trying URL
'https://cran.rstudio.com/bin/windows/contrib/3.4/h2o_3.10.5.3.zip'
Content type 'application/zip' length 73400625 bytes (70.0 MB)
downloaded 70.0 MB
package 'h2o' successfully unpacked and MD5 sums checked
The downloaded binary packages are in
  C:\Users\Giuseppe\AppData\Local\Temp\RtmpGEc5iI\downloaded_packages
```

To test the package, let's go through the following example that uses the popular dataset named Irisdataset. I'm referring to the Iris flower dataset, a multivariate dataset introduced by the British statistician and biologist Ronald Fisher in his 1936 paper *The use of multiple measurements in taxonomic problems* as an example of linear discriminant analysis.

The dataset contains *50* samples from each of the three species of Iris (Iris `setosa`, Iris `virginica`, and Iris `versicolor`). Four features were measured from each sample: the length and the width of the sepals and petals, in centimeters.

The following variables are contained:

- `Sepal.Length` in centimeter
- `Sepal.Width` in centimeter
- `Petal.Length` in centimeter
- `Petal.Width` in centimeter
- Class: `setosa, versicolour, virginica`

The following figure shows a compactly display the structure of the `iris` dataset:

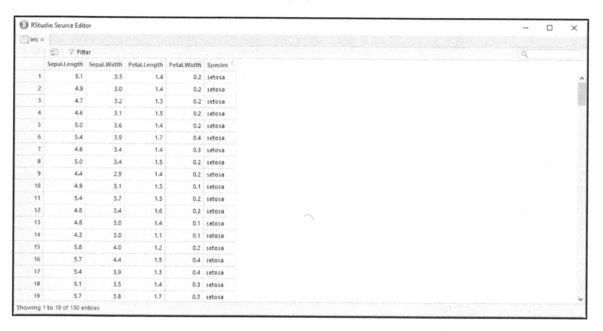

We want to build a classifier that, depending on the size of the sepal and petal, is able to classify the flower species:

```
#########################################################################
################Chapter 3 - Deep Learning with H2O and R################
#########################################################################

library(h2o)

c1=h2o.init(max_mem_size = "2G",
       nthreads = 2,
       ip = "localhost",
       port = 54321)

data(iris)
summary(iris)

iris_d1 <- h2o.deeplearning(1:4,5,
                as.h2o(iris),hidden=c(5,5),
                export_weights_and_biases=T)
iris_d1
plot(iris_d1)

h2o.weights(iris_d1, matrix_id=1)
h2o.weights(iris_d1, matrix_id=2)
h2o.weights(iris_d1, matrix_id=3)
h2o.biases(iris_d1, vector_id=1)
h2o.biases(iris_d1, vector_id=2)
h2o.biases(iris_d1, vector_id=3)

#plot weights connecting `Sepal.Length` to first hidden neurons
plot(as.data.frame(h2o.weights(iris_d1, matrix_id=1))[,1])

#########################################################################
```

Now, let's go through the code to understand how to apply the h2o package to solve a pattern recognition problem.

 Before proceeding, it is necessary to specify that running h2o on R requires Java 8 runtime. Verify the Java version installed on your machine beforehand and eventually download Java version 8 from https://www.java.com/en/download/win10.jsp.

The following figure shows the Java download page from Oracle's site:

Furthermore, the h2o package is built with some required packages; so in order to properly install the h2o package, remember to install the following dependencies, all of which are available in CRAN:

- RCurl
- bitops
- rjson
- jsonlite
- statmod
- tools

After we have successfully installed the h2o package, we can proceed with loading the library:

```
library(h2o)
```

This command loads the library in R environment. The following messages are returned:

```
Your next step is to start H2O:
 > h2o.init()
For H2O package documentation, ask for help:
 > ??h2o
After starting H2O, you can use the Web UI at http://localhost:54321
For more information visit http://docs.h2o.ai
c1=h2o.init(max_mem_size = "2G",
       nthreads = 2,
       ip = "localhost",
       port = 54321)
```

We follow the directions on the R prompt:

```
c1=h2o.init(max_mem_size = "2G",
       nthreads = 2,
       ip = "localhost",
       port = 54321)
```

The h20.init function initiates the h2o engine with a maximum memory size of 2 GB and two parallel cores. The console for h2o is initialized and we get the following messages once we run this script:

```
> c1=h2o.init(max_mem_size = "2G", nthreads = 2)
H2O is not running yet, starting it now...

Note: In case of errors look at the following log files:
C:\Users\Giuseppe\AppData\Local\Temp\RtmpU3xPvT/h2o_Giuseppe_started_from_r
.out
C:\Users\Giuseppe\AppData\Local\Temp\RtmpU3xPvT/h2o_Giuseppe_started_from_r
.err

java version "1.8.0_144"
Java(TM) SE Runtime Environment (build 1.8.0_144-b01)
Java HotSpot(TM) 64-Bit Server VM (build 25.144-b01, mixed mode)

Starting H2O JVM and connecting: . Connection successful!

R is connected to the H2O cluster:
    H2O cluster uptime:         6 seconds 912 milliseconds
    H2O cluster version:        3.10.5.3
    H2O cluster version age:    2 months and 9 days
    H2O cluster name:           H2O_started_from_R_Giuseppe_woc815
    H2O cluster total nodes:    1
    H2O cluster total memory:   1.78 GB
    H2O cluster total cores:    4
    H2O cluster allowed cores:  2
```

```
H2O cluster healthy: TRUE
H2O Connection ip: localhost
H2O Connection port: 54321
H2O Connection proxy: NA
H2O Internal Security: FALSE
R Version: R version 3.4.1 (2017-06-30)
```

Once `h2o` is initiated, the console can be viewed from any browser by pointing to `localhost:54321`. The `h2o` library runs on a JVM and the console allows:

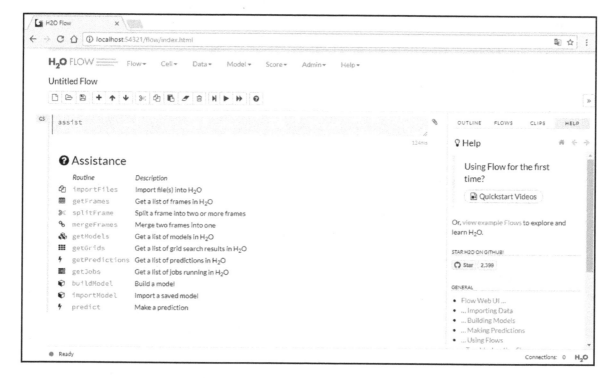

The console is intuitive and provides an interface to interact with the h_2o engine. We can train and test models and run predictions on top of them. The first textbox, labeled **CS**, allows us to enter routines for execution. The `assist` command gives the list of the routines available. Let us continue to analyze the following sample code.

```
data(iris)
summary(iris)
```

The first command loads the `iris` dataset, which is contained in the datasets library, and saves it in a given dataframe. Then we use the `summary` function to produce result summaries of the results of the dataset. The function invokes particular methods which depend on the class of the first argument. The results are shown as follows:

```
> summary(iris)
  Sepal.Length      Sepal.Width      Petal.Length      Petal.Width
 Min.   :4.300    Min.   :2.000    Min.   :1.000    Min.   :0.100
 1st Qu.:5.100    1st Qu.:2.800    1st Qu.:1.600    1st Qu.:0.300
 Median :5.800    Median :3.000    Median :4.350    Median :1.300
 Mean   :5.843    Mean   :3.057    Mean   :3.758    Mean   :1.199
 3rd Qu.:6.400    3rd Qu.:3.300    3rd Qu.:5.100    3rd Qu.:1.800
 Max.   :7.900    Max.   :4.400    Max.   :6.900    Max.   :2.500
       Species
 setosa    :50
 versicolor:50
 virginica :50
```

Let's analyze the next lines of code:

```
iris_d1 <- h2o.deeplearning(1:4,5,
              as.h2o(iris),hidden=c(5,5),
              export_weights_and_biases=T)
```

The `h2o.deeplearning` function is an important function within h2o and can be used for variety of operations. This function builds a DNN model using CPUs builds a feed-forward multilayer ANN on an `H2OFrame`. The `hidden` argument is used to set the number of hidden layers and the number of neurons for each hidden layer. In our case, we have set up a DNN with two hidden layers and 5 neurons for each hidden layer. Finally, the parameter `export_weights_and_biases` tells us that the weights and biases can be stored in `H2OFrame` and can be accessed like other dataframes for further processing.

Before proceeding with the code analysis, a clarification should be made. The attentive reader can ask that on the basis of which evaluation we have chosen the number of hidden layers and the number of neurons for each hidden layer. Unfortunately, there is no precise rule or even a mathematical formula that allows us to determine which numbers are appropriate for that specific problem. This is because every problem is different from each other and each network approximates a system differently. So what makes the difference between one model and another? The answer is obvious and once again very clear: the researcher's experience.

The advice I can give, which stems from the vast experience in data analysis, is to try, try, and try again. The secret to experimental activity is just that. In the case of neural networks, this results in trying to set up different networks and then verifying their performance. For example, in our case, we could have started from a network with two hidden layers and *100* neurons per hidden layer, then progressively reduced those values, and then arrive at those that I proposed in the example. This procedure can be automated with the use of the iterative structures that R owns.

However, some things can be said, for example, for the optimum choice of the number of neurons we need to know that:

- Small number of neurons will lead to high error for your system, as the predictive factors might be too complex for a small number of neurons to capture
- Large number of neurons will overfit to your training data and not generalize well
- The number of neurons in each hidden layer should be somewhere between the size of the input and the output layer, potentially the mean
- The number of neurons in each hidden layer shouldn't exceed twice the number of input neurons, as you are probably grossly overfit at this point

That said, we return to the code:

```
iris_d1
```

At the R prompt, this command prints a brief description of the features of the model we just created, as shown in the following figure:

```
> iris_d1
Model Details:
==============

H2OMultinomialModel: deeplearning
Model ID:  DeepLearning_model_R_1504963874193_14
Status of Neuron Layers: predicting Species, 3-class classification, multinomial distribution, CrossEntropy loss, 73 weights/biases, 4,5 KB, 1.500 training samples, mini-batc
h size 1
  layer units     type dropout        l1          l2 mean_rate rate_rms momentum mean_weight weight_rms mean_bias bias_rms
1     1     4    Input  0.00 %
2     2     5 Rectifier  0.00 % 0.000000 0.000000  0.002308 0.001675 0.000000   -0.094025   0.463426  0.531955 0.115960
3     3     5 Rectifier  0.00 % 0.000000 0.000000  0.005277 0.006356 0.000000   -0.009886   0.411969  1.106424 0.372346
4     4     3   Softmax         0.000000 0.000000  0.002974 0.002250 0.000000    0.707930   1.763234 -0.032859 0.108779


H2OMultinomialMetrics: deeplearning
** Reported on training data. **
** Metrics reported on full training frame **

Training Set Metrics:
=====================

Extract training frame with `h2o.getFrame("iris")`
MSE: (Extract with `h2o.mse`) 0.06007149
RMSE: (Extract with `h2o.rmse`) 0.2450949
Logloss: (Extract with `h2o.logloss`) 0.2303247
Mean Per-Class Error: 0.02666667
Confusion Matrix: Extract with `h2o.confusionMatrix(<model>,train = TRUE)`)
===========================================================================
Confusion Matrix: Row labels: Actual class; Column labels: Predicted class
           setosa versicolor virginica  Error      Rate
setosa         50          0         0 0.0000 =  0 / 50
versicolor      0         48         2 0.0400 =  2 / 50
virginica       0          2        48 0.0400 =  2 / 50
Totals         50         50        50 0.0267 =  4 / 150

Hit Ratio Table: Extract with `h2o.hit_ratio_table(<model>,train = TRUE)`)
=========================================================================
Top-3 Hit Ratios:
  k hit_ratio
1 1  0.973333
2 2  1.000000
3 3  1.000000
```

By carefully analyzing the previous figure, we can clearly distinguish the details of the model along with the confusion matrix. Let's now look at how the training process went on:

```
plot(iris_d1)
```

The `plot` method dispatches on the type of h2o model to select the correct scoring history. The arguments are restricted to what is available in the scoring history for a particular type of model, as shown in the following figure:

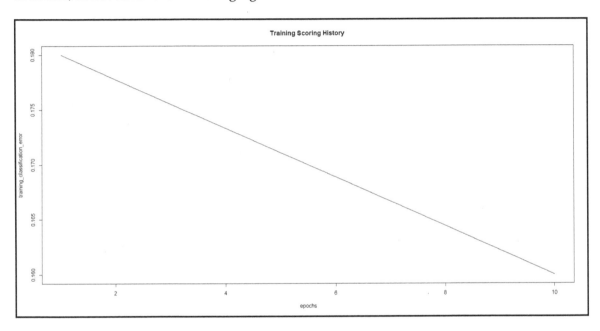

In this plot are shown the training classification errors versus epochs, as we can see that the gradient descents and the errors decrease as we progress in the epochs. How many times the dataset should be iterated (streamed) can be fractional. It defaults to `10`:

```
h2o.weights(iris_d1, matrix_id=1)
h2o.weights(iris_d1, matrix_id=2)
h2o.weights(iris_d1, matrix_id=3)
h2o.biases(iris_d1, vector_id=1)
h2o.biases(iris_d1, vector_id=2)
h2o.biases(iris_d1, vector_id=3)
```

The last six lines of the code simply print a short summary of the weights and biases for the three species of iris flower, as is shown next:

```
> h2o.weights(iris_d1, matrix_id=1)
  Sepal.Length Sepal.Width Petal.Length  Petal.Width
1 -0.013207575 -0.06818321  -0.02756812  0.092810206
2  0.036195096  0.02568028   0.05634377  0.035429616
3 -0.002411760 -0.11541270   0.08219513  0.001957144
4  0.091338813 -0.03271343  -0.25603485 -0.205898494
6 -0.151234403  0.01785624  -0.11815275 -0.110585481
[200 rows x 4 columns]

> h2o.biases(iris_d1, vector_id=1)
C11 0.48224932 0.47699773 0.48994124 0.49552965 0.48991496 0.4739439
[200 rows x 1 column]
```

We have restricted ourselves to seeing weights and biases only for the setosa species, for space reasons. In the following code we use the plot function again:

```
plot(as.data.frame(h2o.weights(iris_d1, matrix_id=1))[,1])
```

This command plots the weights of the first hidden layer neurons versus sepal lengths, as is shown in the following figure:

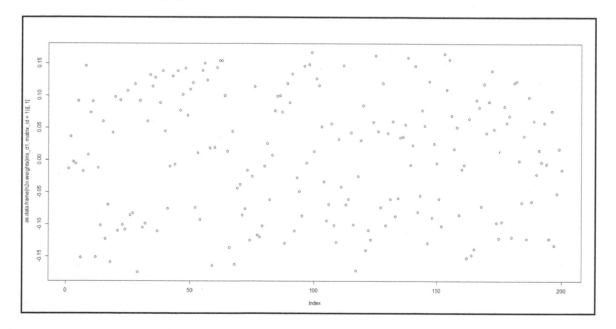

Now, let us dedicate some time to the analysis of the results; in particular, we recover the confusion matrix that we just glimpsed in the model summary screen, shown earlier. To invoke the confusion matrix, we can use the h2o.confusionMatrix function as shown in the following code sample, which retrieves either single or multiple confusion matrices from the h2o objects.

```
> h2o.confusionMatrix(iris_d1)
Confusion Matrix: Row labels: Actual class; Column labels: Predicted class
           setosa versicolor virginica  Error       Rate
setosa         50          0         0 0.0000 =   0 / 50
versicolor      0         48         2 0.0400 =   2 / 50
virginica       0          2        48 0.0400 =   2 / 50
Totals         50         50        50 0.0267 =   4 / 150
```

From the analysis of the confusion matrix, it can be seen that the model manages to correctly classify the three floral species by committing only four errors. These errors are fairly divided among only two species: versicolor, and virginica. However, the setosa species is correctly classified in all 50 occurrences. But why is this happening? To understand, let's take a look at the starting data. In the case of multidimensional data, the best way to do this is to plot a scatterplot matrix of selected variables in a dataset:

```
> pairs(iris[1:4], main = "Scatterplot matrices of Iris Data", pch = 21, bg
= c("red", "green3", "blue")[unclass(iris$Species)])
```

The results are shown in the following figure:

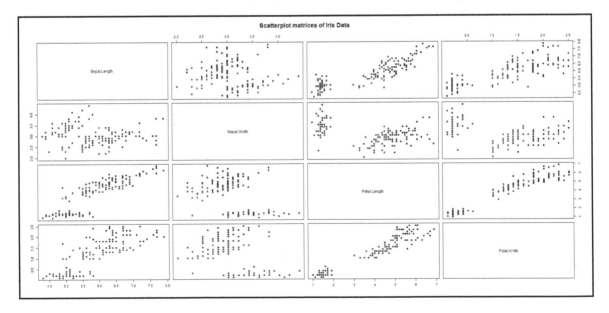

Let's analyze in detail the plot just proposed. The variables are written in a diagonal line from top left to bottom right. Then each variable is plotted against each other. For example, the second box in the first column is an individual scatterplot of Sepal.Length versus Sepal.Width, with Sepal.Length as the *X* axis and Sepal.Width as the *Y* axis. This same plot is replicated in the first plot of the second column. In essence, the boxes on the upper right hand side of the whole scatterplot are mirror images of the plots on the lower left hand.

From the analysis of the figure just seen, it can be seen that the versicolor and virginica species show overlapping boundaries. This makes us understand that the model's attempt to classify it when it falls into that area can cause errors. We can see what happens for the setosa species, which instead has far distant borders from other floral species without any classification error.

That said, we evaluate the accuracy of the model in classifying floral species on the basis of the size of petals and sepals:

```
> h2o.hit_ratio_table(iris_d1)
Top-3 Hit Ratios:
 k hit_ratio
1 1  0.973333
2 2  1.000000
3 3  1.000000
```

The results show that the simulation, based on the first hypothesis, ranked the species with *97* percent accuracy. I would say that is a good result; the model fit the data very well. But how can we measure this feature? One method to find a better fit is to calculate the coefficient of determination (R-squared). To calculate R-squared in h2o, we can use the h2o.r2 method:

```
> h2o.r2(iris_d1)
[1] 0.9596034
```

Now let's understand what we've calculated and how to read the result. R-squared measures how well a model can predict the data, and falls between zero and one. The higher the value of coefficient of determination, the better the model is at predicting the data.

We got a value of *0.96*, so according to what we have said, this is a great result. To get a confirmation of this, we have to compare it with the result of another simulation model. So, we build a linear regression model based on the same data, that is the iris dataset.

To build a linear regression model, we can use the `glm` function. This function is used to fit generalized linear models, specified by giving a symbolic description of the linear predictor and a description of the error distribution:

```
m=iris.lm <- h2o.glm(x=2:5,y=1,training_frame=as.h2o(iris))
```

Now we calculate the model's coefficient of determination:

```
> h2o.r2(m)
[1] 0.8667852
```

Now we can make a comparison between the model based on DNNs and the linear regression model. DNN had provided a R-squared value of *0.96*, while the resulting regression model provided a R-squared value of *0.87*. It is clear that DNN provides much better performance.

Finally, it may be useful to analyze the parameters that are important for a neural network specialist, as shown in the following table:

Argument	Description
x	A vector containing the names or indices of the predictor variables to use in building a model. If x is missing, then all columns except y are used.
y	The name of the response variable in a model. If the data does not contain a header, this is the first column index, increasing from left to right (the response must be either an integer or a categorical variable).
model_id	This is the destination id for a model; it is autogenerated if not specified.
standardize	It is a logical function. If enabled, it automatically standardizes the data. If disabled, the user must provide properly scaled input data. It defaults to TRUE.
activation	It is an activation function. It must be one of Tanh, TanhWithDropout, Rectifier, RectifierWithDropout, Maxout, or MaxoutWithDropout. It defaults to Rectifier.
hidden	This argument specifies hidden layer sizes (for example, [100, 100]). It defaults to [200, 200].

epochs	How many times the dataset should be iterated (streamed) can be fractional. It defaults to `10`.
adaptive_rate	It is a logical argument specifying the Adaptive learning rate. It defaults to `TRUE`.
rho	This describes the adaptive learning rate time decay factor (similar to prior updates). It defaults to `0.99`.
rate_annealing	Learning rate annealing is given by `rate/(1 + rate_annealing * samples)`. It defaults to `1e- 06`.
rate_decay	This is the learning rate decay factor between layers (N^{th} layer: `rate * rate_decay ^ (n - 1)`. It defaults to `1`.
input_dropout_ratio	Input layer dropout ratio (can improve generalization, try `0.1` or `0.2`). It defaults to `0`.
hidden_dropout_ratios	Hidden layer dropout ratios can improve generalization. Specify one value per hidden layer. It defaults to `0.5`.
l1	L1 regularization can add stability and improve generalization, and it causes many weights to become `0`. It defaults to `0`.
l2	L2 regularization can add stability and improve generalization, and it causes many weights to be small. It defaults to `0`.
initial_weights	This is a list of the `H2OFrame` IDs to initialize the weight matrices of this model with.
initial_biases	It is a list of the `H2OFrame` IDs to initialize the bias vectors of this model with.
loss	The loss function must be one of `Automatic`, `CrossEntropy`, `Quadratic`, `Huber`, `Absolute`, or `Quantile`. It defaults to `Automatic`.
distribution	The distribution function must be one of `AUTO`, `bernoulli`, `multinomial`, `gaussian`, `poisson`, `gamma`, `tweedie`, `laplace`, `quantile`, or `huber`. It defaults to `AUTO`.
score_training_samples	It is the number of training set samples for scoring (0 for all). It defaults to `10000`.

`score_validation_samples`	It is the number of validation set samples for scoring (0 for all). It defaults to `0`.
`classification_stop`	The stopping criterion for the classification error fraction on training data (-1 to disable). It defaults to `0`.
`regression_stop`	It is the stopping criterion for the regression error (MSE) on training data (`-1` to disable). It defaults to `1e-06`.
`stopping_rounds`	Early stopping based on convergence of `stopping_metric`. Stop if simple moving average of length `k` of the `stopping_metric` does not improve for `k:=stopping_rounds` scoring events (0 to disable) It defaults to `5`.
`max_runtime_secs`	It is maximum allowed runtime in seconds for model training. Use `0` to disable it. It defaults to `0`.
`diagnostics`	It enables diagnostics for hidden layers. It defaults to `TRUE`.
`fast_mode`	It enables fast mode (minor approximation in backpropagation). It defaults to `TRUE`.
`replicate_training_data`	It replicates the entire training dataset on every node for faster training on small datasets. It defaults to `TRUE`.
`single_node_mode`	It runs on a single node for fine-tuning of model parameters. It defaults to `FALSE`.
`shuffle_training_data`	It enables shuffling of training data (recommended if training data is replicated and `train_samples_per_iteration` is close to `#nodes x #rows`, or if using `balance_classes`). It defaults to `FALSE`.
`missing_values_handling`	Handling of missing values must be one of `MeanImputation` or `Skip`. It defaults to `MeanImputation`.
`quiet_mode`	It enables quiet mode for less output to standard output. It defaults to `FALSE`.

verbose	It prints scoring history to the console (metrics per tree for GBM, DRF, and XGBoost; metrics per epoch for deep learning. It defaults to `False`
autoencoder	Logical autoencoder defaults to `FALSE`
export_weights_and_biases	Whether to export neural network weights and biases to `H2OFrame`. It defaults to `FALSE`.
mini_batch_size	Mini-batch size (smaller leads to better fit, whereas larger can speed up and generalize better). It defaults to `1`.

There are other functions related to R with `h2o` for deep learning. Some useful ones are listed as follows:

Function	**Description**
predict.H2Omodel	Returns an `H2OFrame` object with probabilities and default predictions.
h2o.deepwater	Builds a deep learning model using multiple native GPU backends. Builds DNN on `H2OFrame` containing various data sources.
as.data.frame.H2OFrame	Converts `H2OFrame` to a dataframe.
h2o.confusionMatrix	Displays the confusion matrix for a classification model.
print.H2OFrame	Prints `H2OFrame`.
h2o.saveModel	Saves an `h2o` model object to disk.
h2o.importFile	Imports a file into h2o.

Deep autoencoders using H2O

Autoencoders are unsupervised learning methods on neural networks. We'll see more of this in Chapter 7, *Use Cases of Neural Networks – Advanced Topics*. h2o can be used to detect an anomaly by using deep autoencoders. To train such a model, the same function, h2o.deeplearning(), is used, with some changes in the parameters:

```
anomaly_model <- h2o.deeplearning(1:4,
                         training_frame = as.h2o(iris),
                         activation = "Tanh",
                         autoencoder = TRUE,
                         hidden = c(50,20,50),
                         sparse = TRUE,
                         l1 = 1e-4,
                         epochs = 100)
```

The autoencoder=TRUE sets the deeplearning method to use the autoencoder technique unsupervised learning method. We are using only the training data, without the test set and the labels. The fact that we need a deep autoencoder instead of a feed-forward network is specified by the autoencoder parameter.

We can choose the number of hidden units to be present in different layers. If we choose an integer value, what we get is called a **naive autoencoder**.

Summary

Deep learning is a subject of importance right from image detection to speech recognition and AI-related activity. There are numerous products and packages in the market for deep learning. Some of these are Keras, TensorFlow, h2o, and many others.

In this chapter, we learned the basics of deep learning, many variations of DNNs, the most important deep learning algorithms, and the basic workflow for deep learning. We explored the different packages available in R to handle DNNs.

To understand how to build and train a DNN, we analyzed a practical example of DNN implementation with the `neuralnet` package. We learned how to normalize data across the various available techniques, to remove data units, allowing you to easily compare data from different locations. We saw how to split the data for the training and testing of the network. We learned to use the `neuralnet` function to build and train a multilayered neural network. So we understood how to use the trained network to make predictions and we learned to use the confusion matrix to evaluate model performance.

We saw some basics of the h2o package. Overall, The `h2o` package is a highly user-friendly package that can be used to train feed-forward networks or deep autoencoders. It supports distributed computations and provides a web interface. By including the `h2o` package like any other package in R, we can do all kinds of modeling and processing of DNNs. The power of h2o can be utilized by the various features available in the package.

In the next chapter, we will understand what a perceptron is and what are the applications that can be built using the basic perceptron. We will learn a simple perceptron implementation function in R environment. We will also learn how to train and model a MLP . We will discover the linear separable classifier.

4
Perceptron Neural Network Modeling – Basic Models

So far, we have seen the basics of neural networks and how the learning portion works. In this chapter, we take a look at one of the basic and simple forms of neural network architecture, the perceptron.

A **perceptron** is defined as a basic building block of a neural network. In machine learning, a perceptron is an algorithm for supervised learning of binary classifiers. They classify an output as binary: TRUE/FALSE or 1/0.

This chapter helps understand the following topics:

- Explanation of the perceptron
- Linear separable classifier
- Simple perceptron implementation function
- **Multi-Layer Perceptrons** (**MLPs**)

By the end of the chapter, we will understand the basic concepts of perceptrons and how they are used in neural network algorithm. We will discover the linear separable classifier. We will learn a simple perceptron implementation function in R environment. We will know how to train and model an MLP.

Perceptrons and their applications

A perceptron can be understood as anything that takes multiple inputs and produces one output. It is the simplest form of a neural network. The perceptron was proposed by Frank Rosenblatt in 1958 as an entity with an input and output layer and a learning rule based on minimizing the error. This learning function called **error backpropagation** alters connective weights (synapses) based on the actual output of the network with respect to a given input, as the difference between the actual output and the desired output.

The enthusiasm was enormous and the cybernetics industry was born. But later, scientists Marvin Minsky and Seymour Papert (1969) demonstrated the limits of the perceptron. Indeed, a perceptron is able to recognize, after a suitable training, only linearly separable functions. For example, the XOR logic function cannot be implemented by a perceptron.

The following image shows Frank Rosenblatt at the Cornell Aeronautical Laboratory (1957-1959), while working on the Mark I Perceptron classifier:

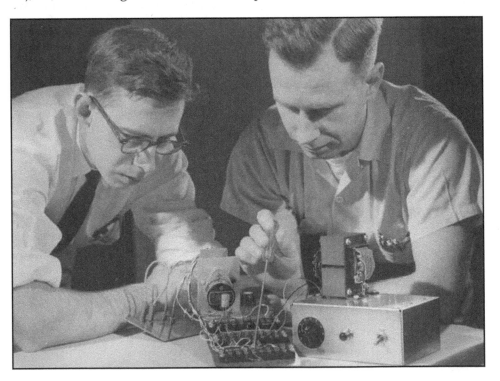

Potentially, a multilevel network of percetters could solve more complex problems, but the increasing computational complexity of training made this path impracticable. Only in recent times have we started to consider the utility of this operational entity.

In the single form, a perceptron has one neuron unit accepting inputs and producing a set of outputs.

For example, let us take a look at the following image:

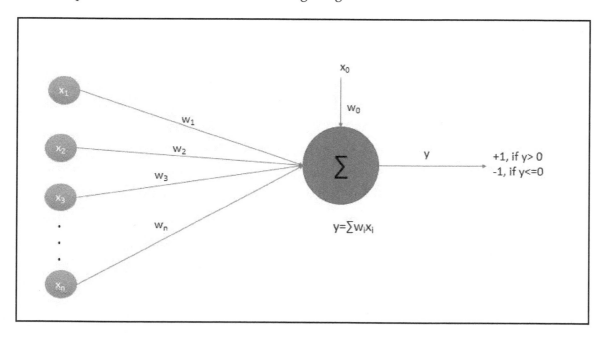

Here $x_1, x_2, .., x_n$ are the set of inputs and x_0 is the bias. x_0 is set to **1**. The output **y** is the sum product of $w_i x_i$. The **signum** function is applied after the sum product has been executed.

It separates the output as:

- If **y>0**, the output is **1**
- If **y<=0**, the output is **-1**

The bias is constant and is associated with weight w_0. This perceptron functions as a linear separator, splitting the output into one category, **-1** or **+1**.

Note that here this is no backpropagation and the weight update updates through steps we will soon see. There is a threshold setup which determines the value of the output. The output here is binary (either **-1** or **+1**), which can be set as zero or one.

Hence, a perceptron is a simple classification function that directly makes its prediction. The core of the functionality lives in the weights and how we update the weights to the best possible prediction of **y**.

This case is a **simple perceptron** or basic perceptron, and the outputs are binary in nature: *0/1 true/false +1/-1.*

There is another type of perceptron called the **multi-class perceptron**, which can classify many possible labels for an animal, such as dog, cat, or bird.

In the following figure is shown a simple perceptron architecture versus multi-class perceptron architecture:

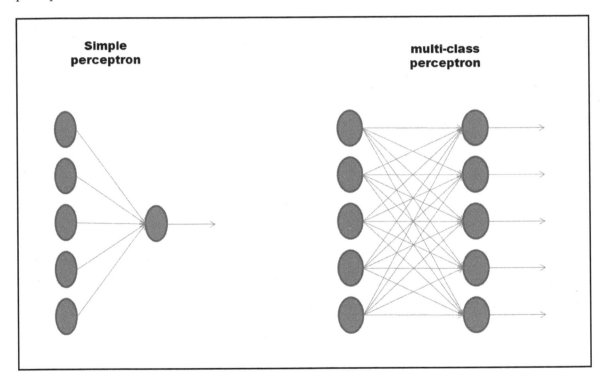

By modifying the weighting vector, we can modify the output of a perceptron to improve the learning or storage properties. For example, we can try to instruct a perceptron such that given an input *x*, output *y* is as close as possible to a given a priori chosen *y* actual value. The computational capabilities of a single perceptron are, however, limited, and the performance that can be obtained depends heavily on both the input choice and the choice of function that you want to implement.

In fact, inputs can be limited to a subset of all the possible inputs, or be randomly extracted according to a certain predetermined probability distribution. To a lesser extent, the performance of such a system also depends on how the distance between the actual outputs and the expected outputs is quantified.

Once you have identified the problem of learning, you can try to find the optimal weight assignment for the given problem.

Simple perceptron – a linear separable classifier

As we saw, a simple perceptron is a single layer neural unit which is a linear classifier. It is a neuron capable of producing only two output patterns, which can be synthesized in *active* or *inactive*. Its decision rule is implemented by a *threshold* behavior: if the sum of the activation patterns of the individual neurons that make up the input layer, weighted for their weights, exceeds a certain threshold, then the output neuron will adopt the output pattern *active*. Conversely, the output neuron will remain in the *inactive* state.

As mentioned, the output is the sum of *weights*inputs* and a function applied on top of it; output is *+1 (y>0)* or *-1(y<=0)*, as shown in the following figure:

$$\text{output} = \begin{cases} -1 & \text{if } w \cdot x + b \leq 0 \\ 1 & \text{if } w \cdot x + b > 0 \end{cases}$$

We can see the linear interaction here; the output *y* is linearly dependent on the inputs.

As with most neural network models, it is possible to realize a learning function based on the modification of synaptic connective weights, even in perceptors. At the beginning of the training phase, weights *w* of perceptron synaptic connections assume completely random values. For training, we have a number of examples with its relative, correct, classification. The network is presented in turn, the different cases to be classified and the network processes each time its response (greater than the threshold or less than the threshold). If the classification is correct (network output is the same as expected), the training algorithm does not make any changes. On the contrary, if the classification is incorrect, the algorithm changes the synaptic weights in an attempt to improve the classification performance of the network.

The single perceptron is an online learner. The weight updates happen through the following steps:

1. Get x and output label y.
2. Update w for $f(x)$.
3. If $f(x)=y$, mark as completed; else, fix it
4. Now adjust score based on error:

    $f(x)= sign(sum\ of\ weights^*inputs)$, the errors are possible

    if $y=+1$ and $f(x)=-1$, w^*x is too small, make it bigger

    if $y=-1$ and $f(x)=+1$, w^*x is too large make it smaller

5. Apply the following rules:

    make $w=w-x$ if $f(f)=+1$ and $y=-1$

    make $w=w+x$ if $f(f)=-1$ and $y=+1$

    $w=w$ if $f(x)=y$

    Or simply, $w=w+yx$ if $f(x)!=y$

6. Repeat steps 3 to 5, until $f(x) = y$.

The perceptron is guaranteed to satisfy all our data, but only for a binary classifier with a single neuron. In step 5, we brought a term called **learning rate**. This helps our model converge. In step 5, w is written as: $w=w+\alpha yx$ if $f(x) != y$, where α is the learning rate chosen.

The bias is also updated as $b=b+ \alpha y$ if $f(x) != y$. The b is actually our w_0.

If the Boolean function is a linear threshold function (that is, if it is linearly separable), then the local perceptron rule can find a set of weights capable of achieving it in a finite number of steps.

This theorem, known as the **perceptron theorem**, is also applicable in the case of the global rule, which modifies the vector of synaptic weights w, not at a single input vector, but depending on the behavior of the perceptron on the whole set of input vectors.

We just mentioned the linearly separable function, but what is meant by this term? We will understand it in the following section.

Linear separation

When a set of output values can be split by a straight line, the output values are said to be linearly separable. Geometrically, this condition describes the situation in which there is a hyperplane that separates, in the vector space of inputs, those that require positive output from those that require a negative output, as shown in the following figure:

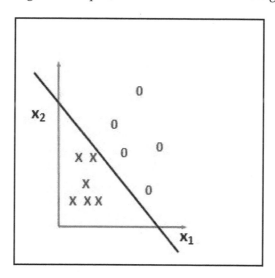

Here, one side of the separator are those predicted to belong to one class whilst those on the other side are predicted to belong to a different class. The decision rule of the Boolean neuron corresponds to the breakdown of the input features space, operated by a hyperplane.

If, in addition to the output neuron, even the input of the neural network is Boolean, then using the neural network to perform a classification is equivalent to determining a Boolean function of the input vector. This function takes the value 1 where it exceeds the threshold value, 0 otherwise. For example, with two input and output Boolean neurons, it is possible to represent, in an extremely intuitive way, the *AND* and *OR* functions.

Indeed, the *AND* gate and *OR* gate are linearly separable. Let's test it in practice by first listing the possible cases in a table and then representing them on a two-dimensional plane.

Let's first do this for the *AND* function. In the following table are listed all the possible cases with the logical results:

x1	x2	y (AND gate)
1	1	1
1	0	0
0	1	0
0	0	0

The following figure shows all the four cases in a two-dimensional plane:

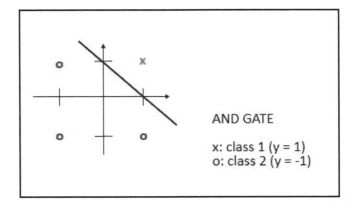

AND GATE

x: class 1 (y = 1)
o: class 2 (y = -1)

All points above the hyperplane are assumed to be *1/TRUE*, while the ones below are assumed to be *0/FALSE*.

Let's do it now for the *OR* function. In the following table are listed all the possible cases with the logical results:

x1	x2	y (OR gate)
1	1	1
1	0	1
0	1	1
0	0	0

The following figure shows all the four cases in a two-dimensional plane:

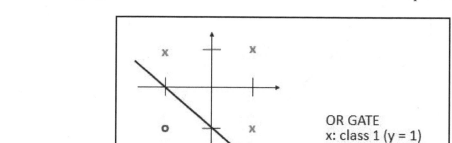

In this case also, all the points above the hyperplane are assumed to be *1/TRUE*, while the ones below are assumed to be *0/FALSE*.

However, some Boolean functions cannot be replicated through a network structure, such as that seen up to here. The *XOR* and identity functions, for example, are not separable: to isolate them, two lines would be needed, which can be implemented only through the use of a more complex network structure.

In the following table are listed all the possible cases with the logical results, for the *XOR* function:

x1	x2	y (XOR gate)
1	1	0
1	0	1
0	1	1
0	0	0

In the following figure are shown all the four cases in a two-dimensional plane:

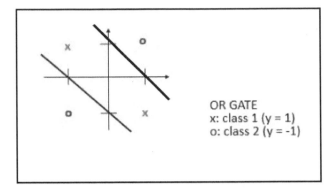

As anticipated, such a function requires two lines to group all possible cases.

After understanding the basics of perceptron theory, we can study a practical case.

The perceptron function in R

In the previous sections, we understood the fundamental concepts underlying the use of a perceptron as a classifier. The time has come to put into practice what has been studied so far. We will do it by analyzing an example in which we will try to classify the floral species on the basis of the size of the petals and sepals of an Iris. As you will recall, the `iris` dataset has already been used in `Chapter 3`, *Deep Learning Using Multilayer Neural Networks*. The reason for its re-use is not only due to the quality of the data contained in it that allows the reader to easily understand the concepts outlined, but also, and more importantly, to be able to compare the different algorithms.

As you will recall, the dataset contains 50 samples from each of three species of Iris (Iris `setosa`, Iris `virginica`, and Iris `versicolor`). Four features were measured from each sample: the length and the width of the sepals and petals, in centimeters.

The following variables are contained:

- Sepal length in cm
- Sepal width in cm
- Petal length in cm
- Petal width in cm
- Class: `setosa`, `versicolour`, `virginica`

In the example presented, we will try to classify the `setosa` and `versicolor` species through linear separation.

Let us implement a perceptron function in R for the `iris` dataset. The code is presented next:

```
####################################################################
###Chapter 4 - Introduction to Neural Networks - using R    #########
###Simple Perceptron implementation function in R - iris dataset  ####
####################################################################

data(iris)
head(iris, n=20)

iris_sub=iris[1:100, c(1, 3, 5)]
names(iris_sub)=c("sepal", "petal", "species")
head(iris_sub)

library(ggplot2)

ggplot(iris_sub, aes(x = sepal, y = petal)) +
 geom_point(aes(colour=species, shape=species), size = 3) +
 xlab("Sepal length") +
 ylab("Petal length") +
 ggtitle("Species vs Sepal and Petal lengths")

euclidean.norm = function(x) {sqrt(sum(x * x))}

distance.from.plane = function(z,w,b) {
 sum(z*w) + b
}

classify.linear = function(x,w,b) {
 distances = apply(x, 1, distance.from.plane, w, b)
 return(ifelse(distances < 0, -1, +1))
}

perceptron = function(x, y, learning.rate=1) {
 w = vector(length = ncol(x)) # initialize weights
 b = 0 # Initialize bias
 k = 0 # count updates
 R = max(apply(x, 1, euclidean.norm))
 mark.complete = TRUE

 while (mark.complete) {
    mark.complete=FALSE
    yc = classify.linear(x,w,b)
    for (i in 1:nrow(x)) {
```

```
            if (y[i] != yc[i]) {
                w = w + learning.rate * y[i]*x[i,]
                b = b + learning.rate * y[i]*R^2
                k = k+1
                mark.complete=TRUE
            }
        }
    }
    s = euclidean.norm(w)
    return(list(w=w/s,b=b/s,updates=k))
}

x = cbind(iris_sub$sepal, iris_sub$petal)

y = ifelse(iris_sub$species == "setosa", +1, -1)

p = perceptron(x,y)

plot(x,cex=0.2)

points(subset(x,Y==1),col="black",pch="+",cex=2)
points(subset(x,Y==-1),col="red",pch="-",cex=2)

intercept = - p$b / p$w[[2]]
slope = - p$w[[1]] /p$ w[[2]]

abline(intercept,slope,col="green")
```

Now, let us go through the code line-by-line. Following the style in the rest of this book, we will present a portion of the code first as follows and then explain it in detail:

```
data(iris)
head(iris, n=20)
```

The first command loads the `iris` dataset, which is contained in the datasets library, and saves it in a given dataframe. Then we use the `head` function to display the first 20 lines of the dataset. Remember, the `head` function returns the first or last parts of a vector, matrix, table, dataframe, or function. In this case, we specify the number of lines that must be displayed (n=20). The following is the result:

```
> head(iris, n=20)
   Sepal.Length Sepal.Width Petal.Length Petal.Width Species
1           5.1         3.5          1.4         0.2  setosa
2           4.9         3.0          1.4         0.2  setosa
3           4.7         3.2          1.3         0.2  setosa
4           4.6         3.1          1.5         0.2  setosa
5           5.0         3.6          1.4         0.2  setosa
```

6	5.4	3.9	1.7	0.4	setosa
7	4.6	3.4	1.4	0.3	setosa
8	5.0	3.4	1.5	0.2	setosa
9	4.4	2.9	1.4	0.2	setosa
10	4.9	3.1	1.5	0.1	setosa
11	5.4	3.7	1.5	0.2	setosa
12	4.8	3.4	1.6	0.2	setosa
13	4.8	3.0	1.4	0.1	setosa
14	4.3	3.0	1.1	0.1	setosa
15	5.8	4.0	1.2	0.2	setosa
16	5.7	4.4	1.5	0.4	setosa
17	5.4	3.9	1.3	0.4	setosa
18	5.1	3.5	1.4	0.3	setosa
19	5.7	3.8	1.7	0.3	setosa
20	5.1	3.8	1.5	0.3	setosa

Let's go back to the code. We will get the binary output by extracting only *100* rows of the `iris` dataset, and extracting only `sepal` length and `petal` length with `species`:

```
iris_sub=iris[1:100, c(1, 3, 5)]
names(iris_sub)=c("sepal", "petal", "species")
head(iris_sub)
```

Here, only the first `100` rows of the `iris` dataset are taken and columns 1,3, and 5 are chosen. This is because the first `100` lines contain the data for the two species (`setosa` and `versicolor`) we are interested in, in the following example. The three columns are `sepal.length(x1)`, `petal.length(x2)`, and `species(y - output)`.

```
library(ggplot2)

ggplot(iris_sub, aes(x = sepal, y = petal)) +
  geom_point(aes(colour=species, shape=species), size = 3) +
  xlab("Sepal length") +
  ylab("Petal length") +
  ggtitle("Species vs Sepal and Petal lengths")
```

First we load the `ggplot2` library, and then we use `ggplot()` to get the scatterplot of the distribution of species with respect to `sepal.length` and `petal.length`. Of course, the library should have been installed beforehand.

Remember, to install a library that is not present in the initial distribution of R, you must use the `install.package` function. This is the main function to install packages. It takes a vector of names and a destination library, downloads the packages from the repositories and installs them.

The objective of the `perceptron` function is to find a linear separation of the `setosa` and `versicolor` species. The following figure shows **Sepal length** versus **Petal length** for the two species of Iris flower:

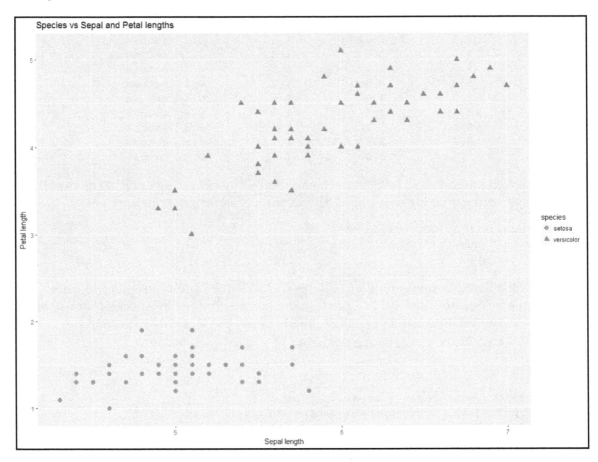

As can be seen, the two species are placed in distinct areas of the plane, so linear separation is possible. At this point, we need to define functions to do the perceptron processing:

```
euclidean.norm = function(x) {sqrt(sum(x * x))}

distance.from.plane = function(z,w,b) {
 sum(z*w) + b
}

classify.linear = function(x,w,b) {
 distances = apply(x, 1, distance.from.plane, w, b)
 return(ifelse(distances < 0, -1, +1))
```

```
}

perceptron = function(x, y, learning.rate=1) {
 w = vector(length = ncol(x)) # initialize weights
 b = 0 # Initialize bias
 k = 0 # count updates
 R = max(apply(x, 1, euclidean.norm))
 mark.complete = TRUE

 while (mark.complete) {
    mark.complete=FALSE
    yc = classify.linear(x,w,b)
    for (i in 1:nrow(x)) {
       if (y[i] != yc[i]) {
          w = w + learning.rate * y[i]*x[i,]
          b = b + learning.rate * y[i]*R^2
          k = k+1
          mark.complete=TRUE
       }
    }
 }
 s = euclidean.norm(w)
 return(list(w=w/s,b=b/s,updates=k))
}
```

We define the `perceptron` function as discussed in the algorithm for perceptron training. We apply `learning.rate` as 1 and try to update the weights in each loop. Once we have the output and the function *(weights*inputs)* equal, we stop the training and move out. The updated weights are returned by the function. The objective of the function is to get a set of optimal weights needed for the model as follows:

```
x = cbind(iris_sub$sepal, iris_sub$petal)

y = ifelse(iris_sub$species == "setosa", +1, -1)

p = perceptron(x,y)
```

With the first line, we set the x inputs as the `sepal` and `petal` lengths. `sepal.length` and `petal.length` form the input matrix. In the second line, we set label output as positive for `setosa` and the rest as negative. The output is either `setosa` or not (+1 or −1). In the third line, we run the `perceptron` function.

We call the `perceptron` function with x and y, which gives the optimal weights for the perceptron as shown in the following code sample:

```
plot(x,cex=0.2)

points(subset(x,Y==1),col="black",pch="+",cex=2)
points(subset(x,Y==-1),col="red",pch="*",cex=2)

intercept = - p$b / p$w[[2]]
slope = - p$w[[1]] /p$ w[[2]]

abline(intercept,slope,col="green")
```

The previous lines of code plot x and y, highlighting `setosa` and `versicolor` as + and * points in the graph. We then find the intercept and slope of the p variable (perceptron), returned by the perceptron. Plotting the linear separation line gives the following graph:

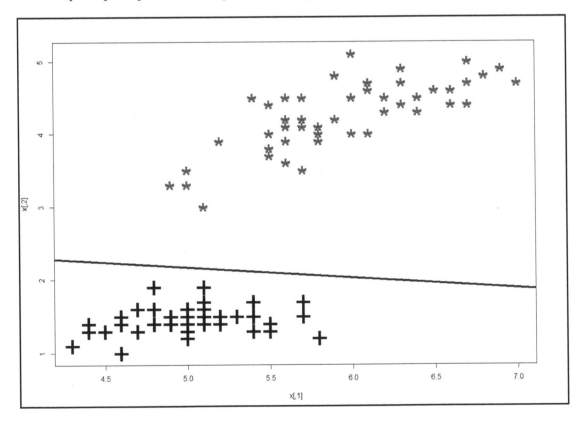

To summarize, we have implemented the perceptron using R code and found optimal weights. The linear separation has been achieved using the perceptron.

Multi-Layer Perceptron

We saw that the *AND* and *OR* gate outputs are linearly separable and perceptron can be used to model this data. However, not all functions are separable. In fact, there are very few and their proportion to the total of achievable functions tends to zero as the number of bits increases. Indeed, as we anticipated, if we take the *XOR* gate, the linear separation is not possible. The crosses and the zeros are in different locations and we cannot put a line to separate them, as shown in the following figure:

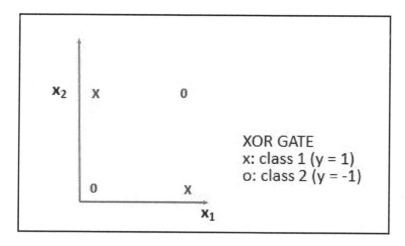

We could think of parsing more perceptrons. The resulting structure could thus learn a greater number of functions, all of which belong to the subset of linearly separable functions.

In order to achieve a wider range of functions, intermediate transmissions must be introduced into the perceptron between the input layer and the output layer, allowing for some kind of internal representation of the input. The resulting perceptron is called MLP.

We have already seen this as feed forward networks in `Chapter 1`, *Neural Network and Artificial Intelligence Concepts*. MLP consists of at least three layers of nodes: input, hidden, and output nodes. Except for the input nodes, each node is a neuron using a non-linear activation function. MLP uses a supervised learning technique and back propagation for training. The multiple layers and non-linear nature distinguishes MLP from simple perceptrons. MLP is specifically used when the data is not linearly separable.

For example, an MLP, such as that shown in the following figure, is able to realize the **XOR** function, which we have previously seen cannot be achieved through a simple perceptron:

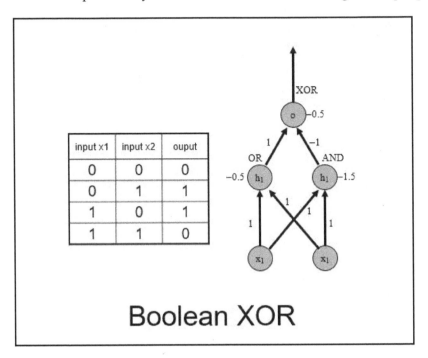

input x1	input x2	ouput
0	0	0
0	1	1
1	0	1
1	1	0

Boolean XOR

XOR is achieved using a three layer network and is a combination of **OR** and **AND** perceptrons. The output layer contains one neuron which gives the **XOR** output. A configuration of this kind allows the two neurons to specialize each on a particular logic function. For example, in the case of **XOR,** the two neurons can respectively carry out the **AND** and **OR** logic functions.

> The term MLP does not refer to a single perceptron that has multiple layers. Rather, it contains many perceptrons that are organized into layers. An alternative is an MLP network.

Applications of MLP are:

- MLPs are extremely useful for complex problems in research.
- MLPs are universal function approximators and they can be used to create mathematical models by regression analysis. MLPs also make good classifier algorithms.

- MLPs are used in diverse fields, such as speech recognition, image recognition, and language translation. They form the basis for deep learning.

We will now implement an MLP using the R package SNNS.

MLP R implementation using RSNNS

The package RSNNS is taken from CRAN for this example of mlp() model build. The SNNS is a library written in C++ and contains many standard implementations of neural networks. This RSNNS package wraps the SNNS functionality to make it available from within R. Using the RSNNS low-level interface, all the algorithmic functionality and flexibility of SNNS can be accessed. The package contains a high-level interface for most commonly used neural network topologies and learning algorithms, which integrate seamlessly into R. A brief description of the RSNNS package, extracted from the official documentation, is shown in the following table:

RSNNS package
Description:
The SNNS is a library containing many standard implementations of neural networks. This package wraps the SNNS functionality to make it available from within R. Using the RSNNS low-level interface, all the algorithmic functionality and flexibility of SNNS can be accessed. Furthermore, the package contains a convenient high-level interface, so that the most common neural network topologies and learning algorithms integrate seamlessly into R.
Details:
Package: RSNNS Type: Package Version: 0.4-9 Date: 2016-12-16 License: LGPL (>=2)
Authors:
Christoph Bergmeir *José M. Benítez*
Usage:

```
mlp(x, y,
size = c(5),
maxit = 100,
initFunc = "Randomize_Weights",
initFuncParams = c(-0.3, 0.3),
learnFunc = "Std_Backpropagation",
learnFuncParams = c(0.2, 0),
updateFunc = "Topological_Order",
updateFuncParams = c(0),
hiddenActFunc = "Act_Logistic",
shufflePatterns = TRUE,
linOut = FALSE,
outputActFunc = if (linOut) "Act_Identity" else "Act_Logistic",
inputsTest = NULL,
targetsTest = NULL,
pruneFunc = NULL,
pruneFuncParams = NULL, ...)
```

We use the `mlp()` function which creates an MLP and trains it. Training is usually performed by backpropagation.

The most commonly used parameters are listed in the following table:

x	A matrix with training inputs for the network
y	The corresponding targets values
size	Number of units in the hidden layers
maxit	Maximum iterations to learn
hiddenActFunc	The activation function of all hidden units
outputActFunc	The activation function of all output units
inputsTest	A matrix with inputs to test the network
targetsTest	The corresponding targets for the test input

Let's see the code for building a SNNS MLP using the full Iris dataset:

```
#############################################################
###Chapter 4 - Introduction to Neural Networks - using R #########
###Simple RSNNS implementation function in R - iris dataset ######
#############################################################

data(iris)

library("RSNNS")

iris = iris[sample(1:nrow(iris),length(1:nrow(iris))),1:ncol(iris)]

irisValues = iris[,1:4]
irisTargets = decodeClassLabels(iris[,5])

iris = splitForTrainingAndTest(irisValues, irisTargets, ratio=0.15)
iris = normTrainingAndTestSet(iris)

model = mlp(iris$inputsTrain,
        iris$targetsTrain,
        size=5,
        learnFuncParams=c(0.1),
        maxit=50,
        inputsTest=iris$inputsTest,
        targetsTest=iris$targetsTest)

summary(model)
weightMatrix(model)

par(mfrow=c(2,2))
plotIterativeError(model)

predictions = predict(model,iris$inputsTest)

plotRegressionError(predictions[,2], iris$targetsTest[,2])

confusionMatrix(iris$targetsTrain,fitted.values(model))
confusionMatrix(iris$targetsTest,predictions)

par(mfrow=c(1,2))
plotROC(fitted.values(model)[,2], iris$targetsTrain[,2])
plotROC(predictions[,2], iris$targetsTest[,2])

confusionMatrix(iris$targetsTrain,
        encodeClassLabels(fitted.values(model),
        method="402040",
        l=0.4,
```

```
      h=0.6))
##################################################################
```

Let's go through the code step-by-step.

This command loads the iris dataset, which is contained in the datasets library, and saves it in a given dataframe. Considering the many times we have used it, I do not think it's necessary to add anything. This loads the RSNNS library for the program:

```
install.packages("RSNNS")
library("RSNNS")
```

Remember, to install a library that is not present in the initial distribution of R, you must use the install.package function. This is the main function to install packages. It takes a vector of names and a destination library, downloads the packages from the repositories and installs them.

In our case, we must use the command install.packages("RSNNS"). The install package is required only the first time, to install the RSNNS package from CRAN.

```
iris = iris[sample(1:nrow(iris),length(1:nrow(iris))),1:ncol(iris)]
```

In this preceding line, the iris dataset is shuffled within rows. This operation makes the order of the rows in the dataset random. In fact, in the original dataset, the observations are ordered by floral species: the first *50* occurrences of the setosa species, followed by the *50* occurrences of the versicolor species, and finally the *50* occurrences of the virginica species. After this operation, the rows happen randomly. To verify this, we print the first 20 lines of the modified dataset:

```
> head(iris, n=20)
     Sepal.Length Sepal.Width Petal.Length Petal.Width    Species
75            6.4         2.9          4.3         1.3 versicolor
112           6.4         2.7          5.3         1.9  virginica
54            5.5         2.3          4.0         1.3 versicolor
36            5.0         3.2          1.2         0.2     setosa
14            4.3         3.0          1.1         0.1     setosa
115           5.8         2.8          5.1         2.4  virginica
125           6.7         3.3          5.7         2.1  virginica
27            5.0         3.4          1.6         0.4     setosa
8             5.0         3.4          1.5         0.2     setosa
41            5.0         3.5          1.3         0.3     setosa
85            5.4         3.0          4.5         1.5 versicolor
64            6.1         2.9          4.7         1.4 versicolor
108           7.3         2.9          6.3         1.8  virginica
65            5.6         2.9          3.6         1.3 versicolor
66            6.7         3.1          4.4         1.4 versicolor
```

98	6.2	2.9	4.3	1.3	versicolor
39	4.4	3.0	1.3	0.2	setosa
84	6.0	2.7	5.1	1.6	versicolor
2	4.9	3.0	1.4	0.2	setosa
142	6.9	3.1	5.1	2.3	virginica

The numbers in the first column are the row numbers of the original dataset. How can we notice the shuffling flawed perfectly. To compare with the original sequence, see the previous example:

```
irisValues = iris[,1:4]
irisTargets = decodeClassLabels(iris[,5])
```

The independent and target variables are set up and assigned to `irisValues` and `irisTargets` respectively:

```
iris = splitForTrainingAndTest(irisValues, irisTargets, ratio=0.15)
iris = normTrainingAndTestSet(iris)
```

In the first line, the training data and the test data is split up through the `splitForTrainingAndTest()` function. This function splits the input and target values to a training and a testing set. A test set is taken from the end of the data. If the data is to be shuffled, this should be done before calling this function. In particular, the data is split as follows: *85* percent for training and *15* percent for testing. In the second line, the data is normalized. To do this, the `normTrainingAndTestSet()` function is used. This function normalizes the training and test set in the following way: The `inputsTrain` member is normalized using `normalizeData` with the parameters given in type. The normalization parameters obtained during this normalization are then used to normalize the `inputsTest` member. If the `dontNormTargets` argument is not set, then the targets are normalized in the same way:

```
model = mlp(iris$inputsTrain,
    iris$targetsTrain,
    size=5,
    learnFuncParams=c(0.1),
    maxit=50,
    inputsTest=iris$inputsTest,
    targetsTest=iris$targetsTest)
```

The `mlp()` function is called with the training dataset to build the model. This function creates an MLP and trains it. MLPs are fully connected feed-forward networks, and probably the most common network architecture in use. Training is usually performed by error backpropagation or a related procedure. The test dataset is also passed to provide the test results:

```
summary(model)
weightMatrix(model)
```

These lines of code allow us to extract useful information from the newly created model. The `summary()` function prints out a summary of the network. The printed information can be either all information of the network in the original SNNS file format, or the information given by `extractNetInfo`. This behavior is controlled with the parameter `origSnnsFormat`, while the `weightMatrix()` function extracts the weight matrix of an `rsnns` object. The following figure shows a screenshot of the summary results:

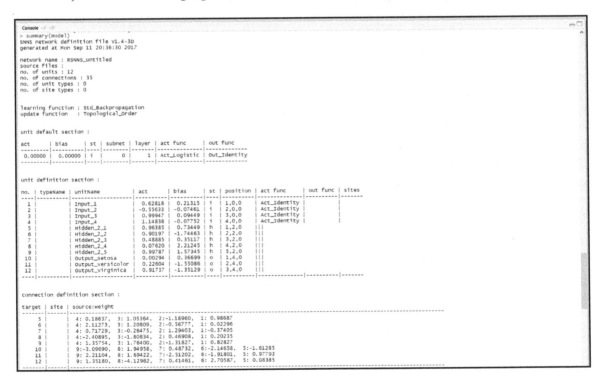

Now we measure the performance of the algorithm in model training:

```
plotIterativeError(model)
```

The `plotIterativeError()` function plots the iterative training and test error of the net of the model. The results are shown in the following figure:

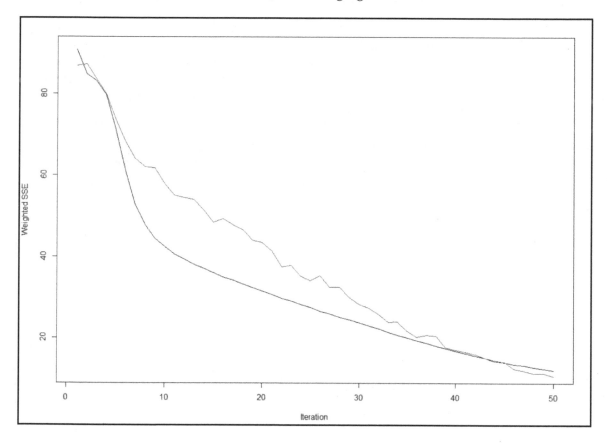

The previous figure showns the iterative fit error as a black line and the iterative test error as a red line. As can be seen, both lines have a strongly decreasing trend, demonstrating that the algorithm quickly converges.

After properly training the model, it is time to use it to make predictions:

```
predictions = predict(model, iris$inputsTest)
```

In this case, we have used the `predict()` function. This is a generic function for predictions from the results of various model fitting functions. The function invokes particular methods which depend on the class of the first argument. We have both the predictions and the actual data; we just have to compare them through the regression error calculus:

```
plotRegressionError(predictions[,2], iris$targetsTest[,2])
```

To plot the regression error, we have used the `plotRegressionError()` function. This function shows target values on the X axis and fitted/predicted values on the Y axis. The optimal fit would yield a line through zero with gradient one. This optimal line is shown in black in the following figure. A linear fit to the actual data is shown in red. The following figure shows the regression error for the model which we previously trained:

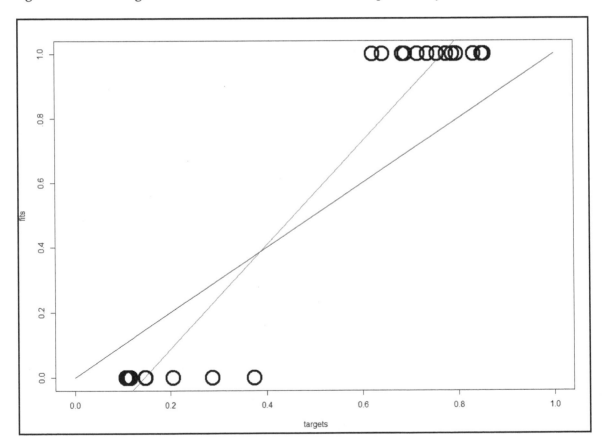

Let's now evaluate the model performance in predicting data by computing the confusion matrix:

```
confusionMatrix(iris$targetsTrain,fitted.values(model))
confusionMatrix(iris$targetsTest,predictions)
```

To compute the confusion matrix, we have used the `confusionMatrix()` function.

 Remember, the confusion matrix shows how many times a pattern with the real class x was classified as class y. A perfect method should result in a diagonal matrix. All values not on the diagonal are errors of the method.

In the first line of the code, we calculated the confusion matrix for the data used in the training (which is *85* percent of the data), while in the second line, we calculated the confusion matrix for the data used in the test (which is the remaining *15* percent of data). The results are as follows:

```
> confusionMatrix(iris$targetsTrain,fitted.values(model))
        predictions
targets  1  2  3
      1 45  0  0
      2  0 34  3
      3  0  1 44
> confusionMatrix(iris$targetsTest,predictions)
        predictions
targets  1  2  3
      1  5  0  0
      2  0 13  0
      3  0  0  5
```

As can be seen, there were four mistakes in the training phase, that only concerned the `versicolor` and `virginica` species. Remember, we obtained the same result in the example presented in Chapter 3, *Deep Learning Using Multilayer Neural Networks*. In the test, however, we did not make any mistakes. I would say very good results, although the processed data is actually small. We graphically evaluate these results:

```
par(mfrow=c(1,2))
plotROC(fitted.values(model)[,2], iris$targetsTrain[,2])
plotROC(predictions[,2], iris$targetsTest[,2])
```

To evaluate network performance, we have plotted the receiver operating characteristic. The previous commands plot the ROC for both the phases (training and testing). The ROC is a metric used to check the quality of classifiers. For each class of a classifier, ROC applies threshold values across the interval *[0,1]* to outputs. The ROC curve is a plot of the TPR versus the FPR, as the threshold is varied. A perfect test would show points in the upper-left corner, with *100* percent sensitivity and *100* percent specificity. The better the lines approach the upper-left corner, the better is the network performance. The following figure shows the ROC curves for both the phases (training to the left and test to the right):

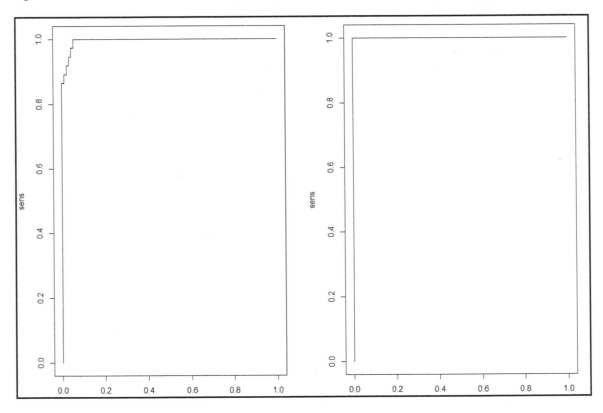

As already mentioned, in the training phase there were errors that are absent in the test.

Note, we used the `par()` function to display both the charts in a single window. In it we have set to display the graphs as a matrix with a row and two columns.

There is no `plot` function within RSNNS, hence we use a `plot` function from GitHub to plot the following MLP for the neural network we just built. There are three classes of output and there are four input nodes:

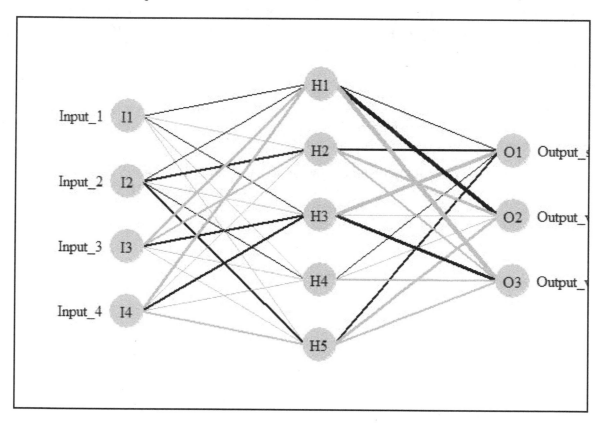

We have seen a simple implementation of an `iris` dataset neural network using RSNNS. The same `mlp()` function can be used for any MLP neural network architecture.

Summary

In this chapter, we introduced you the concept of perceptrons, which are the basic building blocks of a neural network. We also saw multi-layer perceptrons and an implementation using RSNNS. The simple perceptron is useful only for a linear separation problem and cannot be used where the output data is not linearly separable. These limits are exceeded by the use of the MLP algorithm.

We understood the basic concepts of perceptron and how they are used in neural network algorithms. We discovered the linear separable classifier and the functions this concept applies to. We learned a simple perceptron implementation function in R environment and then we learnt how to train and model an MLP.

In the next chapter, we will understand how to train, test, and evaluate a dataset using the neural network model. We will learn how to visualize the neural network model in R environment. We will cover concepts like early stopping, avoiding overfitting, generalization of neural network, and scaling of neural network parameters.

5
Training and Visualizing a Neural Network in R

As seen in Chapters 1, *Neural Network and Artificial Intelligence Concepts*, and Chapter 2, *Learning Process in Neural Networks*, training a neural network model forms the basis for building a neural network.

Feed-forward and backpropagation are the techniques used to determine the weights and biases of the model. The weights can never be zero but the biases can be zero. To start with, the weights are initialized a random number, and by gradient descent, the errors are minimized; we get a set of best possible weights and biases for the model.

Once the model is trained using any of the R functions, we can pass on the independent variables to predict the target or unknown variable. In this chapter, we will use a publicly available dataset to train, test, and visualize a neural network model. The following items will be covered:

- Training, testing, and evaluating a dataset using NN model
- Visualizing the NN model
- Early stopping
- Avoiding overfitting
- Generalization of NN
- Scaling of NN parameters
- Ensemble models

By the end of the chapter, we will understand how to train, test, and evaluate a dataset using NN model. We will learn how to visualize the NN model in R environment. We will cover the concepts like early stopping, avoiding overfitting, generalization of NN, and scaling of NN parameters.

Data fitting with neural network

Data fitting is the process of building a curve or a mathematical function that has the best match with a set of previously collected points. The curve fitting can relate to both interpolations, where exact data points are required, and smoothing, where a flat function is built that approximates the data. The approximate curves obtained from the data fitting can be used to help display data, to predict the values of a function where no data is available, and to summarize the relationship between two or more variables. In the following figure is shown a linear interpolation of collected data:

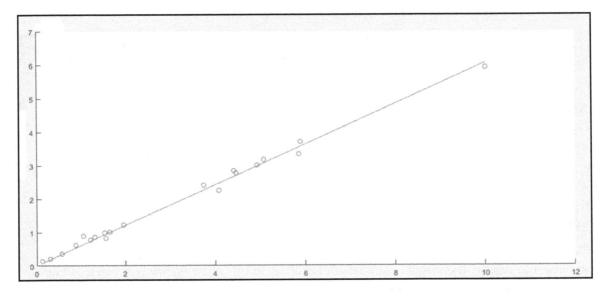

Data fitting is the process of training a neural network on a set of inputs in order to produce an associated set of target outputs. Once the neural network has fit the data, it forms a generalization of the input-output relationship and can be used to generate outputs for inputs it was not trained on.

The fuel consumption of vehicles has always been studied by the major manufacturers of the entire planet. In an era characterized by oil refueling problems and even greater air pollution problems, fuel consumption by vehicles has become a key factor. In this example, we will build a neural network with the purpose of predicting the fuel consumption of the vehicles according to certain characteristics.

To do this, use the `Auto` dataset contained in the `ISLR` package that we have already used in an example in Chapter 3, *Deep Learning Using Multilayer Neural Networks*. The `Auto` dataset contain gas mileage, horsepower, and other information for 392 vehicles. It is a data frame with 392 observations on the following nine variables:

- `mpg`: Miles per gallon
- `cylinders`: Number of cylinders between 4 and 8
- `displacement`: Engine displacement (cubic inches)
- `horsepower`: Engine horsepower
- `weight`: Vehicle weight (lbs)
- `acceleration`: Time to accelerate from 0 to 60 mph (sec)
- `year`: Model year (modulo 100)
- `origin`: Origin of car (American, European, Japanese)
- `name`: Vehicle name

The following is the code that we will use in this example:

```
###############################################################################
########Chapter 5 - Introduction to Neural Networks - using R#############
##########R program to build, train and test neural networks#############
###############################################################################
library("neuralnet")
library("ISLR")

data = Auto
View(data)

plot(data$weight, data$mpg, pch=data$origin,cex=2)
par(mfrow=c(2,2))
plot(data$cylinders, data$mpg, pch=data$origin,cex=1)
plot(data$displacement, data$mpg, pch=data$origin,cex=1)
plot(data$horsepower, data$mpg, pch=data$origin,cex=1)
plot(data$acceleration, data$mpg, pch=data$origin,cex=1)

mean_data <- apply(data[1:6], 2, mean)
sd_data <- apply(data[1:6], 2, sd)

data_scaled <- as.data.frame(scale(data[,1:6],center = mean_data, scale = sd_data))
head(data_scaled, n=20)

index = sample(1:nrow(data),round(0.70*nrow(data)))
train_data <- as.data.frame(data_scaled[index,])
test_data <- as.data.frame(data_scaled[-index,])
```

```
n = names(data_scaled)
f = as.formula(paste("mpg ~", paste(n[!n %in% "mpg"], collapse = " + ")))

net = neuralnet(f,data=train_data,hidden=3,linear.output=TRUE)
plot(net)

predict_net_test <- compute(net,test_data[,2:6])
MSE.net <- sum((test_data$mpg -
predict_net_test$net.result)^2)/nrow(test_data)

Lm_Mod <- lm(mpg~., data=train_data)
summary(Lm_Mod)
predict_lm <- predict(Lm_Mod,test_data)
MSE.lm <- sum((predict_lm - test_data$mpg)^2)/nrow(test_data)

par(mfrow=c(1,2))
plot(test_data$mpg,predict_net_test$net.result,col='black',main='Real vs
predicted for neural network',pch=18,cex=4)
abline(0,1,lwd=5)
plot(test_data$mpg,predict_lm,col='black',main='Real vs predicted for
linear regression',pch=18,cex=4)
abline(0,1,lwd=5)
##############################################################################
```

As usual, we will analyze the code line-by-line, by explaining in detail all the features applied to capture the results.

```
library("neuralnet")
library("ISLR")
```

The first two lines of the initial code are used to load the libraries needed to run the analysis.

> Remember, to install a library that is not present in the initial distribution of R, you must use the `install.package` function. This is the main function to install packages. It takes a vector of names and a destination library, downloads the packages from the repositories and installs them. This function should be used only once and not every time you run the code.

The `neuralnet` library is used to train neural networks using backpropagation, **resilient backpropagation (RPROP)** with or without weight backtracking, or the modified **globally convergent version (GRPROP)**. The function allows flexible settings through custom-choice of error and activation function. Furthermore, the calculation of generalized weights is implemented.

The ISLR library contains a set of datasets freely usable for our examples. This is a series of data collected during major studies conducted by research centers.

```
data = Auto
View(data)
```

This command loads the Auto dataset, which, as we anticipated, is contained in the ISLR library, and saves it in a given dataframe. Use the View function to view a compact display of the structure of an arbitrary R object. The following screenshot shows some of the data contained in the Auto dataset:

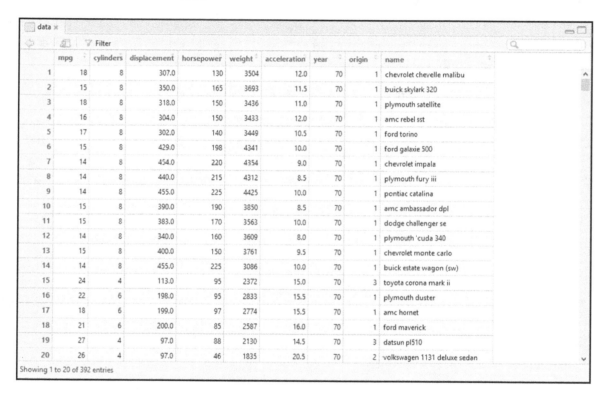

As you can see, the database consists of 392 rows and 9 columns. The rows represent 392 commercial vehicles from 1970 to 1982. The columns represent the 9 characteristics collected for each car, in order: mpg, cylinders, displacement, horsepower, weight, acceleration, year, origin, and name.

Exploratory analysis

Before starting with data analysis through the building and training of a neural network, we conduct an exploratory analysis to understand how data is distributed and extract preliminary knowledge.

We can begin our explorative analysis by tracing a plot of predictors versus target. We recall in this respect that in our analysis, the predictors are the following variables: cylinders, displacement, horsepower, weight, acceleration, year, origin, and name. The target is the mpg variable that contains measurements of the miles per gallon of 392 sample cars.

Suppose we want to examine the weight and mileage of cars from three different origins, as shown in the next graph, using the following code:

```
plot(data$weight, data$mpg, pch=data$origin,cex=2)
```

To plot the chart, we used the plot() function, specifying what to point on the *x* axis (weight), what to point on the *y* axis (mpg), and finally, based on which variable to group the data (origin), as shown in the following graph:

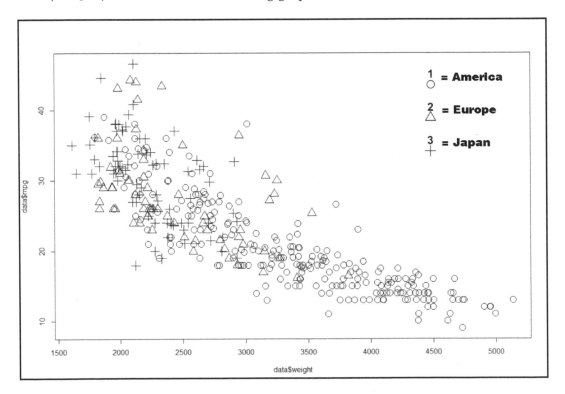

Remember the number in the origin column correspond at the following zone: 1= America, 2=Europe, and 3=Japan). From the analysis of the previous graph, we can find that fuel consumption increases with weight gain. Let's remember that the target measures the miles per gallon, so how many miles are going with a gallon of fuel. It follows that the greater the value of mpg (miles per gallon), the lower the fuel consumption.

Another consideration that comes from plot analysis is that cars produced in America are heavier. In fact, in the right part of the chart (which corresponds to higher values of weight), there are only cars produced in that area.

Finally, if we focus our analysis on the left of the graph, in the upper part that corresponds to the lowest fuel consumption, we find in most cases Japanese and European cars. In conclusion, we can note that cars that have the lowest fuel consumption are Japanese.

Now, let's see the other graphs, that is, what we get if we plot the remaining numeric predictors (cylinders, displacement, horsepower, and acceleration) versus target (mpg).

```
par(mfrow=c(2,2))
plot(data$cylinders, data$mpg, pch=data$origin,cex=1)
plot(data$displacement, data$mpg, pch=data$origin,cex=1)
plot(data$horsepower, data$mpg, pch=data$origin,cex=1)
plot(data$acceleration, data$mpg, pch=data$origin,cex=1)
```

For space reasons, we decided to place the four charts in one. R makes it easy to combine multiple plots into one general graph, using the par() function. Using the par() function, we can include the option mfrow=c(nrows, ncols) to create a matrix of nrows x ncols plots that are filled in by row. For example the option mfrow=c(3,2) creates a matrix plot with 3 rows and 2 columns. In addition, the option mfcol=c(nrows, ncols) fills in the matrix by columns.

In the following figure are shown 4 plot arranged in a matrix of 2 rows and two columns:

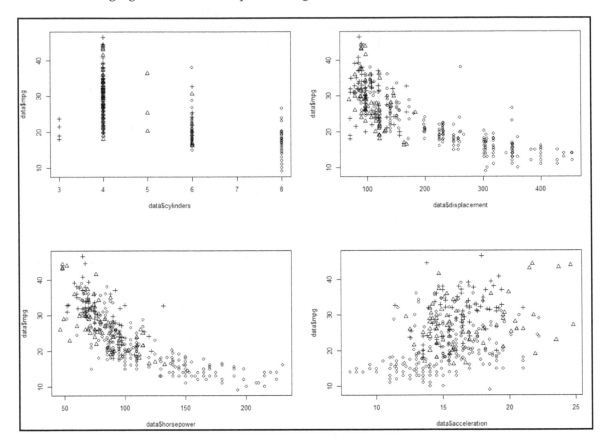

From the analysis of the previous figure, we find confirmation of what has already been mentioned earlier. We can note that cars with higher horsepower have higher fuel consumption. The same thing we can say about the engine displacement; also in this case, vehicles with higher displacement have higher fuel consumption. Again, cars with higher horsepower and displacement values are produced in America.

Conversely, cars with higher acceleration values have lower fuel consumption. This fact is due to the lesser weight that such cars have. Usually, heavy cars are slower in acceleration.

Neural network model

In Chapter 2, *Learning Process in Neural Networks*, we scaled the data before building the network. On that occasion, we pointed out that it is good practice to normalize the data before training a neural network. With normalization, data units are eliminated, allowing you to easily compare data from different locations.

It is not always necessary to normalize numeric data. However, it has been shown that when numeric values are normalized, neural network formation is often more efficient and leads to better prediction. In fact, if numeric data are not normalized and the sizes of two predictors are very distant, a change in the value of a neural network weight has much more relative influence on higher value.

There are several standardization techniques; in Chapter 2, *Learning Process in Neural Networks*, we adopted min-max standardization. In this case, we will adopt Z-scores normalization. This technique consists of subtracting the mean of the column to each value in a column, and then dividing the result for the standard deviation of the column. The formula to achieve this is the following:

$$x_{scaled} = \frac{x - mean}{sd}$$

In summary, the Z score (also called standard score) represents the number of standard deviations with which the value of an observation point or data is greater than the mean value of what is observed or measured. Values above the mean have positive Z-scores, while values below the mean have negative Z-scores. The Z-score is a quantity without dimension, obtained by subtracting the population mean from a single rough score and then dividing the difference for the standard deviation of the population.

Before applying the method chosen for normalization, you must calculate the mean and standard deviation values of each database column. To do this, we use the apply function. This function returns a vector or an array or a list of values obtained by applying a function to margins of an array or matrix. Let's understand the meaning of the arguments used.

```
mean_data <- apply(data[1:6], 2, mean)
sd_data <- apply(data[1:6], 2, sd)
```

The first line allows us to calculate the mean of each variable going to the second line, allowing us to calculate the standard deviation of each variable. Let's see how we used the function `apply()`. The first argument of the apply function specifies the dataset to apply the function to, in our case, the dataset named data. In particular, we have only considered the first six numeric variables; the other ones we will use for other purposes. The second argument must contain a vector giving the subscripts which the function will be applied over. In our case, one indicates rows and two indicates columns. The third argument must contain the function to be applied; in our case, the `mean()` function in the first row and the `sd()` function in the second row. The results are shown as follows:

```
> mean_data
          mpg    cylinders displacement   horsepower      weight
    23.445918     5.471939   194.411990   104.469388 2977.584184
acceleration
    15.541327

> sd_data
          mpg    cylinders displacement   horsepower      weight
     7.805007     1.705783    04.644004    38.491160  849.402560
acceleration
     2.758864
```

To normalize the data, we use the `scale()` function, which is a generic function whose default method centers and/or scales the columns of a numeric matrix:

```
data_scaled <- as.data.frame(scale(data[,1:6],center = mean_data, scale = sd_data))
```

Let's take a look at the data transformed by normalization:

```
head(data_scaled, n=20)
```

The results are as follows:

```
> head(data_scaled, n=20)
          mpg cylinders displacement horsepower      weight acceleration
1  -0.69774672 1.4820530   1.07591459  0.6632851   0.6197483  -1.28361760
2  -1.08211534 1.4820530   1.48683159  1.5725848   0.8422577  -1.46485160
3  -0.69774672 1.4820530   1.18103289  1.1828849   0.5396921  -1.64608561
4  -0.95399247 1.4820530   1.04724596  1.1828849   0.5361602  -1.28361760
5  -0.82586959 1.4820530   1.02813354  0.9230850   0.5549969  -1.82731962
6  -1.08211534 1.4820530   2.24177212  2.4299245   1.6051468  -2.00855363
7  -1.21023822 1.4820530   2.48067735  3.0014843   1.6204517  -2.37102164
8  -1.21023822 1.4820530   2.34689042  2.8715843   1.5710052  -2.55225565
9  -1.21023822 1.4820530   2.49023356  3.1313843   1.7040399  -2.00855363
10 -1.08211534 1.4820530   1.86907996  2.2220846   1.0270935  -2.55225565
11 -1.08211534 1.4820530   1.80218649  1.7024847   0.6892089  -2.00855363
```

```
12 -1.21023822  1.4820530   1.39126949  1.4426848  0.7433646  -2.73348966
13 -1.08211534  1.4820530   1.96464205  1.1828849  0.9223139  -2.18978763
14 -1.21023822  1.4820530   2.49023356  3.1313843  0.1276377  -2.00855363
15  0.07099053 -0.8629108  -0.77799001 -0.2460146 -0.7129531  -0.19621355
16 -0.18525522  0.3095711   0.03428778 -0.2460146 -0.1702187  -0.01497955
17 -0.69774672  0.3095711   0.04384399 -0.1940546 -0.2396793  -0.01497955
18 -0.31337809  0.3095711   0.05340019 -0.5058145 -0.4598340   0.16625446
19  0.45535916 -0.8629108  -0.93088936 -0.4278746 -0.9978592  -0.37744756
20  0.32723628 -0.8629108  -0.93088936 -1.5190342 -1.3451622   1.79736053
```

Let's now split the data for the training and the test:

```
index = sample(1:nrow(data),round(0.70*nrow(data)))
train_data <- as.data.frame(data_scaled[index,])
test_data <- as.data.frame(data_scaled[-index,])
```

In the first line of the code just suggested, the dataset is split into 70:30, with the intention of using 70 percent of the data at our disposal to train the network and the remaining 30 percent to test the network. In the second and third lines, the data of the dataframe named data is subdivided into two new dataframes, called `train_data` and `test_data`. Now we have to build the function to be submitted to the network:

```
n = names(data_scaled)
f = as.formula(paste("mpg ~", paste(n[!n %in% "mpg"], collapse = " + ")))
```

In the first line, we recover all the variable names in the `data_scaled` dataframe, using the `names()` function. In the second line, we build formula that we will use to train the network. What does this formula represent?

The models fitted by the `neuralnet()` function are specified in a compact symbolic form. The ~ operator is basic in the formation of such models. An expression of the form y ~ model is interpreted as a specification that the response y is modelled by a predictor specified symbolically by model. Such a model consists of a series of terms separated by + operators. The terms themselves consist of variable and factor names separated by : operators. Such a term is interpreted as the interaction of all the variables and factors appearing in the term. Let's look at the formula we set:

```
> f
mpg ~ cylinders + displacement + horsepower + weight + acceleration
```

Now we can build and train the network.

In Chapter 3, *Deep Learning Using Multilayer Neural Networks*, we said that to choose the optimal number of neurons, we need to know that:

- Small number of neurons will lead to high error for your system, as the predictive factors might be too complex for a small number of neurons to capture
- Large number of neurons will overfit your training data and not generalize well
- The number of neurons in each hidden layer should be somewhere between the size of the input and the output layer, potentially the mean
- The number of neurons in each hidden layer shouldn't exceed twice the number of input neurons, as you are probably grossly overfit at this point

In this case, we have five input variables (cylinders, displacement, horsepower, weight, and acceleration) and one variable output (mpg). We choose to set three neurons in the hidden layer.

```
net = neuralnet(f,data=train_data,hidden=3,linear.output=TRUE)
```

The hidden argument accepts a vector with the number of neurons for each hidden layer, while the argument linear.output is used to specify whether we want to do regression (linear.output=TRUE) or classification (linear.output=FALSE).

The algorithm used in neuralnet(), by default, is based on the resilient backpropagation without weight backtracking and additionally modifies one learning rate, either the learning rate associated with the smallest absolute gradient (sag) or the smallest learning rate (slr) itself. The neuralnet() function returns an object of class nn. An object of class nn is a list containing at most the components shown in the following table:

Components	Description
call	The matched call.
response	Extracted from the data argument.
covariate	The variables extracted from the data argument.
model.list	A list containing the covariates and the response variables extracted from the formula argument.
err.fct	The error function.
act.fct	The activation function.
data	The data argument.

net.result	A list containing the overall result of the neural network for every repetition.
weights	A list containing the fitted weights of the neural network for every repetition.
generalized.weights	A list containing the generalized weights of the neural network for every repetition.
result.matrix	A matrix containing the reached threshold, needed steps, error, AIC and BIC (if computed), and weights for every repetition. Each column represents one repetition.
startweights	A list containing the startweights of the neural network for every repetition.

To produce result summaries of the results of the model, we use the summary() function:

```
> summary(net)
                     Length Class      Mode
call                 5      -none-     call
response             274    -none-     numeric
covariate            1370   -none-     numeric
model.list           2      -none-     list
err.fct              1      -none-     function
act.fct              1      -none-     function
linear.output        1      -none-     logical
data                 6      data.frame list
net.result           1      -none-     list
weights              1      -none-     list
startweights         1      -none-     list
generalized.weights  1      -none-     list
result.matrix        25     -none-     numeric
```

For each component of the neural network model are displayed three features:

- **Length**: This is component length, that is how many elements of this type are contained in it
- **Class**: This contains specific indication on the component class
- **Mode**: This is the type of component (numeric, list, function, logical, and so on)

To plot the graphical representation of the model with the weights on each connection, we can use the `plot()` function. The `plot()` function is a generic function for the representation of objects in R. Generic function means that it is suitable for different types of objects, from variables to tables to complex function outputs, producing different results. Applied to a nominal variable, it will produce a bar graph. Applied to a cardinal variable, it will produce a scatterplot. Applied to the same variable, but tabulated, that is, to its frequency distribution, it will produce a histogram. Finally, applied to two variables, a nominal and a cardinal, it will produce a boxplot.

```
plot(net)
```

The neural network plot is shown in the following graph:

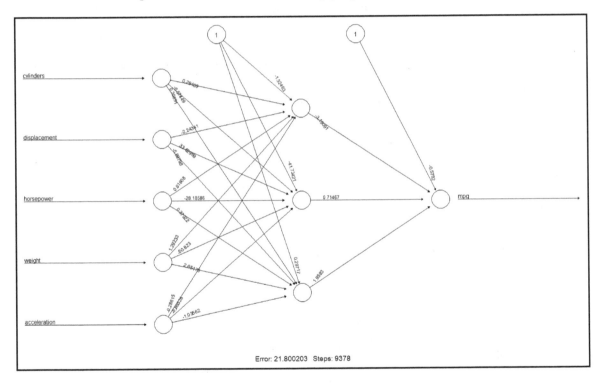

In the previous graph, the black lines (these lines start from input nodes) show the connections between each layer and the weights on each connection, while the blue lines (these lines start from bias nodes which are distinguished by number 1) show the bias term added in each step. The bias can be thought of as the intercept of a linear model.

Though over time we have understood a lot about the mechanics that are the basis of the neural networks, in many respects, the model we have built and trained remains a black box. The fitting, weights, and model are not clear enough. We can be satisfied that the training algorithm is convergent and then the model is ready to be used.

We can print on video, the weights and biases:

```
> net$result.matrix
                                          1
error                      21.800203210980
reached.threshold           0.009985137179
steps                    9378.000000000000
Intercept.to.1layhid1      -1.324633695625
cylinders.to.1layhid1       0.291091600669
displacement.to.1layhid1   -2.243406161080
horsepower.to.1layhid1      0.616083122568
weight.to.1layhid1          1.292334492287
acceleration.to.1layhid1   -0.286145921068
Intercept.to.1layhid2     -41.734205163355
cylinders.to.1layhid2      -5.574494023650
displacement.to.1layhid2   33.629686446649
horsepower.to.1layhid2    -28.185856598271
weight.to.1layhid2        -50.822997942647
acceleration.to.1layhid2   -5.865256284330
Intercept.to.1layhid3       0.297173606203
cylinders.to.1layhid3       0.306910802417
displacement.to.1layhid3   -5.897977831914
horsepower.to.1layhid3      0.379215333054
weight.to.1layhid3          2.651777936654
acceleration.to.1layhid3   -1.035618563747
Intercept.to.mpg           -0.578197055155
1layhid.1.to.mpg           -3.190914666614
1layhid.2.to.mpg            0.714673177354
1layhid.3.to.mpg            1.958297807266
```

As can be seen, these are the same values that we can read in the network plot. For example, `cylinders.to.1layhid1 = 0.291091600669` is the weight for the connection between the input cylinders and the first node of the hidden layer.

Now we can use the network to make predictions. For this, we had set aside 30 percent of the data in the `test_data` dataframe. It is time to use it.

```
predict_net_test <- compute(net,test_data[,2:6])
```

In our case, we applied the function to the `test_data` dataset, using only the columns from 2 to 6, representing the input variables of the network. To evaluate the network performance, we can use the **Mean Squared Error** (**MSE**) as a measure of how far away our predictions are from the real data.

```
MSE.net <- sum((test_data$mpg -
predict_net_test$net.result)^2)/nrow(test_data)
```

Here `test_data$mpg` is the actual data and `predict_net_test$net.result` is the predicted data for the target of the analysis. Following is the result:

```
> MSE.net
[1] 0.2591064572
```

It looks like a good result, but what do we compare it with? To get an idea of the accuracy of the network prediction, we can build a linear regression model:

```
Lm_Mod <- lm(mpg~., data=train_data)
summary(Lm_Mod)
```

We build a linear regression model using the `lm` function. This function is used to fit linear models. It can be used to perform regression, single stratum analysis of variance, and analysis of covariance. To produce a summary of the results of model fitting obtained, we have used the `summary()` function, which returns the following results:

```
> summary(Lm_Mod)
Call:
lm(formula = mpg ~ ., data = train_data)
Residuals:
        Min          1Q      Median          3Q         Max
-1.48013031 -0.34128989 -0.04310873  0.27697893  1.77674878
Coefficients:
                Estimate  Std. Error  t value       Pr(>|t|)
(Intercept)    0.01457260  0.03268643  0.44583       0.656080
cylinders     -0.14056198  0.10067461 -1.39620       0.163809
displacement   0.06316568  0.13405986  0.47118       0.637899
horsepower    -0.16993594  0.09180870 -1.85098       0.065273 .
weight        -0.59531412  0.09982123 -5.96380 0.0000000077563 ***
acceleration   0.03096675  0.05166132  0.59942       0.549400
----
Signif. codes:  0 '***' 0.001 '**' 0.01 '*' 0.05 '.' 0.1 ' ' 1
Residual standard error: 0.5392526 on 268 degrees of freedom
Multiple R-squared:  0.7183376, Adjusted R-squared:  0.7130827
F-statistic: 136.6987 on 5 and 268 DF,  p-value: < 0.00000000000000022204
```

Now we make the prediction with the linear regression model using the data contained in the `test_data` dataframe:

```
predict_lm <- predict(Lm_Mod,test_data)
```

Finally, we calculate the MSE for the regression model:

```
MSE.lm <- sum((predict_lm - test_data$mpg)^2)/nrow(test_data)
```

Following is the result:

```
> MSE.lm
[1] 0.3124200509
```

From the comparison between the two models (neural network model versus linear regression model), once again the neural network wins (0.26 versus 0.31).

We now perform a visual comparison by drawing on a graph the actual value versus the predicted value, first for neural network and then for linear regression model:

```
par(mfrow=c(1,2))

plot(test_data$mpg,predict_net_test$net.result,col='black',main='Real vs
predicted for neural network',pch=18,cex=4)
abline(0,1,lwd=5)

plot(test_data$mpg,predict_lm,col='black',main='Real vs predicted for
linear regression',pch=18,cex=4)
abline(0,1,lwd=5)
```

The comparison between the performance of the neural network model (to the left) and the linear regression model (to the right) on the test set is plotted in the following graph:

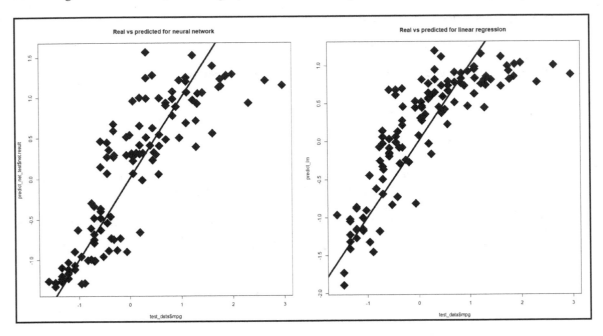

As we can see, the predictions by the neural network are more concentrated around the line than those by the linear regression model, even if you do not note a big difference.

Classifing breast cancer with a neural network

The breast is made up of a set of glands and adipose tissue and is placed between the skin and the chest wall. In fact, it is not a single gland, but a set of glandular structures, called lobules, joined together to form a lobe. In a breast, there are 15 to 20 lobes. The milk reaches the nipple from the lobules through small tubes called milk ducts.

Breast cancer is a potentially serious disease if it is not detected and treated for a long time. It is caused by uncontrolled multiplication of some cells in the mammary gland that are transformed into malignant cells. This means that they have the ability to detach themselves from the tissue that has generated them to invade the surrounding tissues and eventually the other organs of the body. In theory, cancers can be formed from all types of breast tissues, but the most common ones are from glandular cells or from those forming the walls of the ducts.

The objective of this example is to identify each of a number of benign or malignant classes. To do this, we will use the data contained in the dataset named BreastCancer (Wisconsin Breast Cancer Database) contained in the mlbench package. This data has been taken from the UCI Repository Of Machine Learning Databases at DNA samples arrive periodically as Dr. Wolberg reports his clinical cases. The database therefore reflects this chronological grouping of the data. This grouping information appears immediately, having been removed from the data itself. Each variable, except for the first, was converted into 11 primitive numerical attributes with values ranging from 0 through 10. There are 16 missing values.

The dataframes contain 699 observations on 11 variables—1 being a character variable, 9 being ordered or nominal, and 1 target class:

- Id: Sample code number
- Cl.thickness: Clump thickness
- Cell.size: Uniformity of cell size
- Cell.shape: Uniformity of cell shape
- Marg.adhesion: Marginal adhesion
- Epith.c.size: Single epithelial cell size
- Bare.nuclei: Bare nuclei
- Bl.cromatin: Bland chromatin
- Normal.nucleoli: Normal nucleoli
- Mitoses: Mitoses
- Class: Class

As said previously, the objective of this example is to identify each of a number of benign or malignant classes. The following is the code that we will use in this example:

```
###############################################################################
########Chapter 5 - Introduction to Neural Networks - using R#############
####################Classifing breast cancer with R######################
###############################################################################

library("mlbench")
library(neuralnet)

data(BreastCancer)
summary(BreastCancer)

mvindex = unique (unlist (lapply (BreastCancer, function (x) which (is.na
(x)))))
data_cleaned <- na.omit (BreastCancer)
```

```
summary(data_cleaned)

boxplot(data_cleaned[,2:10])
hist(as.numeric(data_cleaned$Mitoses))

par(mfrow=c(3, 3))
hist(as.numeric(data_cleaned$Cl.thickness))
hist(as.numeric(data_cleaned$Cell.size))
hist(as.numeric(data_cleaned$Cell.shape))
hist(as.numeric(data_cleaned$Marg.adhesion))
hist(as.numeric(data_cleaned$Epith.c.size))
hist(as.numeric(data_cleaned$Bare.nuclei))
hist(as.numeric(data_cleaned$Bl.cromatin))
hist(as.numeric(data_cleaned$Normal.nucleoli))
hist(as.numeric(data_cleaned$Mitoses))

str(data_cleaned)
input<-data_cleaned[,2:10]
indx <- sapply(input, is.factor)
input <- as.data.frame(lapply(input, function(x)
as.numeric(as.character(x))))

max_data <- apply(input, 2, max)
min_data <- apply(input, 2, min)
input_scaled <- as.data.frame(scale(input,center = min_data, scale =
max_data - min_data))
View(input_scaled)

Cancer<-data_cleaned$Class
Cancer<-as.data.frame(Cancer)
Cancer<-with(Cancer, data.frame(model.matrix(~Cancer+0)))

final_data<-as.data.frame(cbind(input_scaled,Cancer))

index = sample(1:nrow(final_data),round(0.70*nrow(final_data)))
train_data <- as.data.frame(final_data[index,])
test_data <- as.data.frame(final_data[-index,])

n = names(final_data[1:9])
f = as.formula(paste("Cancerbenign + Cancermalignant ~", paste(n, collapse
= " + ")))

net = neuralnet(f,data=train_data,hidden=5,linear.output=FALSE)
plot(net)

predict_net_test <- compute(net,test_data[,1:9])
predict_result<-round(predict_net_test$net.result, digits = 0)
net.prediction = c("benign", "malignant")[apply(predict_result, 1,
```

```
which.max)]
predict.table = table(data_cleaned$Class[-index], net.prediction)
predict.table

library(gmodels)
CrossTable(x = data_cleaned$Class[-index], y = net.prediction,
 prop.chisq=FALSE)
##################################################################
```

We begin analyzing the code line-by-line, by explaining in detail all the features applied to capture the results.

```
library("mlbench")
library("neuralnet")
```

The first two lines of the initial code are used to load the libraries needed to run the analysis.

 Remember, to install a library that is not present in the initial distribution of R, you must use the `install.package` function. This is the main function to install packages. It takes a vector of names and a destination library, downloads the packages from the repositories and installs them. This function should be used only once and not every time you run the code.

The `mlbench` library contains a collection of artificial and real-world machine learning benchmark problems, including, for example, several datasets from the UCI Repository.

The `neuralnet` library is used to train neural networks using backpropagation, RPROP with or without weight backtracking, or the modified GRPROP. The function allows flexible settings through custom-choice of error and activation function. Furthermore, the calculation of generalized weights is implemented. A brief description of the nnet package, extracted from the official documentation, is shown in the following table:

`neuralnet`: **Training of neural networks**
Description:
Training of neural networks using backpropagation, resilient backpropagation with (Riedmiller, 1994), or without weight backtracking (Riedmiller and Braun, 1993), or the modified globally convergent version by Anastasiadis et al. (2005). The package allows flexible settings through custom-choice of error and activation function.
Details:

Package: `neuralnet` Type: Package Version: 1.33 Date: 2016-08-05 License: GPL-2
Author(s):
Stefan Fritsch Frauke Guenther Marc Suling Sebastian M. Mueller

Returning to the code, at this point we have to load the data to be analyzed:

```
data(BreastCancer)
```

With this command, we upload the data set named `BreastCancer`, as mentioned, in the `mlbench` library.

Exploratory analysis

Before starting with data analysis through the build and training of a neural network, we conduct an exploratory analysis to understand how the data is distributed and extract preliminary knowledge.

```
summary(BreastCancer)
```

With this command, we will see a brief summary using the `summary()` function.

Remember, the `summary()` function is a generic function used to produce result summaries of the results of various model fitting functions. The function invokes particular methods which depend on the class of the first argument.

In this case, the function was applied to a dataframe and the results are shown in the following screenshot:

```
> summary(BreastCancer)
      Id              Cl.thickness    Cell.size      Cell.shape    Marg.adhesion   Epith.c.size
 Length:699           1      :145    1      :384    1      :353    1      :407    2      :386
 Class :character     5      :130    10     : 67    2      : 59    2      : 58    3      : 72
 Mode  :character     3      :108    3      : 52    10     : 58    3      : 58    4      : 48
                      4      : 80    2      : 45    3      : 56    10     : 55    1      : 47
                      10     : 69    4      : 40    4      : 44    4      : 33    6      : 41
                      2      : 50    5      : 30    5      : 34    8      : 25    5      : 39
                      (Other):117    (Other): 81    (Other): 95    (Other): 63    (Other): 66
  Bare.nuclei      Bl.cromatin    Normal.nucleoli     Mitoses            Class
 1      :402    2      :166    1      :443    1      :579    benign   :458
 10     :132    3      :165    10     : 61    2      : 35    malignant:241
 2      : 30    1      :152    3      : 44    3      : 33
 5      : 30    7      : 73    2      : 36    10     : 14
 3      : 28    4      : 40    8      : 24    4      : 12
 (Other): 61    5      : 34    6      : 22    7      :  9
 NA's   : 16    (Other): 69    (Other): 69    (Other): 17
```

The `summary()` function returns a set of statistics for each variable. In particular, it is useful to highlight the result provided for the `class` variable that contains the diagnosis of the cancer mass. In this case, 458 cases of benign `class` and 241 cases of `malignant` class were detected. Another feature to highlight is the Bare.nuclei variable. For this variable, 16 cases of missing value were detected.

A missing value is one whose value is unknown. Missing values are represented in R by the `NA` symbol. `NA` is a special value whose properties are different from other values. `NA` is one of the very few reserved words in R; you cannot give anything this name. `NA` can arise when you read in an Excel spreadsheet with empty cells, for example. You will also see `NA` when you try certain operations that are illegal or don't make sense. Missing values do not necessarily arise from an error; often in real life, there is a lack of detection.

A question arises spontaneously: do we have to worry about the presence of missing value? Unfortunately, yes, and this is due to the fact that almost every operation performed on an `NA` produces an `NA`. Then the presence of missing values in our dataset can cause errors in the calculations we will make later. This is why we are forced to remove the missing values.

To remove missing values, we must first identify them. The is.na() function finds missing values for us; this function returns a logical vector of the same length as its argument, with *T* for missing values and *F* for non-missing. It's fairly common to want to know the index of the missing values, and the which() function helps do this for us. To find all the rows in a dataframe with at least one NA, try this:

```
mvindex = unique (unlist (lapply (BreastCancer, function (x) which (is.na
(x)))))
```

The lapply() function applies the function to each column and returns a list whose *i*-th element is a vector containing the indices of the elements which have missing values in column *i*. The unlist() function turns that list into a vector and unique() gets rid of the duplicates.

Now we have the number of lines where the missing value (NA) appears, as we can see next:

```
> mvindex
[1]  24  41 140 146 159 165 236 250 276 293 295 298 316 322 412 618
```

Now we know there are missing values in our database and we know where they are. We just have to remove those lines from the original dataset. To do this, we can use the following functions:

- na.omit: Drops out any rows with missing values anywhere in them and forgets them forever
- na.exclude: Drops out rows with missing values, but keeps track of where they were, so that when you make predictions, for example, you end up with a vector whose length is that of the original response

We will use the first option, so as to eliminate them forever:

```
data_cleaned <- na.omit (BreastCancer)
```

To confirm the removal of the rows where the missing values appeared, apply the summary() function again:

```
summary (data_cleaned)
```

The results are shown in the following screenshot:

```
> summary(data_cleaned)
      Id            Cl.thickness   Cell.size    Cell.shape   Marg.adhesion  Epith.c.size
Length:683          1    :139    1    :373    1    :346    1    :393    2    :376
Class :character    5    :128   10    : 67    2    : 58    2    : 58    3    : 71
Mode  :character    3    :104    3    : 52   10    : 58    3    : 58    4    : 48
                    4    : 79    2    : 45    3    : 53   10    : 55    1    : 44
                   10    : 69    4    : 38    4    : 43    4    : 33    6    : 40
                    2    : 50    5    : 30    5    : 32    8    : 25    5    : 39
                 (Other):114 (Other): 78  (Other): 93  (Other): 61  (Other): 65
   Bare.nuclei    Bl.cromatin   Normal.nucleoli    Mitoses          Class
1    :402    3    :161    1    :432    1    :563    benign   :444
10   :132    2    :160   10    : 60    2    : 35    malignant:239
2    : 30    1    :150    3    : 42    3    : 33
5    : 30    7    : 71    2    : 36   10    : 14
3    : 28    4    : 39    8    : 23    4    : 12
8    : 21    5    : 34    6    : 22    7    :  9
(Other): 40 (Other): 68 (Other): 68 (Other): 17
```

As you can see now, there is no missing value anymore.

Now, let's go into our exploratory analysis. The first thing we can do is to plot the boxplots of the variables. A first idea is already made by looking at the results of the `summary()` function. Naturally, we will limit ourselves to numeric variables only.

```
boxplot(data_cleaned[,2:10])
```

In the following graph, the boxplots of the numeric variables (from 2° to 10°) contained in the cleaned dataset (`data_cleaned`) are shown:

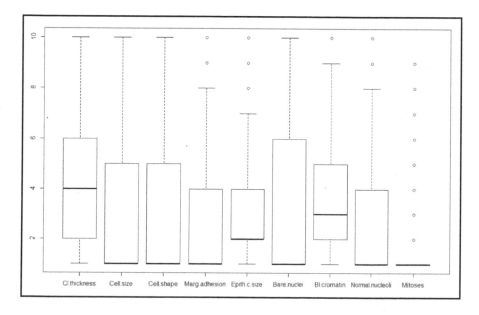

From the analysis of the previous graph, we can note that several variables have outliers, with the variable Mitoses being the one that has the largest number.

Outlier values are numerically different from the rest of the collected data. Statistics derived from samples containing outliers can be misleading.

To better identify the presence of outlier, we can plot histograms of the variables in the database. A histogram is an accurate graphical representation of the distribution of numerical data. It is an estimate of the probability distribution of a continuous variable. To construct a histogram, the first step is to specify the range of values (that is, divide the entire range of values into a series of intervals), and then count how many values fall into each interval. The bins are usually specified as consecutive, non-overlapping intervals of a variable. The bins must be adjacent, and are often of equal size. With histogram, we can see where the middle is in your data distribution, how close the data lies around this middle, and where possible outliers are to be found.

In R environment, we can simply make a histogram by using the hist() function, which computes a histogram of the given data values. We must put the name of the dataset in between the parentheses of this function. To plot many graphs in the same window, we will use the par() function, already used in the previous examples:

```
par(mfrow=c(3, 3))
hist(as.numeric(data_cleaned$Cl.thickness))
hist(as.numeric(data_cleaned$Cell.size))
hist(as.numeric(data_cleaned$Cell.shape))
hist(as.numeric(data_cleaned$Marg.adhesion))
hist(as.numeric(data_cleaned$Epith.c.size))
hist(as.numeric(data_cleaned$Bare.nuclei))
hist(as.numeric(data_cleaned$Bl.cromatin))
hist(as.numeric(data_cleaned$Normal.nucleoli))
hist(as.numeric(data_cleaned$Mitoses))
```

Since the function hist() requires a vector as argument, we have transformed the values contained in the dataset columns into numeric vectors using the as.numeric() function. This function creates or coerces objects of type numeric. In the following graphs are shown the histograms of the numeric variables (from 2° to 10°) contained in the cleaned dataset (data_cleaned):

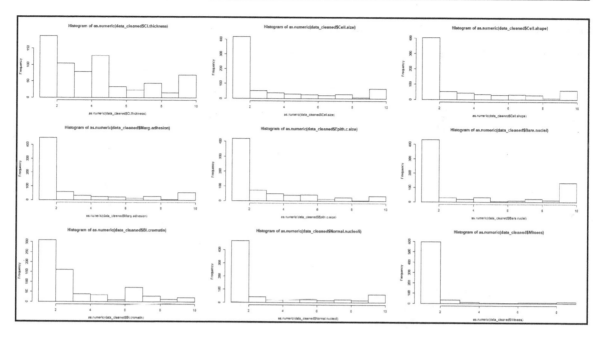

From the analysis of the histograms, it is possible to note that some variables have outliers.

Neural network model

As we did in the previous example, before building and training the network, we have to run the standardization of data. In this case, we will adopt min-max standardization.

Remember, it is good practice to normalize the data before training a neural network. With normalization, data units are eliminated, allowing you to easily compare data from different locations.

Before we begin, make a further check by using the str() function. This function provides a compact display of the internal structure of an object, a diagnostic function, and an alternative to the summary() function. Ideally, only one line for each basic structure is displayed. It is especially well suited to compactly display the (abbreviated) contents of (possibly nested) lists. The idea is to give reasonable output for any R object.

```
str(data_cleaned)
```

The results are shown in the following screenshot:

```
> str(data_cleaned)
'data.frame':     683 obs. of  11 variables:
 $ Id             : chr  "1000025" "1002945" "1015425" "1016277" ...
 $ Cl.thickness   : Ord.factor w/ 10 levels "1"<"2"<"3"<"4"<..: 5 5 3 6 4 8 1 2 2 4 ...
 $ cell.size      : Ord.factor w/ 10 levels "1"<"2"<"3"<"4"<..: 1 4 1 8 1 10 1 1 1 2 ...
 $ cell.shape     : Ord.factor w/ 10 levels "1"<"2"<"3"<"4"<..: 1 4 1 8 1 10 1 2 1 1 ...
 $ Marg.adhesion  : Ord.factor w/ 10 levels "1"<"2"<"3"<"4"<..: 1 5 1 1 3 8 1 1 1 1 ...
 $ Epith.c.size   : Ord.factor w/ 10 levels "1"<"2"<"3"<"4"<..: 2 7 2 3 2 7 2 2 2 2 ...
 $ Bare.nuclei    : Factor w/ 10 levels "1","2","3","4",..: 1 10 2 4 1 10 10 1 1 1 ...
 $ Bl.cromatin    : Factor w/ 10 levels "1","2","3","4",..: 3 3 3 3 9 3 3 1 2 ...
 $ Normal.nucleoli: Factor w/ 10 levels "1","2","3","4",..: 1 2 1 7 1 7 1 1 1 1 ...
 $ Mitoses        : Factor w/ 9 levels "1","2","3","4",..: 1 1 1 1 1 1 1 5 1 ...
 $ Class          : Factor w/ 2 levels "benign","malignant": 1 1 1 1 1 2 1 1 1 1 ...
 - attr(*, "na.action")=Class 'omit'  Named int [1:16] 24 41 140 146 159 165 236 250 276 293 ...
 .. ..- attr(*, "names")= chr [1:16] "24" "41" "140" "146" ...
```

As it is possible to note, the variables are present as a factor. We need to make a transformation for our calculations.

```
input<-data_cleaned[,2:10]
indx <- sapply(input, is.factor)
input <- as.data.frame(lapply(input, function(x)
as.numeric(as.character(x))))
```

We first identified the variables of the factor type and then we transformed them into numeric type. We can now standardize.

For this example, we will use the min-max method (usually called feature scaling) to get all the scaled data in the range *[0, 1]*. The formula to achieve this is the following:

$$X_{scaled} = \frac{x - x_{min}}{x_{max} - x_{min}}$$

Before applying the method chosen for normalization, you must calculate the minimum and maximum values of each database column. To do this, we use the `apply()` function. This function returns a vector or an array or a list of values obtained by applying a function to margins of an array or matrix. Let's understand the meaning of the arguments used.

```
max_data <- apply(data_cleaned[,2:10], 2, max)
```

The first argument of the apply function specifies the dataset to apply the function to, in our case, the dataset named `data`. The second argument must contain a vector giving the subscripts which the function will be applied over. In our case, one indicates rows and two indicates columns. The third argument must contain the function to be applied; in our case, the max function. What we will do next is to calculate the minimums for each column:

```
min_data <- apply(data_cleaned[,2:10], 2, min)
```

Finally, to normalize the data, we use the `scale()` function, which is a generic function whose default method centers and/or scales the columns of a numeric matrix, as shown in the following code:

```
data_scaled <- scale(data_cleaned[,2:10],center = min_data, scale =
max_data - min_data)
```

To confirm the standardization of data, let's see the first 20 lines of the new matrix we created. To do this, we will use the `View()` function:

	Cl.thickness	Cell.size	Cell.shape	Marg.adhesion	Epith.c.size	Bare.nuclei	Bl.cromatin	Normal.nucleoli	Mitoses
1	0.4444444	0.0000000	0.0000000	0.0000000	0.1111111	0.0000000	0.2222222	0.0000000	0.0000000
2	0.4444444	0.3333333	0.3333333	0.4444444	0.6666667	1.0000000	0.2222222	0.1111111	0.0000000
3	0.2222222	0.0000000	0.0000000	0.0000000	0.1111111	0.1111111	0.2222222	0.0000000	0.0000000
4	0.5555556	0.7777778	0.7777778	0.0000000	0.2222222	0.3333333	0.2222222	0.6666667	0.0000000
5	0.3333333	0.0000000	0.0000000	0.2222222	0.1111111	0.0000000	0.2222222	0.0000000	0.0000000
6	0.7777778	1.0000000	1.0000000	0.7777778	0.6666667	1.0000000	0.8888889	0.6666667	0.0000000
7	0.0000000	0.0000000	0.0000000	0.0000000	0.1111111	1.0000000	0.2222222	0.0000000	0.0000000
8	0.1111111	0.0000000	0.1111111	0.0000000	0.1111111	0.0000000	0.2222222	0.0000000	0.0000000
9	0.1111111	0.0000000	0.0000000	0.0000000	0.1111111	0.0000000	0.0000000	0.0000000	0.4444444
10	0.3333333	0.1111111	0.0000000	0.0000000	0.1111111	0.0000000	0.1111111	0.0000000	0.0000000
11	0.0000000	0.0000000	0.0000000	0.0000000	0.0000000	0.0000000	0.2222222	0.0000000	0.0000000
12	0.1111111	0.0000000	0.0000000	0.0000000	0.1111111	0.0000000	0.1111111	0.0000000	0.0000000
13	0.4444444	0.2222222	0.2222222	0.2222222	0.1111111	0.2222222	0.3333333	0.3333333	0.0000000
14	0.0000000	0.0000000	0.0000000	0.0000000	0.1111111	0.2222222	0.2222222	0.0000000	0.0000000
15	0.7777778	0.6666667	0.4444444	1.0000000	0.6666667	0.8888889	0.4444444	0.4444444	0.3333333
16	0.6666667	0.3333333	0.5555556	0.3333333	0.5555556	0.0000000	0.3333333	0.2222222	0.0000000
17	0.3333333	0.0000000	0.0000000	0.0000000	0.1111111	0.0000000	0.1111111	0.0000000	0.0000000
18	0.3333333	0.0000000	0.0000000	0.0000000	0.1111111	0.0000000	0.2222222	0.0000000	0.0000000
19	1.0000000	0.6666667	0.6666667	0.5555556	0.3333333	1.0000000	0.3333333	0.0000000	0.1111111
20	0.5555556	0.0000000	0.0000000	0.0000000	0.1111111	0.0000000	0.2222222	0.0000000	0.0000000

Showing 1 to 20 of 683 entries

As you can see now, the data is between zero and one. At this point, we reconstruct the dataset, adding our target (that is the `class` variable), which represents the diagnosis of the cancer (`benign` or `malignant`). This topic requires our attention: as we have seen before, this variable (`class`) is categorical. Particularly in the data frame is present as a factor, so that we can properly use int the network we must necessarily transform it. Our target is a dichotomous variable (only two values: `benign` and `malignant`), so it can easily be transformed into two dummy variables.

> A dummy variable is one that takes the value 0 or 1 to indicate the absence or presence of some categorical effect that may be expected to shift the outcome.

What we will do is create two new variables (`Cancerbenign` and `Cancermalignant`), starting with the `Class` variable representing our target. The `Cancerbenign` variable will contain values of one at each occurrence of the `benign` value present in the `Class` variable, and values of zero in other cases. In contrast, the `Cancermalignant` variable will contain values of one at each occurrence of the `malignant` value present in the `Class` variable and values of zero in other cases.

```
Cancer<-data_cleaned$Class
Cancer<-as.data.frame(Cancer)
Cancer<-with(Cancer, data.frame(model.matrix(~Cancer+0)))
```

To get the two new dummy variables, we used the `model.matrix()` function. This function creates a model matrix by expanding factors to a set of dummy variables (depending on the contrasts), and expanding interactions similarly. Finally, we add the new variables to the dataset:

```
final_data<-as.data.frame(cbind(input_scaled,Cancer))
```

The time has come to train the network.

The network training phase

The artificial neural networks are composed of simple elements operating in parallel. Connections between network elements are fundamental as they decide network functions. These connections affect the result through its weight, which is regulated in the neural network training phase. In the following diagram is shown a comparison between serial and parallel processing:

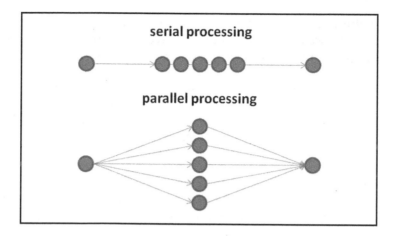

Then, in the training phase, the network is regulated by changing the connection weights, so that a particular input will lead to a specific destination. For example, the network can be adjusted by comparing the output (what we calculate practically) and the target (what we want to get), until the network output matches the target. To get sufficiently reliable results, many input/target pairs are needed to form a network. In the following diagram is shown a simple flow chart of the training phase:

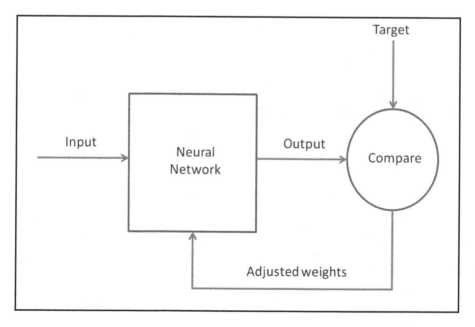

The way these weights are adjusted is defined by the particular algorithm we adopt. After highlighting the importance of the algorithm in network training, much interest must be placed in the preparation of the data to be provided to the network.

In the network training, the weights and bias must be tuned to optimize the network performance. It represents the most important phase of the whole process, as the better the network is, the better the generalization will be able to operate with new data, unknown to it. At this stage, part of the collected data is taken randomly (usually 70 percent of the available cases).

After the neural network training, we can use the network, in that phase a part of the collected data taken randomly (usually 30 perecnt of the available cases) is passed to the network to test it. Then the neural network object can be saved and used as many times as you want with any new data. In the following figure is shown how an original dataset has been divided:

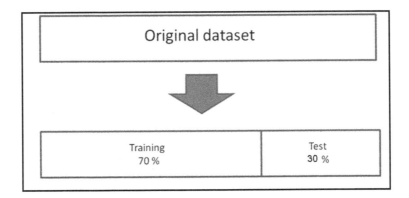

This subdivision of data in code looks like this:

```
index = sample(1:nrow(final_data),round(0.70*nrow(final_data)))
train_data <- as.data.frame(final_data[index,])
test_data <- as.data.frame(final_data[-index,])
```

In the first line of the code just suggested, the dataset is split into 70:30, with the intention of using 70 percent of the data at our disposal to train the network and the remaining 30 percent to test the network. In the second and third lines, the data of the dataframe named data is subdivided into two new dataframes, called train_data and test_data. Now we have to build the function to be submitted to the network:

```
n = names(final_data[1:9])
f = as.formula(paste("Cancerbenign + Cancermalignant ~", paste(n, collapse
= " + ")))
```

In the first line, we recover the names of the first nine variables in the `data_scaled` dataframe, using the `names()` function. In the second line, we build formula that we will use to train the network. What does this formula represent?

The models fitted by the `neuralnet()` function are specified in a compact symbolic form. The ~ operator is basic in the formation of such models. An expression of the form y ~ model is interpreted as a specification that the response y is modelled by a predictor specified symbolically by model. Such a model consists of a series of terms separated by + operators. The terms themselves consist of variable and factor names separated by : operators. Such a term is interpreted as the interaction of all the variables and factors appearing in the term. Let's look at the formula we set:

```
> f
Cancerbenign + Cancermalignant ~ Cl.thickness + Cell.size + Cell.shape +
    Marg.adhesion + Epith.c.size + Bare.nuclei + Bl.cromatin +
    Normal.nucleoli + Mitoses
```

We now have everything we need, we can create and train the network. We recall the advice we gave in the previous example for the correct choice of number of neurons in the hidden layer. We have eight input variables (`Cl.thickness`, `Cell.size`, `Cell.shape`, `Marg.adhesion`, `Epith.c.size`, `Bare.nuclei`, `Bl.cromatin`, `Normal.nucleoli`, and `Mitoses`) and one variable output (`Cancer`). Then we choose to set five neurons in the hidden layer:

```
net = neuralnet(f,data=train_data,hidden=5,linear.output=FALSE)
```

The `hidden` argument accepts a vector with the number of neurons for each hidden layer, while the argument `linear.output` is used to specify whether we want to do regression (`linear.output=TRUE`) or classification (`linear.output=FALSE` (our case)).

The algorithm used in `neuralnet()`, by default, is based on the resilient backpropagation without weight backtracking, and additionally modifies one learning rate, either the learning rate associated with the smallest absolute gradient (`sag`) or the smallest learning rate (`slr`) itself.

To plot the graphical representation of the model with the weights on each connection, we can use the `plot()` function, already widely explained in the previous section:

```
plot(net)
```

The neural network plot is shown in the following graph:

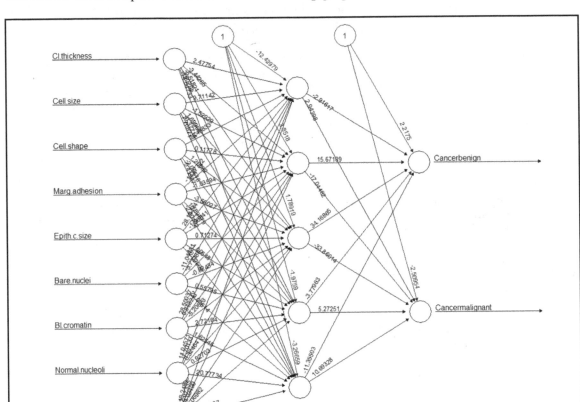

In the previous graph, the black lines (these lines start from input nodes) show the connections between each layer and the weights on each connection, while the blue lines (these lines start from bias nodes which are distinguished by number one) show the bias term added in each step. The bias can be thought of as the intercept of a linear model.

Testing the network

We finally have the network trained and ready for use. Now, we can use it to make our predictions. Remember, we've set aside 30 percent of available data and then use them to test the network. It's time to use it.

```
predict_net_test <- compute(net,test_data[,1:9])
```

To predict data, we have used the compute function, which computes the outputs of all neurons for specific arbitrary covariate vectors, given a trained neural network. Let's look at the results by printing the first ten lines:

```
> head(predict_net_test$net.result,n=10)
              [,1]                        [,2]
1   0.9999999935589190  0.0000000035872535l0720848
2   0.0000011083596034  0.9999993767645581899ll725
4   0.9792070465712006  0.0171647096645310796858S6
5   0.9999999746453074  0.0000000021909385204003642
9   0.9999993390597798  0.0000003272985966S8228207
14  0.9999999999953126  0.0000000000000889095157872
17  0.9999999999989946  0.0000000000000442776879837
19  0.0000001409393993  0.9999999200067661853097343
21  0.0000024771345578  0.9999985539645399601482322
23  0.9999999999999967  0.0000000000000001305142352
```

As we can see, these are real numbers with several decimals. In order to compare them with the data contained in the dataset, we have to round them to the nearest integer. To do this, we will use the round() function that rounds the values in its first argument to the specified number of decimal places (default zero).

```
predict_result<-round(predict_net_test$net.result, digits = 0)
```

We now rebuild the starting variable. We no longer need the two dummy variables; they have done their job well, but now we no longer need them.

```
net.prediction = c("benign", "malignant")[apply(predict_result, 1,
which.max)]
```

Now, we can build the confusion matrix to check the performance of our classifier.

```
predict.table = table(data_cleaned$Class[-index], net.prediction)
```

The confusion matrix is shown as follows:

```
> predict.table
          net.prediction
           benign malignant
  benign      132         5
  malignant     3        65
```

Although in a simple way, the matrix tells us that we only made eight errors. For more information about the confusion matrix, we can use the `CrossTable()` function contained in the `gmodels` package. As always, before loading the book, you need to install it.

```
library(gmodels)
CrossTable(x = data_cleaned$Class[-index], y = net.prediction,
           prop.chisq=FALSE)
```

The confusion matrix obtained by using the `CrossTable()` function is shown in the following screenshot:

```
  Cell Contents
|-----------------------|
|                     N |
|         N / Row Total |
|         N / Col Total |
|       N / Table Total |
|-----------------------|


Total Observations in Table:   205


                          | net.prediction
data_cleaned$Class[-index] |    benign | malignant | Row Total |
--------------------------|-----------|-----------|-----------|
                   benign |       132 |         5 |       137 |
                          |     0.964 |     0.036 |     0.668 |
                          | TN  0.978 |  FP 0.071 |           |
                          |     0.644 |     0.024 |           |
--------------------------|-----------|-----------|-----------|
                malignant |         3 |        65 |        68 |
                          |     0.044 |     0.956 |     0.332 |
                          | FN  0.022 |  TP 0.929 |           |
                          |     0.015 |     0.317 |           |
--------------------------|-----------|-----------|-----------|
             Column Total |       135 |        70 |       205 |
                          |     0.659 |     0.341 |           |
--------------------------|-----------|-----------|-----------|
```

The cells falling on the main diagonal contain counts of examples where the classifier correctly categorized the examples. In the top-left cell, labeled TN, are the true negative results. These 132 of 205 values indicate cases where the cancer was benign, and the algorithm correctly identified it as such. The bottom-right cell, labeled TP, indicates the true positive results, where the classifier and the clinically determined label agree that the mass is malignant. A total of 65 of 205 predictions were true positives.

The cells falling on the other diagonal contain counts of examples where the classifier incorrectly categorized the examples. The three examples in the lower-left FN cell are false negative results; in this case, the predicted value was benign but the cancer was actually malignant. Errors in this direction could be extremely costly, as they might lead a patient to believe that she is cancer-free, when in reality the disease may continue to spread. The cell labeled FP would contain the false positive results, if there were any. These values occur when the model classifies a cancer as malignant when in reality it was benign. Although such errors are less dangerous than a false negative result, they should also be avoided as they could lead to additional financial burden on the health care system, or additional stress for the patient, as additional tests or treatment may have to be provided.

Early stopping in neural network training

The epoch is a measure of each round trip from the forward propagation training and backpropagation update of weights and biases. The round trip of training has to stop once we have convergence (minimal error terms) or after a preset number of iterations.

Early stopping is a technique used to deal with overfitting of the model (more on overfitting in the next few pages). The training set is separated into two parts: one of them is to be used for training, while the other one is meant for validation purposes. We had separated our IRIS dataset into two parts: one 75 percent and another 25 percent.

With the training data, we compute the gradient and update the network weights and biases. The second set of data, the testing or validation data, is used to validate the model overfitting. If the error during validation increases for a specified number of iterations (nnet.abstol/reltol), the training is stopped and the weights and biases at that point are used by the model. This method is called *early stopping.*

An early stopping neural network ensemble generalization error is comparable with an individual neural network of optimal architecture that is trained by a traditional algorithm. The individual neural network needs a complex and perfect tuning to attain this generalization without early stopping.

Avoiding overfitting in the model

The fitting of the training data causes the model to determine the weights and biases along with the activation function values. When the algorithm does too well in some training dataset, it is said to be too much aligned to that particular dataset. This leads to high variance in the output values when the test data is very different from the training data. This high estimate variance is called **overfitting**. The predictions are affected due to the training data provided.

There are many possible ways to handle overfitting in neural networks. The first is regularization, similar to regression. There are two kinds of regularizations:

- L1 or lasso regularization
- L2 or ridge regularization
- Max norm constraints
- Dropouts in neural networks

Regularization introduces a cost term to impact the activation function. It tries to change most of the coefficients by bringing in more features with the objective function. Hence, it tries to push the coefficients for many variables to zero and reduce the cost term.

- **Lasso or L1 regularization or L1 penalty**: This has a penalty term, which uses the sum of absolute weights, so that the weights are optimized to reduce overfitting. **Least Absolute Shrinkage And Selection Operator** (**LASSO**) introduces the penalty weight to shrink the network weights towards zero.
- **L2 penalty or ridge regression**: This is similar to L1, but the penalty is based on squared weights instead of the sum of absolute weights. Larger weights get more penalty.

For both cases, only weights are considered for optimization, and biases (or offsets or intercepts) are excluded from the exercise.

- **Max norm constraints**: This is another regularization technique, whereby we enforce an absolute upper bound on the magnitude of the incoming weight vector for every neuron and the projected gradient descent cannot modify the weights due to the constraint. Here, the parameter vector cannot grow out of control (even if the learning rates are too high) because the updates to the weights are always bounded.

- **Dropout**: This is another overfitting prevention technique. While training, dropout is implemented by keeping a neuron active with some probability p (a hyperparameter) or setting it to zero otherwise. This means that some neurons may not be present during training and hence dropout. The network is unaffected and becomes more accurate even in the absence of certain information. This prevents the network from becoming too dependent on any one (or any small combination) of the neurons. The process of dropout is explained in the following diagram. The red (or dark) neurons are the ones dropped out, and the neural network model survives without these neurons and offers less overfitting and greater accuracy:

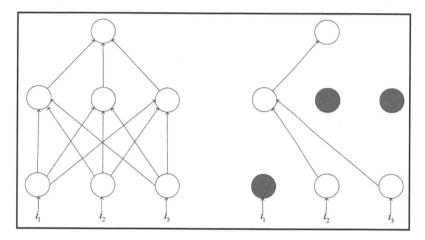

Generalization of neural networks

Generalization is aimed at fitting the training data. It is an extension of the training we have done on the neural networks model. It seeks to minimize the sum of squared errors of the model on the training data (such as using ordinary least squares) and reduce the complexity of the model.

The methods of generalization are listed here:

- Early stopping of training
- Retraining neural networks with different training data
    - Using random sampling, stratified sampling, or any good mix of target data
- Training multiple neural networks and averaging out their outputs

Scaling of data in neural network models

Data scaling or normalization is a process of making model data in a standard format so that the training is improved, accurate, and faster. The method of scaling data in neural networks is similar to data normalization in any machine learning problem.

Some simple methods of data normalization are listed here:

- **Z-score normalization**: As anticipated in previous sections, the arithmetic mean and standard deviation of the given data are calculated first. The standardized score or Z-score is then calculated as follows:

$$z = (X - \mu) / \sigma$$

  Here, X is the value of the data element, μ is the mean, and σ is the standard deviation. The Z-score or standard score indicates how many standard deviations the data element is from the mean. Since mean and standard deviation are sensitive to outliers, this standardization is sensitive to outliers.

- **Min-max normalization**: This calculates the following for each data element:

$$z_i = \frac{x_i - \min(x)}{\max(x) - \min(x)}$$

  Here, x_i is the data element, *min(x)* is the minimum of all data values, and *max(x)* is the maximum of all data values. This method transforms all the scores into a common range of [0, 1]. However, it suffers from outlier sensitivity.

- **Median and MAD**: The median and median absolute deviation (MAD) normalization calculates the normalized data value using the following formula:

$$\frac{x_i - median\left(X^{(j)}\right)}{MAD^{(j)}}$$

Here, x_i represents each data value. This method is insensitive to outliers and the points in the extreme tails of the distribution, and therefore it is robust. However, this technique does not retain the input distribution and does not transform the scores into a common numerical range.

Ensemble predictions using neural networks

Another approach to regularization involves combining neural network models and averaging out the results. The resultant model is the most accurate one.

A neural network ensemble is a set of neural network models taking a decision by averaging the results of individual models. Ensemble technique is a simple way to improve generalization, especially when caused by noisy data or a small dataset. We train multiple neural networks and average their outputs.

As an example, we take 20 neural networks for the same learning problem, we adjust the various parameters in the training processing, and then the mean squared errors are compared with the mean squared errors of their average.

The following are the steps followed:

1. The dataset is loaded and divided into a train and test set. The percentage split can be varied for different neural net models.
2. Multiple models are created with the different training sets and by adjusting the parameters in the nnet() function.
3. All the models are trained and errors in each model are tabulated.
4. The average error is found for each row in test data and the mean square error is calculated for each model.
5. The mean square error is compared with the mean square error of the average.
6. The best model is chosen from the comparison and is used further for prediction.

This method allows us to play with the data and the function parameters to arrive at the optimal setting of the model. We can choose any number of models in the ensemble and do parallel processing of the models using R.

Overfitting is highly reduced and the best parameters of the model are arrived at here.

Summary

In this chapter, we covered the training and visualization of a simple neural network using R. Here, we can change the number of neurons, the number of hidden layers, the activation functions, and so on, to determine the training of the model.

While dealing with a regression problem, the last layer is a single unit, which will give continuous values. For a classification problem, there are n terminal units, each representing the class of output with its probability. The breast cancer example had two output neurons to represent the two classes of values that are output from the neural network.

We have learned how to train, test, and evaluate a dataset using NN model. We have also learned how to visualize the NN model in R environment. We have covered the concepts like early stopping, avoiding overfitting, generalization of NN, and scaling of NN parameters.

6
Recurrent and Convolutional Neural Networks

Until now, we have been studying feed-forward networks, where the data moves in one direction and there is no interconnection of nodes in each layer. In the presence of basic hypotheses that interact with some problems, the intrinsic unidirectional structure of feed-forward networks is strongly limiting. However, it is possible to start from it and create networks in which the results of computing one unit affect the computational process of the other. It is evident that algorithms that manage the dynamics of these networks must meet new convergence criteria.

In this chapter, we will introduce **Recurrent Neural Networks (RNN)**, which are networks with cyclic data flows. We will also see **Convolutional Neural Networks (CNN)**, which are standardized neural networks mainly used for image recognition. For both of these types of networks, we will do some sample implementations in R. The following topics are covered:

- RNN
- The rnn package
- **Long Short-Term Memory (LSTM)** model
- CNN
- Common CNN architecture--**LeNet**

At the end of the chapter, we will understand training, testing, and evaluating an RNN. We will learn how to visualize the RNN model in R environment. We will also be able to train an LSTM model. We will cover the concepts as CNN and common CNN architecture--LeNet.

Recurrent Neural Network

Within the set of **Artificial Neural Networks (ANN)**, there are several variants based on the number of hidden layers and data flow. One of the variants is RNN, where the connections between neurons can form a cycle. Unlike feed-forward networks, RNNs can use internal memory for their processing. RNNs are a class of ANNs that feature connections between hidden layers that are propagated through time in order to learn sequences. RNN use cases include the following fields:

- Stock market predictions
- Image captioning
- Weather forecast
- Time-series-based forecasts
- Language translation
- Speech recognition
- Handwriting recognition
- Audio or video processing
- Robotics action sequencing

The networks we have studied so far (feed-forward networks) are based on input data that is powered to the network and converted into output. If it is a supervised learning algorithm, the output is a label that can recognize the input. Basically, these algorithms connect raw data to specific categories by recognizing patterns.

Recurrent networks, on the other hand, take as their input not only current input data that is powered to the network but also what they have experienced over time.

The decision made by a recurrent network at a specific instant affects the decision it will reach immediately afterwards. So, recurrent networks have two input sources--the present and the recent past--that combine to determine how they respond to new data, just as people do in life everyday.

Recurrent networks are distinguished from feed-forward networks thanks to the feedback loop linked to their past decisions, thus accepting their output momentarily as inputs. This feature can be emphasized by saying that recurrent networks have memory. Adding memory to neural networks has a purpose: there is information in the sequence itself and recurrent networks use it to perform the tasks that feed-forward networks cannot.

RNN is a class of neural network where there are connections between neurons that form a directed cycle. A typical RNN is represented in the following figure:

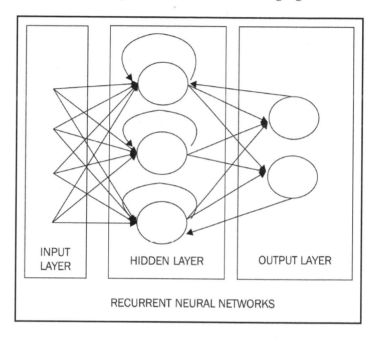

Here, the output of one instance is taken as input for the next instance for the same neuron. The way the data is kept in memory and flows at different time periods makes RNNs powerful and successful.

Under RNNs, there are more variants in the way the data flows backwards:

- Fully recurrent
- Recursive
- Hopfield
- Elman and Jordan networks
- Neural history compressor
- LSTM
- **Gated Recurrent Unit (GRU)**
- Bidirectional
- Recurrent MLP

Recurrent networks are designed to recognize patterns as a sequence of data and are helpful in prediction and forecasting. They can work on text, images, speech, and time series data. RNNs are among the powerful ANNs and represent the biological brain, including memory with processing power. Recurrent networks take inputs from the current input (like a feed-forward network) and the output that was calculated previously:

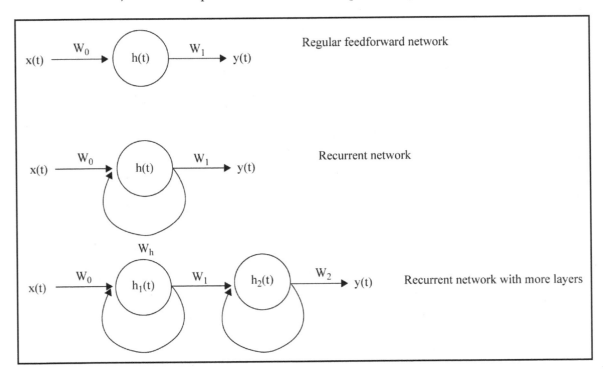

To understand this better, we consider the RNN as a network of neural networks, and the cyclic nature is **unfolded** in the following manner. The state of a neuron h is considered at different time periods (*-t-1, t, t+1* and so on) until convergence or the total number of epochs is reached.

Vanilla is the first model of recurrent ANNs that was introduced. A vanilla RNN is shown in the following figure:

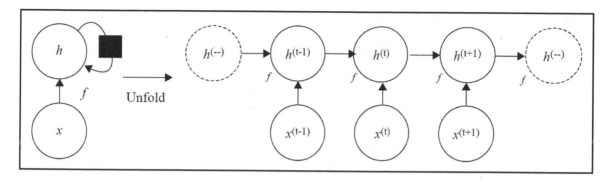

Other variants such as GRU or LSTM networks are more widespread given the simplicity of implementation, and they have demonstrated remarkable performance in a wide range of applications involving sequences such as language modeling, speech recognition, image captioning, and automatic translation.

RNNs can be implemented in R through the following packages:

- `rnn`
- `MxNetR`
- `TensorFlow` for R

RNNs are mainly used for sequence modeling. The inputs and outputs are treated as vectors (a matrix of numbers). For another level of understanding of RNNs, I advise you to go through the character sequencing example by Andrej Karpathy.

The features of RNN make it like an ANN with memory. The ANN memory is more like the human brain. With memory, we can make machines think from scratch and learn from their "memory." RNNs are basically ANNs with loops that allow information to persist in the network. The looping allows information to be passed from state t to state *t+1*.

As seen in the preceding diagram, RNNs can be thought of as multiple copies of the same ANN, with the output of one passing on as input to the next one. When we persist the information, as the patterns change, RNN is able to predict the *t+1* value. This is particularly useful for analyzing time-series-based problems.

There is no specific labeling required; the value that is part of the input forms the time series variable, and RNN can learn the pattern and do the prediction.

The internal state of the RNN is updated for every time step of the learning process. The feed-forward mechanism in RNN is similar to ANN; however, the backpropagation is an error term correction following something called **Backpropagation Through Time (BPTT)**.

Backpropagation through time follows this pseudocode:

1. Unfold the RNN to contain n feed-forward networks.
2. Initialize the weights w to random values.
3. Perform the following until the stopping criteria is met or you are done with the required number of epochs.
4. Set inputs to each network with values as x_i.
5. Forward-propagate the inputs over the whole unfolded network.
6. Back-propagate the error over the unfolded network.
7. Update all the weights in the network.
8. Average out the weights to find the final weight in the folded network.

The rnn package in R

To implement RNN in an R environment, we can use the `rnn` package available through CRAN. This package is widely used to implement an RNN. A brief description of the `rnn` package, extracted from the official documentation, is shown in the following table:

rnn: Recurrent Neural Network
Description:
Implementation of an RNN in R
Details:
Package: `rnn` Type: Package Version: 0.8.0 Date: 2016-09-11 License: GPL-3
Authors:
Bastiaan Quast Dimitri Fichou

The main functions used from the `rnn` package are shown in this table:

`predict_rnn`	Predicts the output of an RNN model: `predict_rnn(model, X, hidden = FALSE, real_output = T, ...)`
`run.rnn_demo`	A function to launch the `rnn_demo` app: `run.rnn_demo(port = NULL)`
`trainr`	This trains the RNN. The model is used by the `predictr` function.
`predictr`	This predicts the output of an RNN model: `predictr(model, X, hidden = FALSE, real_output = T, ...)`

As always, to be able to use a library, we must first install and then load it into our script.

Remember, to install a library that is not present in the initial distribution of R, you must use the `install.package` function. This is the main function to install packages. It takes a vector of names and a destination library, downloads the packages from the repositories and installs them. This function should be used only once and not every time you run the code.

So let's install and load the library:

```
install.packages("rnn")
library("rnn")
```

When we load the library (`library("rnn")`), we may receive the following error:

```
> library("rnn")
Error: package or namespace load failed for 'rnn' in get(Info[i, 1], envir =
env):
  cannot open file 'C:/Users/Giuseppe/Documents/R/win-
library/3.4/digest/R/digest.rdb': No such file or directory
```

Do not worry, as it's nothing serious! R is just saying that, in order to run the `rnn` library, you also need to install the `digest` library. Remember it; in future, if such a problem happens, you now know how to solve it. Just add the following command:

```
install.packages("digest")
```

Now we can launch the demo:

```
run.rnn_demo()
```

When we run `run.rnn_demo()` after installing the `rnn` package, we can access a web page through `127.0.0.1:5876`, which allows us to run a demo of an RNN with preset values and also visually see how the parameters influence an RNN, as shown in the following figure:

At this point, we will be able to set the parameters of our network and choose the appropriate values to be inserted into the boxes via its labels. The following parameters must be set correctly:

- `time dimension`
- `training sample dimension`
- `testing sample dimension`
- `number of hidden layers`
- `Number of unit in the layer number 1`
- `Number of unit in the layer number 2`
- `learningrate`
- `batchsize`
- `numepochs`
- `momentum`
- `learningrate_decay`

After doing this, we just have to click on the train button and the command will be built and trained.

The following figure shows the results of the simulation:

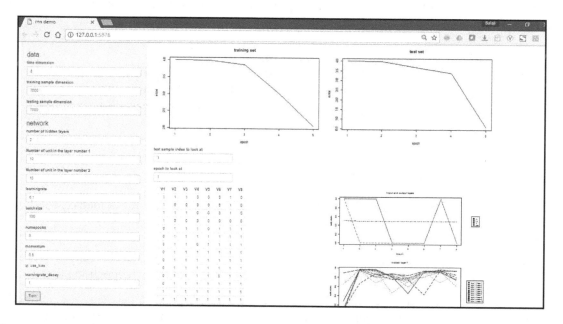

The `trainr` and `predictr` functions are the most important functions in the `rnn` package. The `trainr()` function trains a model with the set of X and Y parameters, which can be used for prediction using the `predictr()` function:

```
trainr(Y, X,
       learningrate,
       learningrate_decay = 1,
       momentum = 0,
       hidden_dim = c(10),
       network_type = "rnn",
       numepochs = 1,
       sigmoid = c("logistic", "Gompertz", "tanh"),
       use_bias = F,
       batch_size = 1,
       seq_to_seq_unsync = F,
       update_rule = "sgd",
       epoch_function = c(epoch_print, epoch_annealing),
       loss_function = loss_L1, ...)

predictr(model,
```

```
X,
hidden = FALSE,
real_output = T,
arguments to pass to sigmoid function)
```

The `trainr()` function takes the following parameters. The output is a model that can be used for prediction:

Y	Array of output values: • `dim` 1: Samples (must be equal to dim 1 of X) • `dim` 2: Time (must be equal to dim 2 of X) • `dim` 3: Variables (could be one or more, if a matrix, will be coerced to an array)
X	Array of input values: • `dim` 1: Samples • `dim` 2: Time • `dim` 3: Variables (could be one or more; if it is a matrix, will be coerced to an array)
`learningrate`	Learning rate to be applied for weight iteration.
`learningrate_decay`	Coefficient to apply to the learning rate at each epoch via the `epoch_annealing` function.
`momemtum`	The coefficient of the last weight iteration to keep for faster learning.
`hidden_dim`	The dimensions of the hidden layers.
`network_type`	The type of network, which could be `rnn`, `gru` or `lstm`.
`numepochs`	The number of iterations, that is, the number of times the whole dataset is presented to the network
`sigmoid`	Method to be passed to the `sigmoid` function.
`batch size`	Number of samples used at each weight iteration. Only one is supported for the moment.
`epoch_function`	Vector of functions to be applied at each epoch loop. Use it to interact with the objects inside the list model or to print and plot at each epoch. It should return the model.
`loss function`	Applied in each sample loop, vocabulary to verify.
`...`	Arguments to be passed to methods, to be used in user defined functions.

Now let's look at a simple example. This example included is in the official documentation of the CRAN rnn package to demonstrate the `trainr` and `predictr` functions and see the accuracy of the predictions.

We have X1 and X with random numbers in the range *0-127*. Y is initialized as X1+X2. After converting X1, X2, and Y to binary values, we use `trainr` to train Y based on X (array of X1 and X2).

Using the model, we predict B based on another sample of A1+A2. The difference of errors is plotted as a histogram:

```
library("rnn")

#Create a set of random numbers in X1 and X2
X1=sample(0:127, 7000, replace=TRUE)
X2=sample(0:127, 7000, replace=TRUE)

#Create training response numbers
Y=X1 + X2

# Convert to binary
X1=int2bin(X1)
X2=int2bin(X2)
Y=int2bin(Y)

# Create 3d array: dim 1: samples; dim 2: time; dim 3: variables.
X=array( c(X1,X2), dim=c(dim(X1),2) )

# Train the model
model <- trainr(Y=Y[,dim(Y)[2]:1],
                X=X[,dim(X)[2]:1,],
                learningrate = 0.1,
                hidden_dim = 10,
                batch_size = 100,
                numepochs = 100)

plot(colMeans(model$error),type='l',xlab='epoch',ylab='errors')

# Create test inputs
A1=int2bin(sample(0:127, 7000, replace=TRUE))
A2=int2bin(sample(0:127, 7000, replace=TRUE))

# Create 3d array: dim 1: samples; dim 2: time; dim 3: variables
A=array( c(A1,A2), dim=c(dim(A1),2) )

# Now, let us run prediction for new A
B=predictr(model,
```

```
  A[,dim(A)[2]:1,] )
B=B[,dim(B)[2]:1]

# Convert back to integers
A1=bin2int(A1)
A2=bin2int(A2)
B=bin2int(B)

# Plot the differences as histogram
hist( B-(A1+A2) )
```

As usual, we will analyze the code line by line, explaining in detail all the features applied to capture the results:

```
library("rnn")
```

The first line of the initial code are used to load the library needed to run the analysis. Let's go to the following commands:

```
X1=sample(0:127, 7000, replace=TRUE)
X2=sample(0:127, 7000, replace=TRUE)
```

These lines create training response numbers; these two vectors will be the inputs of the network we are about to build. We have used the sample() function to take a sample of the specified size from the elements of x either with or without replacement. The two vectors contain 7,000 random integer values between 1 and 127.

```
Y = X1 + X2
```

This command creates training response numbers; this is our target, or what we want to predict with the help of the network.

```
X1=int2bin(X1)
X2=int2bin(X2)
Y=int2bin(Y)
```

These three lines of code convert integers into binary sequences. We need to transform numbers into binaries before adding bit by bit. In the end, we get a sequence of eight values for each value, these values being 0 or 1. To understand the transformation we analyze a preview of one of these variables:

```
> head(X1,n=10)
     [,1] [,2] [,3] [,4] [,5] [,6] [,7] [,8]
[1,]    1    1    1    0    0    1    0    0
[2,]    0    0    0    1    0    0    0    0
[3,]    1    0    0    0    1    0    1    0
[4,]    0    0    0    0    0    0    1    0
```

```
[5,]    0    1    0    0    0    0    0    0
[6,]    0    0    0    1    1    1    0    0
[7,]    1    0    1    1    0    1    1    0
[8,]    1    1    0    0    0    1    0    0
[9,]    1    0    1    0    0    0    0    0
[10,]   0    0    0    1    0    0    0    0
```

Let's go back to analyze the code:

```
X=array( c(X1,X2), dim=c(dim(X1),2) )
```

This code creates a 3D array as required by the `trainr()` function. In this array, we have the following:

- `dim 1`: Samples (must be equal to `dim 1` of inputs)
- `dim 2`: Time (must be equal to `dim 2` of inputs)
- `dim 3`: Variables (could be one or more; if it is a matrix, this will be coerced to the array)

```
model <- trainr(Y=Y[,dim(Y)[2]:1],
                X=X[,dim(X)[2]:1,],
                learningrate = 0.1,
                hidden_dim = 10,
                batch_size = 100,
                numepochs = 100)
```

The `trainr()` function trains an RNN in native R. It takes a few minutes as the training happens based on X and Y. The following code shows the last 10 trained epoch results displayed on the R prompt:

```
Trained epoch: 90 - Learning rate: 0.1
Epoch error: 3.42915263914405
Trained epoch: 91 - Learning rate: 0.1
Epoch error: 3.44100549476955
Trained epoch: 92 - Learning rate: 0.1
Epoch error: 3.43627697030863
Trained epoch: 93 - Learning rate: 0.1
Epoch error: 3.43541472188254
Trained epoch: 94 - Learning rate: 0.1
Epoch error: 3.43753094787383
Trained epoch: 95 - Learning rate: 0.1
Epoch error: 3.43622412149714
Trained epoch: 96 - Learning rate: 0.1
Epoch error: 3.43604894997742
Trained epoch: 97 - Learning rate: 0.1
Epoch error: 3.4407798878595
Trained epoch: 98 - Learning rate: 0.1
```

```
Epoch error: 3.4472752590403
Trained epoch: 99 - Learning rate: 0.1
Epoch error: 3.43720125450988
Trained epoch: 100 - Learning rate: 0.1
Epoch error: 3.43542353819336
```

We can see the evolution of the algorithm by charting the error made by the algorithm to subsequent epochs:

```
plot(colMeans(model$error),type='l',xlab='epoch',ylab='errors')
```

This graph shows the epoch versus error:

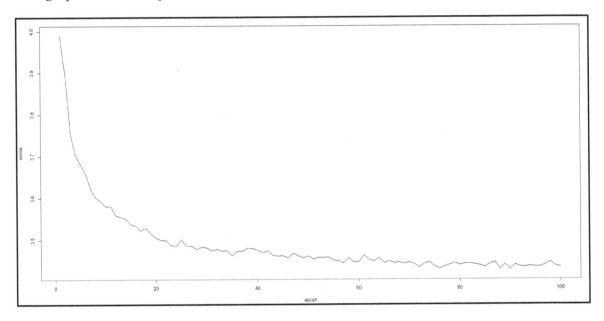

Now the model is ready and we can use it to test the network. But first, we need to create some test data:

```
A1=int2bin(sample(0:127, 7000, replace=TRUE))
A2=int2bin(sample(0:127, 7000, replace=TRUE))
A=array( c(A1,A2), dim=c(dim(A1),2) )
```

Now, let us run the prediction for new data:

```
B=predictr(model, A[,dim(A)[2]:1,] )
B=B[,dim(B)[2]:1]
```

Convert back to integers:

```
A1=bin2int(A1)
A2=bin2int(A2)
B=bin2int(B)
```

Finally, plot the differences as a histogram:

```
hist( B-(A1+A2) )
```

The histogram of errors is shown as follows:

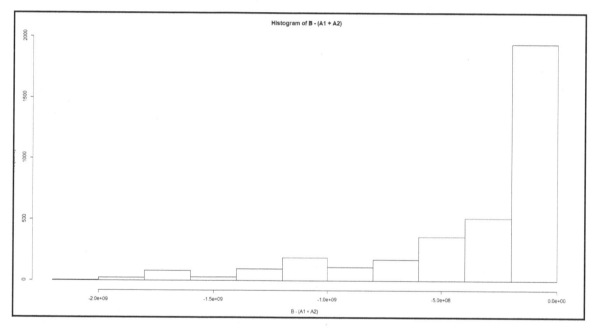

As can be seen here, the bin with more frequent is near zero to indicate that in most cases, the predictions coincide with the current values. All the other bins are related to the errors. We can therefore say that the network simulates the system with good performance.

LSTM model

We have seen that RNNs have a memory that uses persistent previous information to be used in the current neural network processing. The previous information is used in the present task. However, the memory is short-term and we do not have a list of all of the previous information available for the neural node.

When we introduce a long-term memory into the RNN, we are able to remember a lot of previous information and use it for the current processing. This concept is called LSTM model of RNN, which has numerous use cases in video, audio, text prediction, and various other applications.

LSTMs were introduced by Hochreiter & Schmidhuber in 1997.

The LSTM network is trained using **Backpropagation Through Time** (**BPTT**) and diminishes the vanishing gradient problem. LSTMs have powerful applications in time series predictions and can create large, recurrent networks to address difficult sequence problems in machine learning.

LSTM have **gates** that make the long/short term memory possible. These are contained in memory blocks connected through layers:

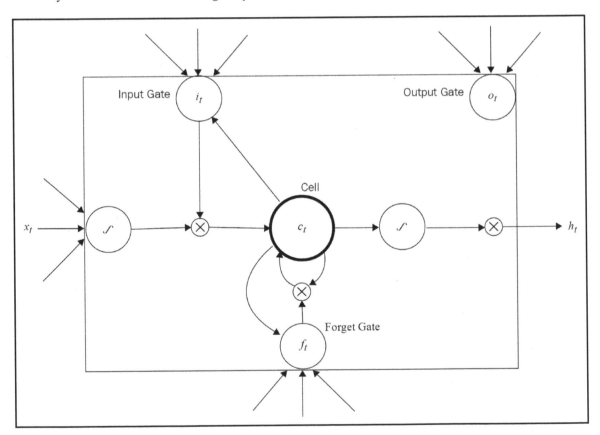

There are three types of gates within a unit:

- **Input Gate:** Scales input to cell (write)
- **Output Gate**: Scales output to cell (read)
- **Forget Gate**: Scales old cell value (reset)

Each gate is like a switch that controls the read/write, thus incorporating the long-term memory function into the LSTM model.

LSTMs can be used to solve the following sequence prediction problems:

- Direct sequence prediction
- Sequence classification
- Sequence generation
- Sequence to sequence prediction

The key differences between GRU and LSTM are:

- A GRU has two gates, whereas an LSTM has three gates.
- GRUs don't possess any internal memory that is different from the exposed hidden state. They don't have the output gate, which is present in LSTMs.
- There is no second nonlinearity applied when computing the output in GRU.

Convolutional Neural Networks

Another important set of neural networks in deep learning is CNN. They are designed specifically for image recognition and classification. CNNs have multiple layers of neural networks that extract information from images and determine the class they fall into.

For example, a CNN can detect whether the image is a cat or not if it is trained with a set of images of cats. We will see the architecture and working of CNN in this section.

For a program, any image is a just a set of RGB numbers in a vector format. If we can make a neural network understand the pattern, it can form a CNN and detect images.

Regular neural nets are universal mathematical approximators that take an input, transform it through a series of functions, and derive the output. However, these regular neural networks do not scale well for an image analysis. For a 32 x 32 pixel RGB image, the hidden layer would have *32*32*3=3072* weights. The regular neural nets work fine for this case. However, when the RGB image is scaled to size *200 x 200* pixel, the number of weights required in the hidden layer is *200*200*3=120,000* and the network does not perform well.

Enter CNN to solve this scalability problem. In CNN, the layers of a CNN have neurons arranged in three dimensions (**height**, **width**, and **depth**).

The following diagram shows a neural net and a CNN:

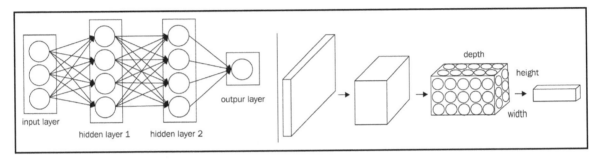

CNN is a sequence of layers of neural nets, wherein each layer transforms one volume of activations to another through a differentiable function. There are three types of layers that build the CNN:

- Convolutional layer
- Pooling layer
- Fully connected layer

Step #1 – filtering

The convolutional layer does the heavy math operations. In computer vision, a typical approach to processing an image is to convolute it with a filter to extract only the salient features in it. This is the first operation in a CNN. The input image is applied a filter logic to create an **activation map** or **feature map**:

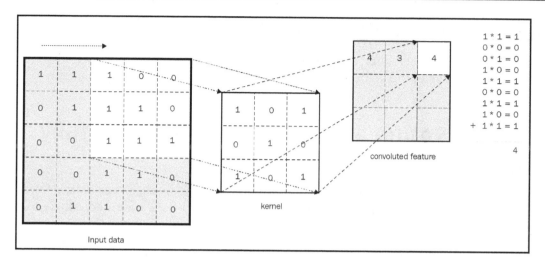

The convoluted feature vector is created by applying the kernel vector on each 3 x 3 vector of the image.

The mathematical steps for filtering are as follows:

1. Line up the feature and the image patch.
2. Multiply each image pixel by the corresponding feature pixel.
3. Add them up.
4. Divide each sum by the total number of pixels in the feature.

Once the filtering is done, the next step is to compress the filtered pixels.

Step #2 – pooling

In this step, we shrink the image stack. For each feature obtained in the convolutional step, we build up a matrix and now find the maximum in each chosen matrix to shrink the entire input. The steps are below:

1. Pick a window size (usually 2 or 3).
2. Pick a stride moving range of pixels (usually 2).
3. Slide the window across the filtered images.
4. For each window, we take the maximum value.

If the slid window does not have the required number of cells as in the previous windows, we take whatever values are available.

Step #3 – ReLU for normalization

In this step, we take the pooling output and for each pixel and apply the ReLU normalization to tweak the values. If any of the values is negative, we make it zero.

Step #4 – voting and classification in the fully connected layer

The final layer is the fully connected layer and there is voting by the set of values to determine the class of the output. The fully connected layer is just a merged matrix of all the previous outputs.

This is the final layer and the output is determined based on the highest voted category.

By stacking up the layers in steps 1, 2, and 3, we form the convolution network, which can reduce the error term with backpropagation to give us the best prediction.

The layers can be repeated multiple times and each layer output forms an input to the next layer.

A classical CNN architecture would look like this:

Input -> Conv -> ReLU -> Conv -> ReLU -> Pool -> ReLU -> Conv -> ReLU -> Pool ->Fully Connected

An example classification prediction using CNN is shown in the following figure:

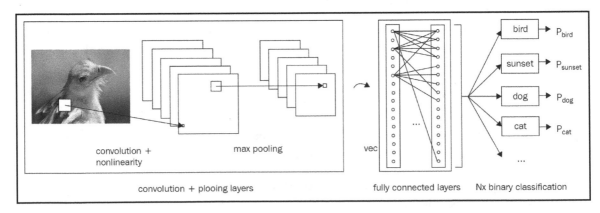

We will see an implementation of CNN using R in `Chapter 7`, *Use Cases of Neural Networks – Advanced Topics*.

Common CNN architecture - LeNet

LeNet-5 is a convolutional network designed by Le Cun in the 1990s for handwritten and machine-printed character recognition.
It is the first successful application of convolutional networks. It has the following architecture:

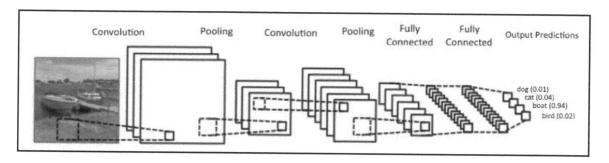

Humidity forecast using RNN

As the first use case of RNNs, we see how we can train and predict an RNN using the `trainr()` function. Our purpose is to forecast the humidity of a certain location as a function of the day. The input file contains daily weather observations from multiple Australian weather stations. These observations are obtained from the Australian Commonwealth Bureau of Meteorology and are subsequently processed to create a relatively large sample dataset for illustrating analytics, data mining, and data science using R and the rattle.data package. The `weatherAUS` dataset is regularly updated and updates of this package usually correspond to updates to this dataset. The data is updated from the Bureau of Meteorology website. The `locationsAUS` dataset records the location of each weather station. The source dataset is copyrighted by the Australian Commonwealth Bureau of Meteorology and is used with permission.

 A CSV version of this dataset is available at the following link:
https://rattle.togaware.com/weatherAUS.csv

The `weatherAUS` dataset is a dataframe containing over 140,000 daily observations from over 45 Australian weather stations. This dataset contains the following variables:

- `Date`: The date of observation (a `Date` object).
- `Location`: The common name of the location of the weather station.
- `MinTemp`: The minimum temperature in degrees celsius.
- `MaxTemp`: The maximum temperature in degrees celsius.
- `Rainfall`: The amount of rainfall recorded for the day in mm.
- `Evaporation`: The so-called class a pan evaporation (mm) in the 24 hours to 9 a.m.
- `Sunshine`: The number of hours of bright sunshine in the day.
- `WindGustDir`: The direction of the strongest wind gust in the 24 hours to midnight.
- `WindGustSpeed`: The speed (km/h) of the strongest wind gust in the 24 hours to midnight.
- `Temp9am`: Temperature (degrees C) at 9 a.m.
- `RelHumid9am`: Relative humidity (percent) at 9 a.m.
- `Cloud9am`: Fraction of the sky obscured by clouds at 9 a.m. This is measured in oktas, which are a unit of eighths. It records how many eighths of the sky are obscured by cloud. A zero measure indicates completely clear sky whilst an 8 indicates that it is completely overcast.
- `WindSpeed9am`: Wind speed (km/hr) averaged over 10 minutes prior to 9 a.m. 6 weatherAUS.
- `Pressure9am`: Atmospheric pressure (hpa) reduced to mean sea level at 9 a.m.
- `Temp3pm`: Temperature (degrees C) at 3 p.m.
- `RelHumid3pm`: Relative humidity (percent) at 3 p.m.
- `Cloud3pm`: Fraction of sky obscured by cloud (in oktas: eighths) at 3 p.m.
- `WindSpeed3pm`: Wind speed (km/hr) averaged over 10 minutes prior to 3 p.m.
- `Pressure3pm`: Atmospheric pressure (hpa) reduced to mean sea level at 3 p.m.
- `ChangeTemp`: Change in temperature.
- `ChangeTempDir`: Direction of change in temperature.
- `ChangeTempMag`: Magnitude of change in temperature.
- `ChangeWindDirect`: Direction of wind change.
- `MaxWindPeriod`: Period of maximum wind.
- `RainToday`: Integer 1 if precipitation (mm) in the 24 hours to 9 a.m. exceeds 1 mm, and 0 otherwise.

- `TempRange`: Difference between minimum and maximum temperatures (degrees C) in the 24 hours to 9 a.m.

- `PressureChange`: Change in pressure.

- `RISK_MM`: The amount of rain. A kind of measure of the risk.

- `RainTomorrow`: The target variable. Will it rain tomorrow?

In our case, we will use only two of the many variables contained in it:

- `Date`: The date of observation (a `Date` object)

- `RelHumid9am`: Relative humidity (percent) at 9 a.m

As said previously, the objective of this example is to forecast the humidity of a certain location as a function of the day. Here is the code that we will use in this example:

```
##############################################################
### Chapter 6 - Introduction to RNNs - using R   #########
########## Humidity forecasting with RNNs################
##############################################################

library("rattle.data")
library("rnn")

data(weatherAUS)
View(weatherAUS)

#extract only 1 and 14 clumn and first 3040 rows (Albury location)
data=weatherAUS[1:3040,c(1,14)]
summary(data)

data_cleaned <- na.omit(data)
data_used=data_cleaned[1:3000]

x=data_cleaned[,1]
y=data_cleaned[,2]

head(x)
head(y)

X=matrix(x, nrow = 30)
Y=matrix(y, nrow = 30)

# Standardize in the interval 0 - 1
Yscaled = (Y - min(Y)) / (max(Y) - min(Y))
Y=t(Yscaled)
```

```
train=1:70
test=71:100

model <- trainr(Y = Y[train,],
                X = Y[train,],
                learningrate = 0.05,
                hidden_dim = 16,
                numepochs = 1000)

plot(colMeans(model$error),type='l',xlab='epoch',ylab='errors')

Yp <- predictr(model, Y[test,])

plot(as.vector(t(Y[test,])), col = 'red', type='l',
     main = "Actual vs Predicted Humidity: testing set",
     ylab = "Y,Yp")
lines(as.vector(t(Yp)), type = 'l', col = 'black')
legend("bottomright", c("Predicted", "Actual"),
       col = c("red","black"),
       lty = c(1,1), lwd = c(1,1))


############################################################
```

We begin analyzing the code line by line, explaining in detail all the features applied to capture the results:

```
library("rattle.data")
library("rnn")
```

The first two lines of the initial code are used to load the libraries needed to run the analysis.

Remember that to install a library that is not present in the initial distribution of R, you must use the `install.package` function. This is the main function to install packages. It takes a vector of names and a destination library, downloads the packages from the repositories and installs them. This function should be used only once and not every time you run the code.

The `rattle.data` library contains the datasets used as default examples by the `rattle` package. The datasets themselves can be used independently of the `rattle` package to illustrate analytics, data mining, and data science tasks.

The `rnn` library contains several functions for implementing an RNN in R:

```
data(weatherAUS)
View(weatherAUS)
```

With this command, we upload the dataset named `weatherAUS`, as mentioned, contained in the `rattle.data` library. In the second line, the `view` function is used to invoke a spreadsheet-style data viewer on the dataframe object, as shown in the following figure:

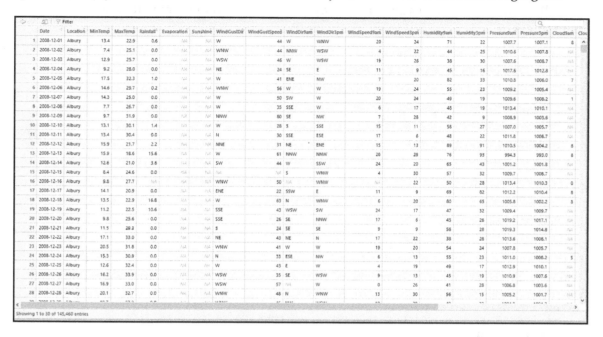

Returning to the code, as before, we use only two variables. In addition, the dataset contains data from different locations in Australia. We will limit our study to the first location (`Albury`):

```
data=weatherAUS[1:3040,c(1,14)]
```

Let's get a preliminary data analysis using the `summary()` function:

```
> summary(data)
       Date               Humidity9am
 Min.   :2008-12-01   Min.   : 18.00
 1st Qu.:2010-12-30   1st Qu.: 61.00
 Median :2013-04-27   Median : 76.00
 Mean   :2013-03-22   Mean   : 74.07
 3rd Qu.:2015-05-27   3rd Qu.: 88.00
 Max.   :2017-06-25   Max.   :100.00
                      NA's   :9
```

The `summary()` function returns a set of statistics for each variable. In particular, it is useful to highlight the result provided for the `Humidity9am` variable; this represents our target. For this variable, nine cases of missing value were detected. To remove the missing values, we will use the `na.omit()` function; it drops any rows with missing values and forgets them forever:

```
data_cleaned <- na.omit(data)
data_used=data_cleaned[1:3000]
```

With the second line of code, we limit our analysis to the first 3000 observations. Now we must set the input and the output data to the format required by the `trainr()` function:

```
x=data_cleaned[,1]
y=data_cleaned[,2]
```

In this way, x will represent our input and y our target:

```
X=matrix(x, nrow = 30)
Y=matrix(y, nrow = 30)
```

With this piece of code we construct a matrix of 30 lines and 100 columns with the data available. Recall is a size setting required for the function we will use for model building. We can now standardize this:

```
Yscaled = (Y - min(Y)) / (max(Y) - min(Y))
Y=t(Yscaled)
```

For this example, we have used the min-max method (usually called feature scaling) to get all the scaled data in the range *[0,1]*. The formula for this is as follows:

$$y_{scaled} = \frac{y - y_{min}}{y_{max} - y_{min}}$$

During the normalization, we must calculate the minimum and maximum values of each database column. Then we transpose the matrix obtained:

```
train=1:70
test=71:100
```

In these lines of code, the dataset is split into 70 : 30, with the intention of using 70 percent of the data at our disposal to train the network and the remaining 30 percent to test the network. Now is the time to build and train the model:

```
model <- trainr(Y = Y[train,],
                X = Y[train,],
                learningrate = 0.05,
                hidden_dim = 16,
                numepochs = 1000)
```

The trainr() function trains an RNN in R environment. We have used 16 neurons in the hidden layer and the number of epochs is 1,000. The trainr() function takes a few minutes as the training happens based on X and Y. Here are the last 10 Trained epoch results as displayed on the R prompt:

```
Trained epoch: 990 - Learning rate: 0.05
Epoch error: 0.382192317958489
Trained epoch: 991 - Learning rate: 0.05
Epoch error: 0.376313106021699
Trained epoch: 992 - Learning rate: 0.05
Epoch error: 0.380178990096884
Trained epoch: 993 - Learning rate: 0.05
Epoch error: 0.379260612039631
Trained epoch: 994 - Learning rate: 0.05
Epoch error: 0.380475314573825
Trained epoch: 995 - Learning rate: 0.05
Epoch error: 0.38169633378182
Trained epoch: 996 - Learning rate: 0.05
Epoch error: 0.373951666567461
Trained epoch: 997 - Learning rate: 0.05
Epoch error: 0.374880624458934
Trained epoch: 998 - Learning rate: 0.05
Epoch error: 0.384185799764121
Trained epoch: 999 - Learning rate: 0.05
Epoch error: 0.381408598560978
Trained epoch: 1000 - Learning rate: 0.05
Epoch error: 0.375245688144538
```

We can see the evolution of the algorithm by charting the error made by the algorithm to subsequent epochs:

```
plot(colMeans(model$error),type='l',xlab='epoch',ylab='errors')
```

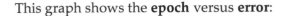
This graph shows the **epoch** versus **error**:

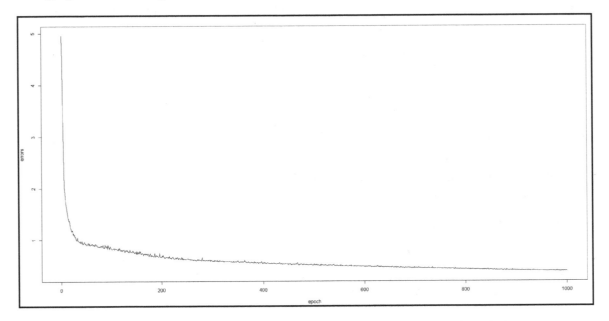

We finally have the network trained and ready for use; now we can use it to make our predictions. Remember, we've set aside 30 percent of the available data to test the network. It's time to use it:

```
Yp <- predictr(model, Y[test,])
```

Finally, to compare the results, let's plot a graph showing the moisture content in the test set and the predicted results in order:

```
plot(as.vector(t(Y[test,])), col = 'red', type='l',
    main = "Actual vs Predicted Humidity: testing set",
    ylab = "Y,Yp")
lines(as.vector(t(Yp)), type = 'l', col = 'black')
legend("bottomright", c("Predicted", "Actual"),
      col = c("red","black"),
      lty = c(1,1), lwd = c(1,1))
```

The following figure shows the actual values and predicted values:

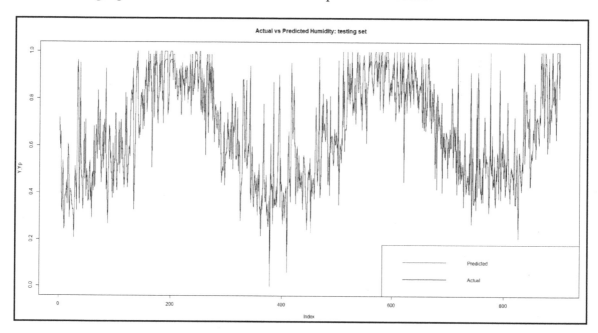

From the analysis of the figure, it is possible to note one thing: the data is adapted to a good approximation to indicate that the model is able to predict the humidity conditions with good performance.

Summary

In this chapter, we saw RNNs and how to use internal memory for their processing. We also covered CNNs, which are standardized neural networks mainly used for image recognition. For RNNs, we studied some sample implementations in R.

We learned how to train, test, and evaluate an RNN. We also learned how to visualize the RNN model in an R environment. We discovered the LSTM model. We introduced the concepts as CNN and a common CNN architecture: LeNet.

In the next chapter, we will see more use cases involving R implementations of neural networks and deep learning.

7
Use Cases of Neural Networks – Advanced Topics

With **Artificial Neural Networks (ANN)**, let's try to simulate typical brain activities such as image perception, pattern recognition, language understanding, sense-motor coordination, and so on. ANN models are composed of a system of nodes, equivalent to neurons of a human brain, which are interconnected by weighted links, equivalent to synapses between neurons. The output of the network is modified iteratively from link weights to convergence.

This final chapter presents ANN applications from different use cases and how neural networks can be used in the AI world. We will see some use cases and their implementation in R. You can adapt the same set of programs for other real work scenarios.

The following topics will be covered:

- TensorFlow integration with R
- Keras integration with R
- Handwritten digit recognition using `MNIST` dataset with `H2O`
- Building LSTM with mxnet
- Clustering data using auto encoders with `H2O`
- **Principal Component Analysis (PCA)** using `H2O`
- Breast cancer detection using the `darch` package

By the end of this chapter, you will have understood the advanced concepts of the learning process and their implementation in the R environment. We will apply different types of algorithms to implement a neural network. We will review how to train, test, and deploy a model. We will look again at how to perform a correct valuation procedure. We will also cover more of deep learning in our use cases as deep learning is the latest thing that is based on advanced neural networks.

TensorFlow integration with R

TensorFlow is an open source numerical computing library provided by Google for machine intelligence. It hides all of the programming required to build deep learning models and gives the developers a black box interface to program. The Keras API for TensorFlow provides a high-level interface for neural networks.

Python is the **de facto** programming language for deep learning, but R is catching up. Deep learning libraries are now available with R and a developer can easily download TensorFlow or Keras similar to other R libraries and use them.

In TensorFlow, nodes in the graph represent mathematical operations, while the graph edges represent the multidimensional data arrays (tensors) communicated between them. TensorFlow was originally developed by the Google Brain Team within Google's machine intelligence research for machine learning and deep neural networks research, but it is now available in the public domain. TensorFlow exploits GPU processing when configured appropriately.

The generic use cases for TensorFlow are as follows:

- Image recognition
- Computer vision
- Voice/sound recognition
- Time series analysis
- Language detection
- Language translation
- Text-based processing
- **Handwriting Recognition (HWR)**
- Many others

In this section, we will see how we can bring TensorFlow libraries into R. This will open up a huge number of possibilities with deep learning using TensorFlow in R. In order to use TensorFlow, we must first install Python. If you don't have a Python installation on your machine, it's time to get it.

Python is a dynamic **Object-Oriented Programming** (**OOP**) language that can be used for many types of software development. It offers strong support for integration with other languages and programs, is provided with a large standard library, and can be learned within a few days. Many Python programmers can confirm a substantial increase in productivity and feel that it encourages the development of higher quality code and maintainability. Python runs on Windows, Linux/Unix, macOS X, OS/2, Amiga, Palm Handhelds, and Nokia phones. It also works on Java and .NET virtual machines. Python is licensed under the OSI-approved open source license; its use is free, including for commercial products.

Python was created in the early 1990s by Guido van Rossum at Stichting Mathematisch Centrum in the Netherlands as a successor of a language called **ABC**. Guido remains Python's principal author, although it includes many contributions from others.

 If you do not know which version to use, there is an (English) document that could help you choose. In principle, if you have to start from scratch, we recommend choosing Python 3, and if you need to use third-party software packages that may not be compatible with Python 3, we recommend using Python 2.7. All information about the available versions and how to install Python is given at https://www.python.org/.

After properly installing the Python version of our machine, we have to worry about installing TensorFlow. We can retrieve all library information and available versions of the operating system from the following link: https://www.tensorflow.org/.

Also, in the install section, we can find a series of guides that explain how to install a version of TensorFlow that allows us to write applications in Python. Guides are available for the following operating systems:

- Installing TensorFlow on Ubuntu
- Installing TensorFlow on macOS X
- Installing TensorFlow on Windows
- Installing TensorFlow from sources

For example, to install Tensorflow on Windows, we must choose one of the following types:

- TensorFlow with CPU support only
- TensorFlow with GPU support

To install TensorFlow, start a terminal with privileges as administrator. Then issue the appropriate `pip3` install command in that terminal. To install the CPU-only version, enter the following command:

```
C:\> pip3 install --upgrade tensorflow
```

A series of code lines will be displayed on the video to keep us informed of the execution of the installation procedure, as shown in the following figure:

At this point, we can return to our favorite environment; I am referring to the R development environment. We will need to install the interface to TensorFlow. The R interface to TensorFlow lets you work productively using the high-level Keras and Estimator APIs, and when you need more control, it provides full access to the core TensorFlow API. To install the R interface to TensorFlow, we will use the following procedure.

First, install the `tensorflow` R package from CRAN as follows:

```
install.packages("tensorflow")
```

Then, use the **install_tensorflow()** function to install TensorFlow (for a proper installation procedure, you must have administrator privileges):

```
library(tensorflow)
install_tensorflow()
```

• We can confirm that the installation succeeded:

```
sess = tf$Session()
hello <- tf$constant('Hello, TensorFlow!')
sess$run(hello)
```

This will provide you with a default installation of TensorFlow suitable for use with the tensorflow R package. Read on if you want to learn about additional installation options, including installing a version of TensorFlow that takes advantage of NVIDIA GPUs if you have the correct CUDA libraries installed. In the following code, we can check the success of the installation:

```
> library(tensorflow)
> sess = tf$Session()
> hello <- tf$constant('Hello, TensorFlow!')
> sess$run(hello)
b'Hello, TensorFlow!'
```

Keras integration with R

Keras is a set of open source neural network libraries coded in Python. It is capable of running on top of MxNet, TensorFlow, or Theano. The steps to install Keras in RStudio are very simple. The following code snippet gives the steps for installation and we can check whether Keras is working by checking the load of the MNIST dataset.

By default, RStudio loads the CPU version of TensorFlow. Once Keras is loaded, we have a powerful set of deep learning libraries that can be utilized by R programmers to execute neural networks and deep learning. To install Keras for R, use this code:

```
install.packages("devtools")
devtools::install_github("rstudio/keras")
```

At this point, we load the `keras` library:

```
library(keras)
```

Finally, we check whether keras is installed correctly by loading the MNIST dataset:

```
> data=dataset_mnist()
```

MNIST HWR using R

Handwriting Recognition (HWR) is a very commonly used procedure in modern technology. The image of the written text can be detected offline from a piece of paper by optical scanning (**optical character recognition** (**OCR**)) or intelligent word recognition. Alternatively, pen tip movements can be detected online (for example, from a pen-computer surface, a task that is generally easier since there are more clues available). Technically, recognition of handwriting is the ability of a computer to receive and interpret a handwritten intelligible input from sources such as paper documents, photos, touchscreens, and other devices.

HWR is performed through various techniques that generally require OCR. However, a complete script recognition system also manages formatting, carries out correct character segmentation, and finds the most plausible words.

Modified National Institute of Standards and Technology (**MNIST**) is a large database of handwritten digits. It has a set of 70,000 examples of data. It is a subset of NIST's larger dataset. The digits are of 28x28 pixel resolution and are stored in a matrix of 70,000 rows and 785 columns; 784 columns form each pixel value from the 28x28 matrix and one value is the actual digit. The digits have been size-normalized and centered in a fixed-size image.

 The digit images in the MNIST set were originally selected and experimented with by Chris Burges and Corinna Cortes using bounding-box normalization and centering. Yann LeCun's version uses centering by center of mass within in a larger window. The data is available on Yann LeCun's website at http://yann.lecun.com/exdb/mnist/.

Each image is created as 28x28. Here is a sample of images of *0-8* from the MNIST dataset:

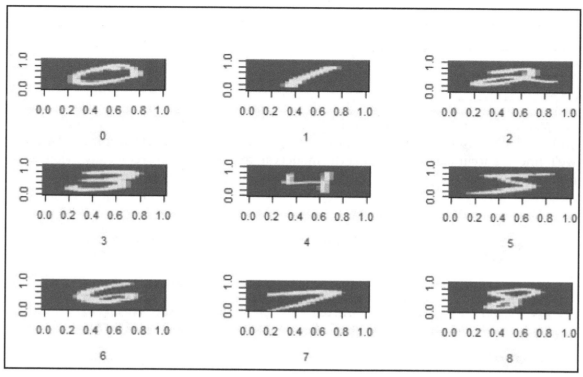

MNIST has a sample of several handwritten digits. This dataset can be fed for our training to an R program and our code can recognize any new handwritten digit that is presented as data for prediction. This is a case where the neural network architecture functions as a computer vision system for an AI application.

The following table shows the distribution of the MNIST dataset available on LeCun's website:

Digit	Count
0	5923
1	6742
2	5958
3	6131
4	5842

5	5421
6	5918
7	6265
8	5851
9	5949

We will not use the h2o package for deep learning to train and test the MNIST dataset. We will split the dataset of 70,000 rows into 60,000 training rows and 10,000 test rows. Then, we'll find the accuracy of the model. The model can then be used to predict any incoming dataset of 28x28 pixel handwritten digits containing numbers between zero and nine. Finally, we will reduce the file size to 100 rows for demo training processing on two datasets in .csv format, named mnist_train_100.csv and mnist_test_10.csv.

For our sample R code, we use a 100-row training dataset and a 10-row test dataset. The R code is presented here:

```
###############################################################
### Chapter 7 - Neural Networks with R - Use cases    ########
### Handwritten digit recognition through MNIST dataset ########
###############################################################

library("h2o")

h2o.init(nthreads=-1,max_mem_size="3G")

setwd ("c://R")

train_mnist=read.csv("mnist_train_100.csv", header=FALSE)
attach(train_mnist)
names(train_mnist)

test_mnist=read.csv("mnist_test_10.csv", header=FALSE)
attach(test_mnist)
names(test_mnist)

m = matrix(unlist(train_mnist[10,-1]),
           nrow = 28,
           byrow = TRUE)

image(m,col=grey.colors(255))

rotate = function(x) t(apply(x, 2, rev))
```

```r
image(rotate(m),col=grey.colors(255))

par(mfrow=c(2,3))
lapply(1:6,
        function(x)  image(
          rotate(matrix(unlist(train_mnist[x,-1]),
                          nrow = 28,
                          byrow = TRUE)),
          col=grey.colors(255),
          xlab=train_mnist[x,1]
        )
)

par(mfrow=c(1,1))

str(train_mnist)

x=2:785
y=1

table(train_mnist[,y])

model=h2o.deeplearning(x,
                        y,
                        as.h2o(train_mnist),
                        model_id="MNIST_deeplearning",
                        seed=405,
                        activation="RectifierWithDropout",
                        l1=0.00001,
                        input_dropout_ratio=0.2,
                        classification_stop = -1,
                        epochs=2000
                        )

summary(model)

h2o.scoreHistory(model)

preds=h2o.performance(model,
                        as.h2o(test_mnist))

newdata = h2o.predict(model,
                        as.h2o(test_mnist))

predictions = cbind(as.data.frame(seq(1,10)),
                        test_mnist[,1],
                        as.data.frame(newdata[,1]))
```

```
names(predictions) = c("Number","Actual","Predicted")

as.matrix(predictions)
##################################################################
```

Now, let's go through the code to learn how to apply the h2o package to solve a HWR problem. We've already properly introduced the h2o package in Chapter 3, *Deep Learning Using Multilayer Neural Networks*. The h2o is included and initiated through the following code:

```
library("h2o")
h2o.init(nthreads=-1,max_mem_size="3G")
```

The following results are displayed in the R prompt:

```
> h2o.init(nthreads=-1,max_mem_size="3G")
H2O is not running yet, starting it now...
Note: In case of errors look at the following log files:
C:\Users\lavoro\AppData\Local\Temp\Rtmpiit6zE/h2o_lavoro_started_from_r.out
C:\Users\lavoro\AppData\Local\Temp\Rtmpiit6zE/h2o_lavoro_started_from_r.err
java version "1.7.0_40"
Java(TM) SE Runtime Environment (build 1.7.0_40-b43)
Java HotSpot(TM) 64-Bit Server VM (build 24.0-b56, mixed mode)
Starting H2O JVM and connecting: ..... Connection successful!
R is connected to the H2O cluster:
 H2O cluster uptime:        15 seconds 229 milliseconds
 H2O cluster version:       3.10.5.3
 H2O cluster version age:   2 months and 18 days
 H2O cluster name:          H2O_started_from_R_lavoro_huu267
 H2O cluster total nodes:   1
 H2O cluster total memory:  2.67 GB
 H2O cluster total cores:   4
 H2O cluster allowed cores: 4
 H2O cluster healthy:       TRUE
 H2O Connection ip:         localhost
 H2O Connection port:       54321
 H2O Connection proxy:      NA
 H2O Internal Security:     FALSE
 R Version:                 R version 3.4.1 (2017-06-30)
```

The training file is opened using a handle. It is set to have 100 rows to simplify the demo work. The complete dataset can be downloaded from the URL suggested before.

```
setwd("C://R")
```

This command sets the working directory where we will have inserted the dataset for the next reading.

```
train_mnist=read.csv("mnist_train_100.csv", header=FALSE)
attach(train_mnist)
names(train_mnist)
```

This piece of code first loads the training dataset of MNIST, reducing the file size to 100 rows for demo training processing. Then we use the attach() function to attach the database to the R search path. This means that the database is searched by R when evaluating a variable, so objects in the database can be accessed by simply giving their names. Finally, we use the names() function to set the names of the dataset. The same thing we will do for the dataset to be used in the testing phase:

```
test_mnist=read.csv("mnist_test_10.csv", header=FALSE)
attach(test_mnist)
names(test_mnist)
```

At this point, we create a 28x28 matrix with pixel color values by taking the tenth row of the dataset, which contains the number zero:

```
m = matrix(unlist(train_mnist[10,-1]),
        + nrow = 28,
        + byrow = TRUE)
```

Let's see what we've got by plotting an object image:

```
image(m,col=grey.colors(255))
```

In the following is shown the image of the handwritten digit:

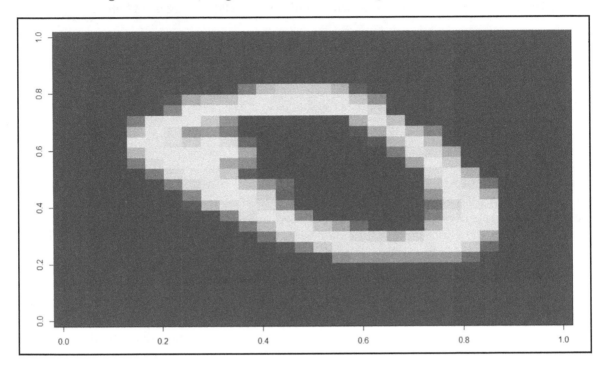

Now let's create a mirror image of the handwritten digit:

```
> rotate = function(x) t(apply(x, 2, rev))
```

Then, view the image to verify the operation just made:

```
> image(rotate(m),col=grey.colors(255))
```

In the following is shown the mirror image:

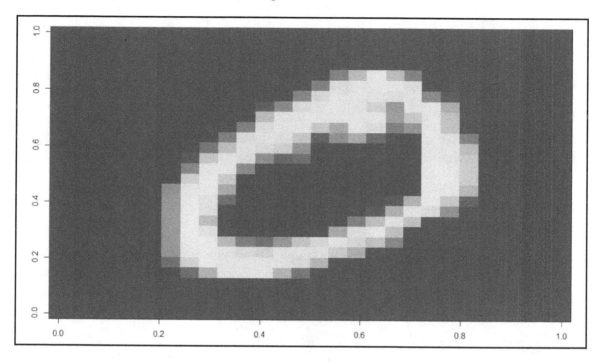

Now, let's do the same for the first six rows in the dataset:

```
par(mfrow=c(2,3))
lapply(1:6,
       function(x) image(
         rotate(matrix(unlist(train_mnist[x,-1]),
                       nrow = 28,
                       byrow = TRUE)),
         col=grey.colors(255),
         xlab=train_mnist[x,1]
       )
)
```

These are the images of the handwritten digits contained in the first six rows of the dataset:

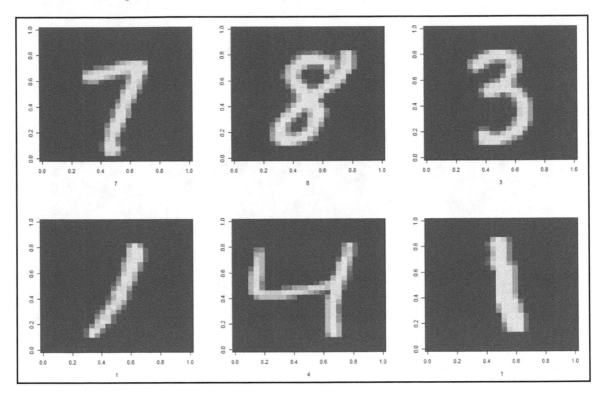

Reset the plot options back to default:

```
par(mfrow=c(1,1))
```

The next command lets us do some explanatory analysis of the training data:

```
str(train_mnist)
x=2:785
y=1
```

This command finds the count of each number in the training matrix:

```
table(train_mnist[,y])
```

The results are shown here:

```
> table(train_mnist[,y])
 0  1  2  3  4  5  6  7  8  9
13 14  6 11 11  5 11 10  8 11
```

Above are displayed the number of occurrences of each digit in the dataset. It's time to build and train the model:

```
model=h2o.deeplearning(x,
                       y,
                       as.h2o(train_mnist),
                       model_id="MNIST_deeplearning",
                       seed=405,
                       activation="RectifierWithDropout",
                       l1=0.00001,
                       input_dropout_ratio=0.2,
                       classification_stop = -1,
                       epochs=2000
)
```

Now, to produce the summaries of the results of the model fitting function, we will use the summary() function:

```
summary(model)
```

The following figure shows some of the results obtained:

```
> summary(model)
Model Details:
==============

H2ORegressionModel: deeplearning
Model Key: MNIST_deeplearning
Status of Neuron Layers: predicting V1, regression, gaussian distribution, Quadratic loss, 140.801 weights/biases, 1,7 MB
, 154.000 training samples, mini-batch size 1
  layer units        type dropout       l1       l2 mean_rate rate_rms momentum mean_weight
1     1   501        Input 20.00 %
2     2   200 RectifierDropout 50.00 % 0.000010 0.000000  0.021286 0.021856 0.000000    0.001784
3     3   200 RectifierDropout 50.00 % 0.000010 0.000000  0.014527 0.020565 0.000000   -0.011704
4     4     1       Linear         0.000010 0.000000  0.000684 0.000148 0.000000    0.000461
  weight_rms mean_bias bias_rms
1
2   0.054456  0.477551 0.033506
3   0.069420  0.953085 0.025633
4   0.055432 -0.025779 0.000000

H2ORegressionMetrics: deeplearning
** Reported on training data. **
** Metrics reported on full training frame **

MSE:   0.1341056
RMSE:  0.3662044
MAE:   0.2928374
RMSLE: 0.2140151
Mean Residual Deviance :  0.1341056
```

We can understand the evolution of the algorithm used, by checking the performance of the training model:

```
preds=h2o.performance(model,
                      as.h2o(test_mnist))
```

At this point, we have a properly trained `model`, so we can use it to make predictions. In our case, we will use it to recognize handwritten digits:

```
newdata = h2o.predict(model,
                    as.h2o(test_mnist))
```

Now that we have used `model`, we need to format the actual and expected matrices to verify the accuracy:

```
predictions = cbind(as.data.frame(seq(1,10)),
                   test_mnist[,1],
                   as.data.frame(newdata[,1]))
```

Enter the names of the variables inserted into the matrix:

```
names(predictions) = c("Number","Actual","Predicted")
```

Finally, check the output:

```
as.matrix(predictions)
```

The results are shown here:

```
> as.matrix(predictions)
       Number Actual    Predicted
 [1,]      1      7   6.90180840
 [2,]      2      3   3.62368445
 [3,]      3      1   0.53782891
 [4,]      4      0  -0.03092147
 [5,]      5      6   5.21024129
 [6,]      6      1   0.30850593
 [7,]      7      6   6.44916207
 [8,]      8      9   3.59962551
 [9,]      9      5   3.17590073
[10,]     10      9   7.35213625
```

As can be seen from the analysis of the table just proposed, for the test data, the model has predicted 60 percent (six out of ten) correctly. This accuracy is only for the small training dataset. The model can be improved further by:

- Increasing the training dataset count
- Tweaking the parameters of the `h20.deeplearning` function
- Allocating more memory to the `h2o` JVM
- Expanding the test dataset

LSTM using the iris dataset

Continuing with the LSTM architecture for RNN introduced in Chapter 6, *Recurrent and Convolutional Neural Networks*, we present the iris dataset processing using the mxnet LSTM function. The function expects all inputs and outputs as numeric. It is particularly useful for processing text sequences, but here we will train an LSTM model on the iris dataset. The input values are petal.length, petal.width, sepal.length, and sepal.width. The output variable is Species, which is converted to a numeric value between one and three. The iris dataset has been detailed in Chapter 4, *Perceptron Neural Network Modeling – Basic Models*:

```
#####################################################################
### Chapter 7 - Neural Networks with R - Use cases      #########
### Prediction using LSTM on IRIS dataset               #########
#####################################################################

##Required one time
library("mxnet")

data(iris)

x = iris[1:5!=5,-5]
y = as.integer(iris$Species)[1:5!=5]

train.x = data.matrix(x)
train.y = y

test.x = data.matrix(iris[1:5==5,-5])
test.y = as.integer(iris$Species)[1:5==5]

model <- mx.mlp(train.x, train.y, hidden_node=10, out_node=3,
out_activation="softmax",
                num.round=20, array.batch.size=15, learning.rate=0.07,
momentum=0.9,
                eval.metric=mx.metric.accuracy)

preds = predict(model, test.x)
pred.label = max.col(t(preds))

test.y
pred.label
#####################################################################
```

The program requires mxnet, which needs to be installed. mxnet for R is available for both CPUs and GPUs and for the following OSes: Linux, macOS, and Windows.

We will only indicate the installation procedures for Windows machines and CPU versions. Refer to the following URL for information on installation procedures for other architectures: `https://mxnet.incubator.apache.org/get_started/install.html`.

To install `mxnet` on a computer with a CPU processor, we use the prebuilt binary package. We can install the package directly on the R console through the following code:

```
cran <- getOption("repos")
cran["dmlc"] <- "https://s3-us-west-2.amazonaws.com/apache-mxnet/R/CRAN/"
options(repos = cran)
install.packages("mxnet")
```

The following packages are installed:

```
package 'bindr' successfully unpacked and MD5 sums checked
package 'brew' successfully unpacked and MD5 sums checked
package 'assertthat' successfully unpacked and MD5 sums checked
package 'bindrcpp' successfully unpacked and MD5 sums checked
package 'glue' successfully unpacked and MD5 sums checked
package 'pkgconfig' successfully unpacked and MD5 sums checked
package 'BH' successfully unpacked and MD5 sums checked
package 'plogr' successfully unpacked and MD5 sums checked
package 'yaml' successfully unpacked and MD5 sums checked
package 'irlba' successfully unpacked and MD5 sums checked
package 'hms' successfully unpacked and MD5 sums checked
package 'XML' successfully unpacked and MD5 sums checked
package 'Rook' successfully unpacked and MD5 sums checked
package 'tidyselect' successfully unpacked and MD5 sums checked
package 'gridExtra' successfully unpacked and MD5 sums checked
package 'dplyr' successfully unpacked and MD5 sums checked
package 'downloader' successfully unpacked and MD5 sums checked
package 'htmltools' successfully unpacked and MD5 sums checked
package 'htmlwidgets' successfully unpacked and MD5 sums checked
package 'igraph' successfully unpacked and MD5 sums checked
package 'influenceR' successfully unpacked and MD5 sums checked
package 'purrr' successfully unpacked and MD5 sums checked
package 'readr' successfully unpacked and MD5 sums checked
package 'rstudioapi' successfully unpacked and MD5 sums checked
package 'rgexf' successfully unpacked and MD5 sums checked
package 'tidyr' successfully unpacked and MD5 sums checked
package 'viridis' successfully unpacked and MD5 sums checked
package 'DiagrammeR' successfully unpacked and MD5 sums checked
package 'visNetwork' successfully unpacked and MD5 sums checked
package 'data.table' successfully unpacked and MD5 sums checked
package 'mxnet' successfully unpacked and MD5 sums checked
```

As you can see the installation of the mxnet package, install in addition to several packages. So, we already have everything we need to proceed. This mxnet library contains the mx.lstm function we are going to use:

```
library("mxnet")
```

In the following code, the internal dataset iris is loaded and the x and y variables are set with independent and target variables, respectively. The Species variable is converted to a number between one and three:

```
data(iris)
x = iris[1:5!=5,-5]
y = as.integer(iris$Species)[1:5!=5]
```

Just an explanation, with the following code:

```
x = iris[1:5!=5,-5]
```

We asked R to select from the iris dataset, which consists of 150 lines and five columns, only lines one to four, leaving out the fifth. This procedure will also be performed for multiples of five, so in the end, we will omit every multiple row of five from our selection. We will also omit the fifth column. At the end, we will get 120 rows and four columns.

We now set the input and output:

```
train.x = data.matrix(x)
train.y = y
```

Then we set the dataframe we will use for the test, by selecting only the lines we had previously omitted:

```
test.x = data.matrix(iris[1:5==5,-5])
test.y = as.integer(iris$Species)[1:5==5]
```

The mx.lstm function is called with the input and output values so that the model is trained with the LSTM on the RNN with the dataset:

```
model <- mx.mlp(train.x, train.y, hidden_node=10, out_node=3,
out_activation="softmax",
                num.round=20, array.batch.size=15, learning.rate=0.07,
momentum=0.9,
                eval.metric=mx.metric.accuracy)
```

Now we can make predictions:

```
preds = predict(model, test.x)
pred.label = max.col(t(preds))
```

Finally, we print the results to compare the model performance:

```
test.y
pred.label
```

Here are the results:

```
> test.y
 [1] 1 1 1 1 1 1 1 1 1 1 2 2 2 2 2 2 2 2 2 2 3 3 3 3 3 3 3 3 3 3
> pred.label
 [1] 2 2 2 2 2 2 2 2 2 3 3 3 3 3 3 3 3 3 3 3 3 3 3 3 3 3 3 3 3 3
```

From the comparison between the test data and those obtained from the forecast it can be noticed that the best results were obtained for the versicolor species. From the results obtained, it is clear that the model needs to be improved because the forecasts it is able to perform are not at the level of those obtained in the models we obtained in the previous examples.

Working with autoencoders

We have seen autoencoders in the deep learning chapter for unsupervised learning. Autoencoders utilize neural networks to perform non-linear dimensionality reduction. They represent data in a better way, by finding latent features in it using universal function approximators. Autoencoders try to combine or compress input data in a different way.

A sample representation using MLP is shown here:

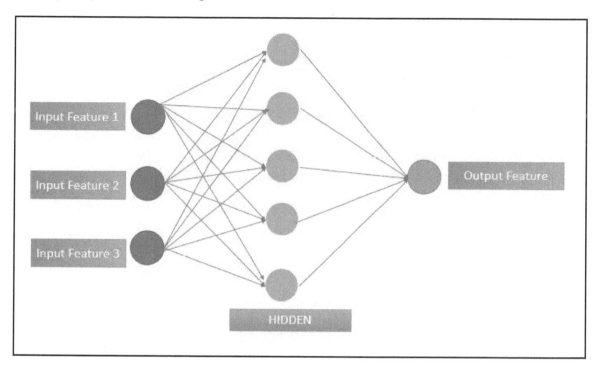

PCA using H2O

One of the greatest difficulties encountered in multivariate statistical analysis is the problem of displaying a dataset with many variables. Fortunately, in datasets with many variables, some pieces of data are often closely related to each other. This is because they actually contain the same information, as they measure the same quantity that governs the behavior of the system. These are therefore redundant variables that add nothing to the model we want to build. We can then simplify the problem by replacing a group of variables with a new variable that encloses the information content.

PCA generates a new set of variables, among them uncorrelated, called principal components; each main component is a linear combination of the original variables. All principal components are orthogonal to each other, so there is no redundant information. The principal components as a whole constitute an orthogonal basis for the data space. The goal of PCA is to explain the maximum amount of variance with the fewest number of principal components. It is a form of multidimensional scaling. It is a linear transformation of the variables into a lower dimensional space that retains the maximum amount of information about the variables. A principal component is therefore a combination of the original variables after a linear transformation.

In the following example, we use `h2o` to achieve PCA. The `prcomp()` function is used find the principal components of a set of input features. This is unsupervised learning:

```r
library(h2o)
h2o.init()

ausPath = system.file("extdata", "australia.csv", package="h2o")
australia.hex = h2o.uploadFile(path = ausPath)
summary(australia.hex)

pca_model=h2o.prcomp(training_frame = australia.hex,
                     k = 8,
                     transform = "STANDARDIZE")

summary(pca_model)
barplot(as.numeric(pca_model@model$importance[2,]),
        main="Pca model",
        xlab="Pca component",
        ylab="Proportion of Variance")
```

Now, let's go through the code to understand how to apply the `h2o` package to apply PCA.

We can proceed with loading the library:

```r
library(h2o)
```

This command loads the library into the R environment. The following function initiates the `h2o` engine with a maximum memory size of 2 GB and two parallel cores:

```r
h2o.init()
```

The following messages are returned:

```
> h2o.init()
 Connection successful!

R is connected to the H2O cluster:
    H2O cluster uptime: 5 hours 40 minutes
    H2O cluster version: 3.10.5.3
    H2O cluster version age: 2 months and 18 days
    H2O cluster name: H2O_started_from_R_lavoro_huu267
    H2O cluster total nodes: 1
    H2O cluster total memory: 2.63 GB
    H2O cluster total cores: 4
    H2O cluster allowed cores: 4
    H2O cluster healthy: TRUE
    H2O Connection ip: localhost
    H2O Connection port: 54321
    H2O Connection proxy: NA
    H2O Internal Security: FALSE
    R Version: R version 3.4.1 (2017-06-30)
```

We follow the directions on the R prompt:

```
c1=h2o.init(max_mem_size = "2G",
        nthreads = 2,
        ip = "localhost",
        port = 54321)
```

The `h2o.init` function initiates the `h2o` engine with a maximum memory size of 2 GB and two parallel cores. The following commands load the data into the R environment:

```
ausPath = system.file("extdata", "australia.csv", package="h2o")
australia.hex = h2o.uploadFile(path = ausPath)
```

The first instruction generates the path that contains the file to upload. To upload a file in a directory local to your `h2o` instance, use `h2o.uploadFile()`, which can also upload data local to your `h2o` instance in addition to your R session. In the parentheses, specify the `h2o` reference object in R and the complete URL or normalized file path for the file. Let's see now that it's inside:

```
summary(australia.hex)
```

Now let's print a brief summary of the dataset:

```
> summary(australia.hex)
 premax            salmax           minairtemp        maxairtemp        maxsst            maxsoilmoist
 Min.   : 18.00    Min.   :3441     Min.   :272.6     Min.   :285.0     Min.   :285697    Min.   : 0.000
 1st Qu.: 74.59    1st Qu.:3490     1st Qu.:277.0     1st Qu.:292.0     1st Qu.:290485    1st Qu.: 0.000
 Median :149.76    Median :3533     Median :278.8     Median :299.9     Median :293635    Median : 4.000
 Mean   :161.46    Mean   :3529     Mean   :279.9     Mean   :297.5     Mean   :295676    Mean   : 5.117
 3rd Qu.:249.98    3rd Qu.:3558     3rd Qu.:282.0     3rd Qu.:302.4     3rd Qu.:301934    3rd Qu.: 8.992
 Max.   :450.00    Max.   :3650     Max.   :290.0     Max.   :310.0     Max.   :303697    Max.   :16.000
 Max_czcs          runoffnew
 Min.   : 0.1600   Min.   :    0.00
 1st Qu.: 0.6308   1st Qu.:    0.00
 Median : 1.0120   Median :   16.81
 Mean   : 1.3694   Mean   :  232.22
 3rd Qu.: 1.7014   3rd Qu.:  297.72
 Max.   :11.3700   Max.   : 2400.00
```

To perform PCA on the given dataset, we will use the `prcomp()` function:

```
pca_model=h2o.prcomp(training_frame = australia.hex,
                     k = 8,
                     transform = "STANDARDIZE")
```

Now let's print a brief `summary` of the model:

```
summary(pca_model)
```

In the following figure, we see a summary of the PCA model:

```
> summary(pca_model)
Model Details:
==============

H2ODimReductionModel: pca
Model Key:  PCA_model_R_1505718700685_6
Importance of components:
                          pc1       pc2       pc3       pc4       pc5       pc6       pc7       pc8
Standard deviation     1.750703  1.512142  1.031181  0.828313  0.608379  0.548136  0.418162  0.231495
Proportion of Variance 0.383120  0.285822  0.132917  0.085763  0.046266  0.037557  0.021857  0.006699
Cumulative Proportion  0.383120  0.668942  0.801859  0.887622  0.933887  0.971444  0.993301  1.000000

H2ODimReductionMetrics: pca

No model metrics available for PCA



Scoring History for GramSVD:
            timestamp    duration iteration
1 2017-09-18 15:02:44   0.005 sec         0
```

To better understand the results, we can make a scree plot of the percent variability explained by each principal component. The percent variability explained is contained in the model importance variables from the PCA model.

The following figure shows a scree plot of the percent variability explained by each principal component:

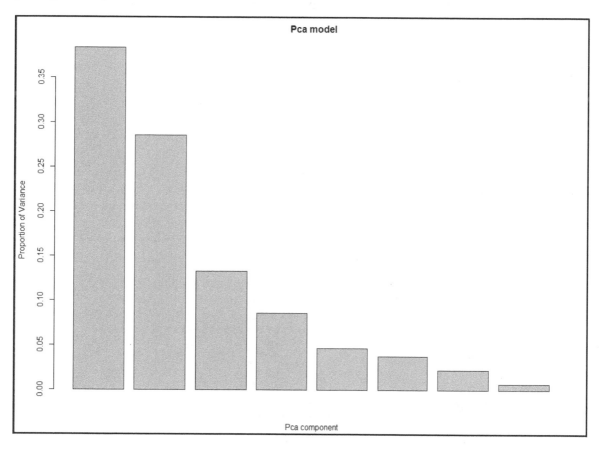

The bar plot shows the proportion of variance for each principal component; as you can see, the first two components have about 70 percent of the variance.

Autoencoders using H2O

An autoencoder is an ANN used for learning without efficient coding control. The purpose of an autoencoder is to learn coding for a set of data, typically to reduce dimensionality. Architecturally, the simplest form of autoencoder is an advanced and non-recurring neural network very similar to the MLP, with an input level, an output layer, and one or more hidden layers that connect them, but with the layer outputs having the same number of input level nodes for rebuilding their inputs.

In the following is proposed an example of autoencoder using h2o on a movie dataset.

 The dataset used in this example is a set of movies and genre taken from https://grouplens.org/datasets/movielens.

We use the movies.csv file, which has three columns:

- movieId
- title
- genres

There are 164,979 rows of data for clustering. We will use h2o.deeplearning to have the autoencoder parameter fix the clusters. The objective of the exercise is to cluster the movies based on genre, which can then be used to recommend similar movies or same-genre movies to the users. The program uses h20.deeplearning, with the autoencoder parameter set to T:

```
################################################################
### Chapter 7 - Neural Networks with R - Use cases    #########
### Autoencoder using H2O on a movie dataset          #########
################################################################

library("h2o")

setwd ("c://R")
#Load the training dataset of movies
movies=read.csv ( "movies.csv", header=TRUE)
head(movies)

model=h2o.deeplearning(2:3,
                       training_frame=as.h2o(movies),
                       hidden=c(2),
                       autoencoder = T,
                       activation="Tanh")

summary(model)

features=h2o.deepfeatures(model,
                          as.h2o(movies),
                          layer=1)

d=as.matrix(features[1:10,])
labels=as.vector(movies[1:10,2])
```

```
plot(d,pch=17)
text(d,labels,pos=3)
```

Now, let's go through the code:

```
library("h2o")
setwd ("c://R")
```

These commands load the library in the R environment and set the working directory where we will have inserted the dataset for the next reading. Then we load the data:

```
movies=read.csv( "movies.csv", header=TRUE)
```

To visualize the type of data contained in the dataset, we analyze a preview of one of these variables:

```
head(movies)
```

The following figure shows the first 20 rows of the `movie` dataset:

```
> head(movies, n=20)
   movieId                                title                                      genres
1        1                     Toy Story (1995) Adventure|Animation|Children|Comedy|Fantasy
2        2                       Jumanji (1995)                   Adventure|Children|Fantasy
3        3              Grumpier Old Men (1995)                               Comedy|Romance
4        4             Waiting to Exhale (1995)                         Comedy|Drama|Romance
5        5   Father of the Bride Part II (1995)                                       Comedy
6        6                          Heat (1995)                        Action|Crime|Thriller
7        7                       Sabrina (1995)                               Comedy|Romance
8        8                  Tom and Huck (1995)                           Adventure|Children
9        9                  Sudden Death (1995)                                       Action
10      10                     GoldenEye (1995)                    Action|Adventure|Thriller
11      11         American President, The (1995)                        Comedy|Drama|Romance
12      12    Dracula: Dead and Loving It (1995)                                Comedy|Horror
13      13                         Balto (1995)                  Adventure|Animation|Children
14      14                         Nixon (1995)                                        Drama
15      15               Cutthroat Island (1995)                     Action|Adventure|Romance
16      16                         Casino (1995)                                  Crime|Drama
17      17         Sense and Sensibility (1995)                                Drama|Romance
18      18                    Four Rooms (1995)                                       Comedy
19      19 Ace Ventura: When Nature Calls (1995)                                       Comedy
20      20                    Money Train (1995)          Action|Comedy|Crime|Drama|Thriller
```

Now we build and train `model`:

```
model=h2o.deeplearning(2:3,
                       training_frame=as.h2o(movies),
                       hidden=c(2),
                       autoencoder = T,
                       activation="Tanh")
```

Let's analyze some of the information contained in `model`:

```
summary(model)
```

This is an extract from the results of the `summary()` function:

```
Scoring History:
                timestamp       duration  training_speed  epochs iterations       samples training_rmse training_mse
1 2017-09-18 15:22:34       56.000 sec 0,00000 obs/sec  0.00000          0      0.000000       0.01413      0.00020
2 2017-09-18 15:24:59 2 min 49.489 sec   1042 obs/sec 10.11068         61 92260.000000       0.01339      0.00018

Variable Importances: (Extract with `h2o.varimp`)
==================================================

Variable Importances:
                        variable relative_importance scaled_importance percentage
1               genres.Comedy              1.000000          1.000000   0.005904
2                genres.Drama              0.791133          0.791133   0.004671
3         genres.Drama|Romance              0.196586          0.196586   0.001161
4        genres.Comedy|Romance              0.187687          0.187687   0.001108
5 genres.Comedy|Fantasy|Romance              0.181368          0.181368   0.001071

---
                              variable relative_importance scaled_importance percentage
10022            title.Speechless (1994)             0.000395          0.000395   0.000002
10023        title.Monsters, Inc. (2001)             0.000374          0.000374   0.000002
10024 title.Lover, The (Amant, L') (1992)             0.000188          0.000188   0.000001
10025          title.Smurfs 2, The (2013)             0.000168          0.000168   0.000001
10026                  title.missing(NA)             0.000000          0.000000   0.000000
10027                 genres.missing(NA)             0.000000          0.000000   0.000000
```

In the next command, we use the `h2o.deepfeatures()` function to extract the non-linear feature from an `h2o` dataset using an H2O deep learning model:

```
features=h2o.deepfeatures(model,
                  as.h2o(movies),
                  layer=1)
```

In the following code, the first six rows of the features extracted from the model are shown:

```
> features
  DF.L1.C1 DF.L1.C2
1 0.2569208 -0.2837829
2 0.3437048 -0.2670669
3 0.2969089 -0.4235294
4 0.3214868 -0.3093819
5 0.5586608 0.5829145
6 0.2479671 -0.2757966
[9125 rows x 2 columns]
```

Finally, we plot a diagram where we want to see how the model grouped the movies through the results obtained from the analysis:

```
d=as.matrix(features[1:10,])
labels=as.vector(movies[1:10,2])
plot(d,pch=17)
text(d,labels,pos=3)
```

The plot of the movies, once clustering is done, is shown next. We have plotted only 100 movie titles due to space issues. We can see some movies being closely placed, meaning they are of the same genre. The titles are clustered based on distances between them, based on genre.

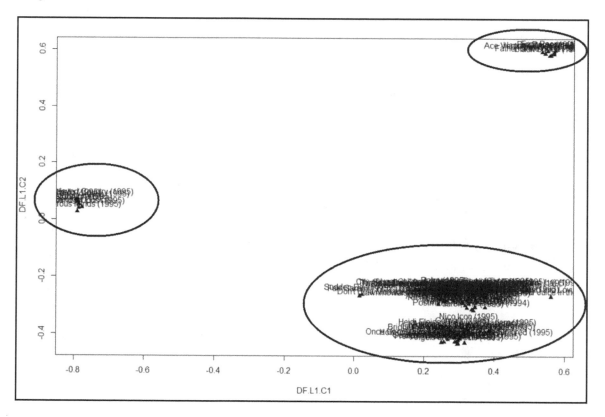

Given the large number of titles, the movie names cannot be distinguished, but what appears to be clear is that the model has grouped the movies into three distinct groups.

Breast cancer detection using darch

In this section, we will use the `darch` package, which is used for deep architectures and **Restricted Boltzmann Machines (RBM)**. The `darch` package is built on the basis of the code from G. E. Hinton and R. R. Salakhutdinov (available under MATLAB code for **Deep Belief Nets (DBN)**). This package is for generating neural networks with many layers (deep architectures) and training them with the method introduced by the authors.

This method includes a pre-training with the contrastive divergence method and fine-tuning with commonly known training algorithms such as backpropagation or conjugate gradients. Additionally, supervised fine-tuning can be enhanced with maxout and dropout, two recently developed techniques used to improve fine-tuning for deep learning.

The basis of the example is classification based on a set of inputs. To do this, we will use the data contained in the dataset named BreastCancer.csv that we just used in Chapter 5, *Training and Visualizing a Neural Network in R*. This data has been taken from the **UCI Repository Of Machine Learning.** The dataset is periodically updated as soon as Dr. Wolberg reports his clinical cases. The data is of breast cancer patients with a classification of benign or malignant tumor based on a set of ten independent variables.

 To get the data, we draw on the large collection of data available in the **UCI Machine Learning Repository** at `http://archive.ics.uci.edu/ml`.

Details of the data are as follows:

- **Number of instances**: 699 (as of 15 July 1992)
- **Number of attributes**: 10 plus the class attribute
- **Attribute information**: The class attribute has been moved to the last column

The description of the attributes is shown here:

```
 #  Attribute                   Domain
 -- ------------------------------------------
 1. Sample code number          id number
 2. Clump Thickness             1 - 10
 3. Uniformity of Cell Size     1 - 10
 4. Uniformity of Cell Shape    1 - 10
 5. Marginal Adhesion           1 - 10
 6. Single Epithelial Cell Size 1 - 10
 7. Bare Nuclei                 1 - 10
 8. Bland Chromatin             1 - 10
 9. Normal Nucleoli             1 - 10
10. Mitoses                     1 - 10
11. Class:                      (2 for benign, 4 for malignant)
```

To understand the `darch` function, we first set up an XOR gate and then use it for training and verification. The `darch` function uses output data and input attributes to build the model, which can be tested internally by `darch` itself. In this case, we achieve 0 percent error and 100 percent accuracy.

Next, we use the breast cancer data to build the `darch` model and then check the accuracy:

```
####################################################################
####Chapter 7 - Neural Networks with R ##########
####Breast Cancer Detection using darch package ##########
####################################################################
library("mlbench")
library("darch")

data(BreastCancer)
summary(BreastCancer)

data_cleaned <- na.omit(BreastCancer)
summary(data_cleaned)

model <- darch(Class ~ ., data_cleaned, layers = c(10, 10, 1),
        darch.numEpochs = 50, darch.stopClassErr = 0, retainData = T)

plot(model)

predictions <- predict(model, newdata = data_cleaned, type = "class")
cat(paste("Incorrect classifications:", sum(predictions !=
data_cleaned[,11])))
table(predictions,data_cleaned[,11])

library(gmodels)
```

```
CrossTable(x = data_cleaned$Class, y = predictions,
           prop.chisq=FALSE)
```

We begin analyzing the code line by line, explaining in detail all the features applied to capture the results:

```
library("mlbench")
library("darch")
```

The first two lines of the initial code are used to load the libraries needed to run the analysis.

> Remember that, to install a library that is not present in the initial distribution of R, you must use the `install.package` function. This is the main function to install packages. It takes a vector of names and a destination library, downloads the packages from the repositories and installs them. This function should be used only once and not every time you run the code.

The `mlbench` library contains a collection of artificial and real-world machine learning benchmark problems, including, for example, several datasets from the UCI repository.

The `darch` library is a package for deep architectures and RBM:

```
data(BreastCancer)
```

With this command, we upload the dataset named `BreastCancer`, as mentioned, in the `mlbench` library. Let's see now that it's inside:

```
summary(BreastCancer)
```

With this command, we see a brief summary by using the `summary()` function.

> Remember, the `summary()` function is a generic function used to produce result summaries of the results of various model fitting functions. The function invokes particular methods that depend on the class of the first argument.

In this case, the function has been applied to a dataframe and the results are listed in the following figure:

```
> summary(BreastCancer)
      Id             Cl.thickness    Cell.size      Cell.shape    Marg.adhesion    Epith.c.size
Length:699         1    :145    1     :384    1     :353    1       :407    2       :386
Class :character   5    :130    10    : 67    2     : 59    2       : 58    3       : 72
Mode  :character   3    :108    3     : 52    10    : 58    3       : 58    4       : 48
                   4    : 80    2     : 45    3     : 56    10      : 55    1       : 47
                   10   : 69    4     : 40    4     : 44    4       : 33    6       : 41
                   2    : 50    5     : 30    5     : 34    8       : 25    5       : 39
                   (Other):117  (Other): 81  (Other): 95  (Other): 63  (Other): 66
  Bare.nuclei    Bl.cromatin    Normal.nucleoli     Mitoses           Class
1     :402    2      :166    1      :443    1      :579    benign   :458
10    :132    3      :165    10     : 61    2      : 35    malignant:241
2     : 30    1      :152    3      : 44    3      : 33
5     : 30    7      : 73    2      : 36    10     : 14
3     : 28    4      : 40    8      : 24    4      : 12
(Other): 61   5      : 34    6      : 22    7      :  9
NA's   : 16   (Other): 69   (Other): 69   (Other): 17
```

The `summary()` function returns a set of statistics for each variable. In particular, it is useful to highlight the result provided for the `Class` variable, which contains the diagnosis of the cancer mass. In this case, `458` cases of `benign` class and `241` cases of `malignant` class were detected. Another feature to highlight is the `Bare.nuclei` variable. For this variable, `16` cases of missing values were detected.

To remove missing values, we can use the `na.omit()` function:

```
data_cleaned <- na.omit(BreastCancer)
```

Now we build and train the model:

```
model <- darch(Class ~ ., data_cleaned, layers = c(10, 10, 1),
        darch.numEpochs = 50, darch.stopClassErr = 0, retainData = T)
```

To evaluate the `model` performance, we can plot the raw network error:

```
plot(model)
```

The plot of error versus epoch is shown in the following figure:

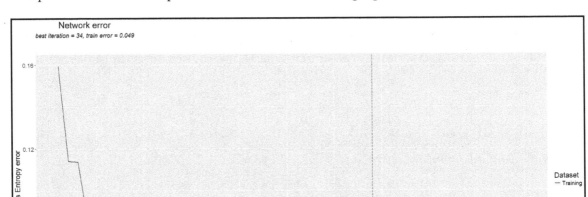

We get the minimum error at 34 epochs.

We finally have the network trained and ready for use; now we can use it to make our predictions:

```
predictions <- predict(model, newdata = data_cleaned, type = "class")
```

We used the entire set of data at our disposal to make our forecast using the model. All we have to do is compare the results obtained with the model predictions and the data available in the dataset:

```
cat(paste("Incorrect classifications:", sum(predictions !=
data_cleaned[,11])))
```

The results are shown as follows:

```
> cat(paste("Incorrect classifications:", sum(predictions !=
data_cleaned[,11])))
Incorrect classifications: 2
```

The results are really good! Only two wrong classifications! I would say that we can be content with the fact that they started from 683 observations. To better understand what the errors were, we build a confusion matrix:

```
table(predictions,data_cleaned[,11])
```

The results are shown here:

```
> table(predictions,data_cleaned[,11])

predictions benign malignant
   benign       443         1
   malignant      1       238
```

Although in a simple way, the matrix tells us that we only made two errors equally distributed between the two values of the class. For more information on the confusion matrix, we can use the CrossTable() function contained in the gmodels package. As always, before loading the book, you need to install it:

```
library(gmodels)
CrossTable(x = data_cleaned$Class, y = predictions,
           prop.chisq=FALSE)
```

The confusion matrix obtained by using the CrossTable() function is shown in the following figure:

```
> CrossTable(x = data_cleaned$Class, y = predictions,
+             prop.chisq=FALSE)

   Cell Contents
|-------------------------|
|                       N |
|           N / Row Total |
|           N / Col Total |
|         N / Table Total |
|-------------------------|

Total Observations in Table:  683

                  | predictions
data_cleaned$Class |    benign | malignant | Row Total |
-------------------|-----------|-----------|-----------|
            benign |       443 |         1 |       444 |
                   |     0.998 |     0.002 |     0.650 |
                   |     0.998 |     0.004 |           |
                   |     0.649 |     0.001 |           |
-------------------|-----------|-----------|-----------|
         malignant |         1 |       238 |       239 |
                   |     0.004 |     0.996 |     0.350 |
                   |     0.002 |     0.996 |           |
                   |     0.001 |     0.348 |           |
-------------------|-----------|-----------|-----------|
      Column Total |       444 |       239 |       683 |
                   |     0.650 |     0.350 |           |
-------------------|-----------|-----------|-----------|
```

As we had anticipated in the classification, our model has only two errors: *FP* and *FN*. Then calculate the accuracy; as indicated in `Chapter 2`, *Learning Processes in Neural Networks*, it is given by the following formula:

$$ACC = \frac{TP+TN}{P+N} = \frac{TP+TN}{TP+TN+FP+FN}$$

Let's calculate the accuracy in R environment:

```
> Accuracy = (443+238)/683
> Accuracy
[1] 0.9970717
```

As mentioned before, the classifier has achieved excellent results.

Summary

In this final chapter, we saw some use cases with neural networks and deep learning. This should form the basis of your future work on neural networks. The usage is common in most cases, with changes in the dataset involved for the model during training and testing.

We saw the following examples in this chapter:

- Integrating TensorFlow and Keras with R, which opens up vast set of use cases to be built using R
- Building a digit recognizer through classification using H2O
- Understanding the LSTM function with MxNet
- PCA using H2O
- Building an autoencoder using H2O
- Usage of `darch` for classification problems

R is a very flexible and a major statistical programming language for data scientists across the world. A grasp of neural networks with R will help the community evolve further and increase the usage of R for deep learning and newer use cases.

Index

CPSIA information can be obtained
at www.ICGtesting.com
Printed in the USA
FSHW010820060819
60748FS